D1521031

Narrative in the Feminine

Daphne Marlatt and
Nicole Brossard

Susan Knutson

Wilfrid Laurier University Press

This book has been published with the help of a grant from the Humanities and Social Sciences Federation of Canada, using funds provided by the Social Sciences and Humanities Research Council of Canada. We acknowledge the support of the Canada Council for the Arts for our publishing program. We acknowledge the financial support of the Government of Canada through the Book Publishing Industry Development Program for our publishing activities.

Canadian Cataloguing in Publication Data

Knutson, Susan Lynne
   Narrative in the feminine : Daphne Marlatt and Nicole Brossard

Includes bibliographical references and index.
ISBN 0-88920-301-6 (bound)

1. Marlatt, Daphne, 1942- . How hug a stone. 2. Brossard, Nicole, 1943- . Picture theory. 3. Canadian literature—Women authors—History and criticism. 4. Narration (Rhetoric). I. Title.

PS8576.A74H683 2000   C810.9′9287   C99-930632-4
PR9199.3.M36H683 2000

Cover design by Leslie Macredie. Front cover photo: *A Hand to Standing Stones, Scotland 1983*, by Marlene Creates (CARfac©Collective).

Printed in Canada

Contents

PART FIVE
Bibliography, Appendix and Index

List of Figures

v

Acknowledgements

Eᴀʀʟɪᴇʀ ᴅʀᴀꜰᴛꜱ ᴏꜰ ꜱᴇᴄᴛɪᴏɴꜱ of this book have appeared in the following articles: "Protean Travelogue in Nicole Brossard's *Picture Theory*: Feminist Desire and Narrative Form," *Modern Language Studies* 27.3, 4 (Winter 1997), 197-211; "Reading Nicole Brossard," *Ellipse* 53 (1995), 9-19; " 'Imagine Her Surprise': The Debate over Feminist Essentialism," *Collaboration in the Feminine: Writings on Women and Culture from Tessera*, edited by Barbara Godard (Toronto: Second Story Press, 1994), 228-36; "Nicole Brossard's Elegant International Play," *Canada: Theoretical Discourse/Discours théoriques*, edited by Terry Goldie, Carmen Lambert and Rowland Lorimer (Montréal: Association for Canadian Studies/Association d'études canadiennes, 1994), 187-202; "Writing Meta-narrative in the Feminine," *Signature: A Journal of Theory and Canadian Literature* 3 (Summer 1990), 28-43; "Challenging the Masculine Generic," *Tessera* 4/*Contemporary Verse 2* 11, 2-3 (Spring/Summer 1988), 76-88. Related material was presented at "Message in a Bottle: The Literature of Small Islands," Charlottetown, P.E.I., June 24-28, 1998; "Transformations," Lancaster University, U.K., July 19, 1997; N.E.M.L.A., Montréal, April 19-20, 1996; A.C.C.U.T.E., Charlottetown, P.E.I., May 1992; and "Theoretical Discourse in the Canadian Intellectual Community," Gray Rocks, Québec, September 24-27, 1992.

Abbreviations

A	Daphne Marlatt's *Ana Historic*
HHS	Daphne Marlatt's *How Hug a Stone*
IASR	Roland Barthes's "Introduction à l'analyse structurale des récits"
MG	Monique Wittig's "The Mark of Gender"
N	Mieke Bal's *Narratology*
NBBW	Alice Parker's "Nicole Brossard's Body Work"
Préface	Louise Forsyth's "Préface" to *Picture Theory*
PT	Nicole Brossard's *Picture Theory*
RI	Nicole Brossard's "De radical à intégrales"
RM	Hélène Cixous's "Le rire de la Méduse"
Touch	Daphne Marlatt's *Touch to My Tongue*
WG	Robert Graves's *The White Goddess*

Preface

THIS BOOK IS COMPOSED of three relatively distinct parts. Although arguments build from chapter to chapter and connections run through the whole, I have tried to write so that sections and chapters can be read on their own.

Part One addresses certain prominent themes within feminist writing theory: French feminism, "essentialism," and gender as a semiotic product. The rapport between language and privilege is explored in relation to the concept of the (masculine) generic, taking account of anti-racist theory and practice. Classical and feminist narrative theory are brought together to articulate the link between narrative grammar and gender, and to introduce key terms and concepts necessary for the feminist narratological readings undertaken in Parts Two and Three.

Part Two reads Daphne Marlatt's *How Hug a Stone* at the three narrative levels of fabula, story and text. At the deepest level of narrative, Marlatt constructs a gender-inclusive human subject which defaults not to the generic masculine but to the feminine, thanks to intense focalization of story and text through the senses of the i-narrator. At the intertextual level, another story unfolds: a subtext that both threatens and restores, and through which the reader comes uncannily close to the Neolithic people who once made Avebury their home.

Part Three proposes a parallel reading of Nicole Brossard's *Picture Theory*—a novel modelled on the hologram, interfacing wave formations and cortical energy fields rearranging reality in the human mind. Intertextual, playful *Picture Theory* draws us into (re-)readings of other Brossardian texts, notably, "De radical à intégrales," and of Djuna Barnes, Monique Wittig, James Joyce, Simone de Beauvoir, Homer, Sappho, Wittgenstein—to name a few. By the end, Brossard has done a remarkable thing: "woman" is readable and reading actively in a reconceived Western civilization.

Chapter 12 closes with a reflection on the expression *écriture au féminin*—a Québécois contribution, I argue, to an international theoretical debate. In what ways are *Picture Theory* and *How Hug a Stone* written in the feminine? Can these texts suggest transitional symbologies-in-evolution to replace the deposed, white, universal man? Evolution itself, imaged as a spiral, is perhaps the concept that best reflects feminist aspirations for life in a life-oriented world, at least in these two texts.

In my study, materials written in French are normally presented in French, with a footnote giving the English translation for phrases longer than one word. Translations are cited in the bibliography; when published translations do not exist, I have translated. Certain texts present exceptions. Monique Wittig writes her own English texts, and may have written "The Mark of Gender" in English; in any case, I have not seen it in French. Neither have I found a French version of "Variations on Some Common Themes," which may have been put together by the editors of *Questions féministes* for the first issue of their journal's English counterpart, *Feminist Issues*. I cite both these texts in English.

My thanks are due to Daphne Marlatt and Nicole Brossard for their solidarity and support for this project, and to Lorraine Weir for teaching me to be more tough-minded. Thanks also to the Social Sciences and Humanities Research Council, the Canadian Federation for the Humanities, Université Sainte-Anne and Wilfrid Laurier University Press. Parts of this book were researched (with great pleasure) at the British Library in London and at the Bibliothèque Marguerite Durand in Paris. I also want to thank for their support my family and friends, especially my son, Nicholas, who has been very patient.

PART ONE

Gender and Narrative Grammar

CHAPTER 1

Writing Women: Some Introductory Questions

No one ever told us we had to study our lives,
make of our lives a study, as if learning natural
history or music.
— Adrienne Rich, *The Dream of a
Common Language*

IN A WIDE RANGE OF DISCIPLINES and discourses, feminist thought has
wrought a sea-change, a fundamental and thoroughgoing transformation
of what we understand and how we understand it. One such domain,
called up by the key words—gender, narrative, writing—is rich with
provocative and difficult questions. In what sense is narrative complicit
with gender? Is it possible to fully imagine a gender-inclusive hero? How
are feminist writers translating theory into practice? Have significant
structural innovations been made in women's writing? Can we formally
describe narrative in the feminine? Perhaps rashly, I have tried to answer
some of these questions, guided by systematic, narratological readings of
Daphne Marlatt's intricate and controversial long poem, *How Hug a
Stone* (1983) and Nicole Brossard's playful, philosophical novel, *Picture
Theory* (1982).

In 1929, Virginia Woolf complained that the nineteenth-century sentence is a "man's sentence ... unsuited for a woman's use" (73). For
women's fiction to have a future, Woolf speculates, "the book has somehow to be adapted to the [female] body" (74). Women poets will devise
new literary forms, "for it is the poetry [in women] which is still denied
outlet" (73-74). In the late 1970s, Woolf's prophecy seemed to have
been fulfilled as readers and writers on both sides of the Atlantic discovered a passion for women's writing. As graduate students in Vancouver, in
the early 1980s, my friends and I passed from hand to hand Michèle
Valiquette's red-jacketed copy of Elaine Marks and Isabelle de
Courtivron's *New French Feminisms*, where we read and reread the

3

English translation of Hélène Cixous's "Le rire de la méduse." "Women must write through their bodies," declares Cixous. Women "must invent the impregnable language that will wreck partitions, classes, and rhetorics, regulations and codes"[1] (256). "Woman must write her self: must write about women and bring women to writing, from which they have been driven away as violently as from their bodies. . . . Woman must put herself into the text—as into the world and into history—by her own movement"[2] (245). And if, as Daphne Marlatt would put it in a 1984 interview with Ellea Wright, the "push" to write with the body came from France, as Canadians we were equally passionate about reading the feminist writers of English Canada and Québec. I myself learned French in order to read Louky Bersianik and the inimitable Nicole Brossard who, in 1977, condensed the matter of women's writing into one revolutionary sentence: "*J'ai tué le ventre et je l'écris*"[3] (*L'amèr* 27). We also treasured the work of Daphne Marlatt, whose extraordinary powers of attention saw how deeply that push towards writing with the body might retune grammar to the frequencies of many women's lives:

> how can the standard sentence structure of English with its linear authority, subject through verb to object, convey the wisdom of endlessly repeating and not exactly repeated cycles her body knows? or the mutuality her body shares embracing other bodies, children, friends, animals, all those she customarily holds and is held by? how can the separate nouns mother and child convey the fusion, bleeding womb-infant mouth, she experiences in those first days of feeding? what syntax can carry the turning herself inside out in love when she is both sucking mouth and hot gush on her lover's tongue?" (*Touch* 47-48)

The female body, the womb itself, would be freed from patriarchally controlled production and put to work on another kind of text, freedom writing, wom(b)en's writing.

Marlatt, Brossard and Cixous, in each of the passages I cite above, go beyond the merely reasonable hypothesis that a woman's experience is reflected in her texts, to theorize a material correspondence between a

---

1 Il faut que la femme écrive par son corps, qu'elle invente la langue imprenable qui crève les cloisonnements, classes et rhétoriques, ordonnances et codes (48).

2 Il faut que la femme s'écrive: que la femme écrive de la femme et fasse venir les femmes à l'écriture, dont elles ont été éloignées aussi violemment qu'elles l'ont été de leurs corps. . . . Il faut que la femme se mette au texte—comme au monde, et à l'histoire—de son propre mouvement (39).

3 *I have murdered the womb and I am writing it* (21).

woman's writing and her gender. An image emerges of the writing woman, tracing her female body in a womanly text: biology signifying in coded tropes, syntax, sounds and words. "Plus corps donc plus écriture"[4] (48) (257), as Cixous maintained. "Elle écrit à l'encre blanche"[5] (44). The metaphor is a potent catalyst of writing and discourse, powered by the oxymoron linking the female body to the Apollonian logos. However, as early as the mid-1970s, the discourse of *writing the body* was criticized for its biological-metaphysical—or, as it has come to be known, essentialist—definition of femininity. Christine Delphy, Emmanuèlle Lesseps and the other members of the editorial collective of the French journal *Questions féministes* were among the first to clearly oppose essentialism, which they counterposed to their own materialist feminist theory. These and other early critics of gender essentialism warned of the inherent dangers to women in any theory that reified women's "difference" from men; their fears were shown to be justified in 1979, when feminist scholarship exploring women's difference was recontextualized against the interests of women in the U.S. District Court of Chicago, and a sex-discrimination case brought against Sears Roebuck and Co. by the Equal Employment Opportunity Commission (McDermott, 149-57) was defeated. Since that time, and in spite of the contributions of scholars such as Barbara Godard, Diana Fuss and Teresa de Lauretis, the debate concerning gender essentialism has become increasingly academic, perhaps, as Christine Delphy suggests, because of widespread misreading of what is known in the United States as French feminism.

As Louise Forsyth notes, Canadian feminists who have followed both the French and the American debates tend to see beyond the theoretical pitfalls which have slowed progress and sown discord in the international feminist movement (*Errant* 10). Efforts to read our leading feminist writers in the light of the American debate have not had much impact. In "Essentialism? A Problem in Discourse," Barbara Godard traces the Canadian debate, noting that essentialism has been a non-issue in Québec, where a strong post-existentialist discursive tradition treats gender as a semiotic product (32). The essentialism/constructionist paradigm does appear in the early 1990s, however—in attacks on lesbian writers. Teresa de Lauretis also remarks that the debate over feminist essentialism obscures feminist critiques of heterosexuality, pointing

---

4 More body, hence more writing (257).
5 She writes in white ink (251).

out that in the United States a direct challenge to the social-symbolic institution of heterosexuality has been made "most articulately by precisely those feminists who are then accused of separatism in their political stance and of essentialism with regard to their epistemological claims. I do not think it is a coincidence" ("The Essence of the Triangle" 32). The relatively tardy appearance of these attacks in Canada may be attributable to a shared perception among Canadian feminists that lesbianism is everybody's issue, as Mariana Valverde suggests (103; see also Knutson "Imagine Her Surprise"). On the other hand, both Marlatt and Brossard have been accused of "feminist essentialism." Does their early leadership of the movement for women's writing make them "guilty" of this curiously serious charge? Could it be their lesbianism which makes them "guilty"? Or does a text written "in the feminine" presume a cultural invariance of gender identification, to paraphrase Judith Butler's influential argument (339)?

The Spring 1989 issue of *Line*, while highlighting Daphne Marlatt's contribution to Canadian letters, also includes articles that criticize her representation of gender. Frank Davey argues that *How Hug a Stone* is a metaphysical text which "places against the categorizing and collecting masculine, an essential feminine" (45). Lola Lemire Tostevin cites a lyrical passage from *Ana Historic* to conclude that when Marlatt refers to "the difference" (*A* 126) she is speaking "within the traditional concept of binary opposition" (38). The debate continues in subsequent issues of what is now *West Coast Line*, notably in *Beyond Tish*, when Brenda Carr interviews Marlatt and rearticulates the essentialism question:

> BC: It is possible to see ... aspect[s] of your work as sliding towards the patriarchal essentialist trap that reduces woman to body/sexuality, erases differences between women, conflates women with nature, and ultimately leaves woman outside of culture and cultural production. In an interview with Janice Williamson, you indicate that you see your use of this imagery as a self-conscious recuperation, a gesture of double decolonization of what has been traditionally devalued as "feminine." Is this eco-feminist position still a necessary corrective in our world that is sometimes seen as "post-colonial" (and I might add "post-feminist")?

> DM: Our world certainly isn't post-colonial or post-feminist. And presuming to speak from a "post" position just blinds us to the fact that things haven't really changed all that much. (104-105)

In pointing to the political necessity for an ongoing critique of patriarchal gender, Marlatt indirectly responds to Tostevin's earlier use of Teresa de

Lauretis's *Technologies of Gender* to support her claim that *Ana Historic* theorizes sexual difference "within the conceptual frame of a universal sex opposition" (Tostevin, 38; de Lauretis, 2). Marlatt notes implicitly that any such reading of de Lauretis overlooks an important qualification of political timing specified clearly in de Lauretis's text: "To pose the question of gender in . . . [binary] terms, *once the critique of patriarchy has been fully outlined*, keeps feminist thinking bound to the terms of Western patriarchy itself" (1; my emphasis).

Sandra Gilbert and Susan Gubar are also invoked in Tostevin's critique of binary gender, and she might have added Julia Kristeva, whose condemnation of male/female gender as "metaphysical" lies behind most contemporary critiques of feminist essentialism, including Toril Moi's influential reading of Elaine Showalter reading Virginia Woolf. In *A Room of One's Own*, Woolf argues that as women overcome impediments to creativity, our writing will more and more resemble that of men. Woolf viewed traces of gender in writing as negative and admired androgyny in writing, considering the great writer to a have a mind which was "woman-manly" or "man-womanly" (94). "It is fatal for anyone who writes to think of their sex" (99). The better women's writing is, the closer it will come to the Shakespearean ideal of the unimpeded, incandescent and androgynous mind (55). Moi argues that Woolf's theory of androgyny "deconstructs" patriarchal gender, and she counters Elaine Showalter's critical point that in theorizing an androgynous writing, Woolf is less than completely enthusiastic about writing as a woman. Moi maintains that for Woolf, androgyny is not "a flight from fixed gender identities, but a recognition of their falsifying metaphysical nature."

> Far from felling such gender identities because she fears them, Woolf rejects them because she has seen them for what they are. She has understood that the goal of the feminist struggle must precisely be to deconstruct the death-dealing binary oppositions of masculinity and femininity. (13)

Moi's argument is framed by her reading of Kristeva, and particularly of Kristeva's three stages of feminism:

> for Julia Kristeva it is not the biological sex of a person, but the subject position she or he takes up, that determines their revolutionary potential. Her views . . . reflect this refusal of biologism and essentialism. The feminist struggle, she argues, must be seen historically and politically as a three-tiered one, which can be schematically summarized as follows:

1. Women demand equal access to the symbolic order. Liberal feminism. Equality.
2. Women reject the male symbolic order in the name of difference. Radical feminism. Femininity extolled.
3. (This is Kristeva's own position). Women reject the dichotomy between masculine and feminine as metaphysical." (Moi, 12)

The adoption of the deconstructive third position does not involve a rejection of stage two, but folds it in; as Moi specifies, it "remains *politically* essential for feminists to defend women *as* women" (13). Similar views on this question are broadly shared by Gayatri Chakravorty Spivak, Teresa de Lauretis and many others. Christine Delphy, for example, also insists that gender is constructed, rather than essential, but she emphasizes that this does not mean that gender isn't a dominant condition of social life. The qualification is important since many critics, in avoiding a reification of gender, seem to reconcile themselves to the relatively invisible norm which is the white, able-bodied, heterosexual and male generic in European-based cultures.

The critique of feminist essentialism should not be interpreted as a ban on the representation of binary gender. Discourse needs to be kept open not only to our impressions of gender difference but also to terms and concepts such as lesbianism and racism which some people find very difficult. Sadly, readers who distrust Marlatt's feminism will also fail to hear her invitation to read into a place "where live things are" (*HHS* 79)—an open space in discourse where both women and men may hope to experience more life-affirming gender relations in the future. Davey entertains the possibility that the "single meaning" (46) of sexist, binary gender is not immanent in the poem as a whole, and he is correct in doing so. Sexist binary gender is *represented* in How Hug a Stone—represented and criticized precisely as prescriptive, as "script" (*HHS* 17). Narratological analysis of the poem shows that traditional gender re-enacts a frightening, incomplete and fossilized closure out of which the narrator *and* her son are finally able to move.

Marlatt's i-narrator, as Davey also notes (41), is associated with an anti-hierarchical textual plurality, quite incompatible with the didacticism he finds in How Hug a Stone (42). In fact, Marlatt's i/eye is a feminist and anti-colonialist response to the dynamics of the imperial ego. Its activity must be interpreted in the context of the ongoing Freudian and feminist critique of the gaze and women's ambiguous relationship to it, as Carr has done in her analysis of *Steveston* and *Salvage* (1989, 92). In the light of what is often understood to be an appropriating masculine gaze, Marlatt's focalizing i/eye asserts a female and feminist subjectivity at the same time that she doubles back to her early grounding in proprioceptive poetics. This can be seen, for example, in the letter to Davey published in the same issue of *Line*, where we find her exploring an interest in the visible whereby the "mind's eye" is noted as the "scene" of poetry (5-7). Reading Marlatt's text through these theoretical frames clarifies how the i-narrator is a necessary component in the textual creation of an integral female subject. Of course, the i-narrator is not the only subject in the poem. Davey is right to note that Kit's maleness is significant, but he misreads Kit's importance for the poem's construction of a generic subjectivity which includes both male and female. In the process, Frank Davey misses Marlatt's gesture of solidarity with her son and—by extension—with other boys and men.

Nicole Brossard has also been accused of essentialism. In *Lesbian Utopics*, Annamarie Jagose argues that leading lesbian feminist theorists and writers, including Brossard, have misled their readers by claiming to be subversive when, in fact, they are complicit with patriarchal law. Of Bonnie Zimmerman and Monique Wittig, for example, Jagose writes, "the utopic theorization of 'lesbian' inadvertently illustrates that what poses as subversion may, in fact, be complicit with that which it purports to subvert" (5-6). Wittig's discursive lesbian is found to maintain and reproduce phallocentrism (7), while her "strategies of emancipation may be entirely complicit with the oppressive structures they are intended to exceed" (7). According to Jagose, Wittig is not alone in saying quite the opposite of what she wishes to say. Marilyn Hacker's sequence of explicitly lesbian love sonnets is found to be a figuration of a "renovated closet" (22). Mary Fallon's "utopic project to write . . . beyond the operation of a regulatory heterosexuality always reinstalls itself within that legislative system" (99). Gloria Anzaldúa's *Borderlands* "replicates the mechanisms of defense that it critiques" (138).

Many of Jagose's most sweeping condemnations are reserved for Brossard, whom Jagose (mis-)takes to be a Québécoise Irigaray (22, 43), an essentialist (45) who "disavows . . . the always already ambiguous and plural nature of language" (66). Brossard is accused of the "unexamined reproduction" of the "problematic concept" of "women" (45). As evidence, Jagose cites Brossard's statement that, "Whatever our ethnic or religious origins, we all belong quite visibly to the category 'women'" (*The Aerial Letter*, 134; cited in Jagose, 45). She argues that Brossard

here implies both "the transcultural notion of patriarchy and the fundamental homogeneity of the category 'women.' In a cunning maneuver, all
the more so for being unacknowledged, the concepts 'patriarchy' and
'women' reinforce each other" (45). Jagose's analysis of Brossard is
apparently based on a partial reading of the English translation of *La lettre áerienne*. If she had read further, she might have learned that to argue
that Brossard is unaware of the plurality of language is nothing short of
absurd, and that Brossard's deployment of the concept "woman" is anything but unexamined. In the passage quoted by Jagose, Brossard is
thinking along the lines of Elizabeth Weed, who notes that although the
term "women" is "unstable and unreliable, there is little danger of laps-
ing into 'sexual indifference' or indifference to gender, because 'women'
are . . . continually produced by social formations" (xix), and Denise
Riley, who characterizes women's history as "the history of feminization"
(138). Women are feminized by the gaze of others; whatever we might
think about it, we belong *visibly* to the category "women."

Brossard's theoretical work on the constitution and nature of the word
"woman" is arguably the most sophisticated in the Western Hemisphere,
although her achievement is to a certain extent shared by all the creators
of Québécois feminism during the years after the Quiet Revolution. The
debate over the nature and status of the word "woman" begins in France
during the 1970s, during the period when French feminism experienced
the unfortunate political and philosophical schisms which so damaged it
that in Paris, in 1986, it was possible for a demonstration of a quarter of
a million people, representing hundreds of progressive organizations, to
not include a single women's group or a single feminist slogan.[6] During a

---

6 In 1986, *Psych et Po* had held for six years a copyright on the expression "MLF" or
   Women's Liberation Movement. Hélène Cixous commanded a significant following
   within the university, where she studied and taught primarily the texts of men.
   Monique Wittig had moved to the United States. Paris, then as now, was home to a
   small independent feminist movement which operated La maison des femmes, a
   slightly dilapidated house in the 20th *arrondisement*, where a handful of volunteers
   duplicated themselves in every committee and program. The *Psych et Po* group, at
   the Librairie des femmes, claimed to be unaware of La maison des femmes and of the
   newsletter, *Paris féministe*, which was/is published there. They did direct me to the
   Bibliothèque Marguerite Durand, a feminist history research library in Paris. I eventually located a women's karate dojo, coffeehouse and bookstore called La mutinerie.
   When I mentioned feminism at the dojo, my new friends told me it wasn't their struggle. They were lesbians, and didn't consider themselves women.
     The split in the French feminist movement is documented in Hélène Cixous, "Ô
   grand-mère que vous avez de beaux concepts!" and "Poésie, e(s)t politique?"; early

research trip to Paris, I met Parisian women who closely resembled Canadian feminists in attitudes and lifestyle but who explained to me that feminism was not their struggle. "On ne s'identifie pas comme femme,"[7] I was told, and the name of Monique Wittig—admired by me precisely as a *feminist* theorist—was invoked. As Jill Vickers has pointed out, feminist theory may not be text-based, but texts become crucial as feminism theorizes lived experience, producing documents that have material consequences.[8] This dialectic is why feminist theory matters; the point could hardly be demonstrated more clearly than it is by the debates in French feminism in the late 1970s and early 1980s.

With respect to the word "woman" or "femme," by 1979, two camps within the French movement had clearly opposing positions. Without too much simplification, it can be said that the group *Psych et Po*, or Psychanalyse et Politique, led by Antoinette Fouque (and with which Cixous was associated), embraced both the word and the idea of woman. They signed their texts "des femmes" or simply with three woman symbols ("la situation et notre politique"); they named their bookstores "Les librairies des femmes" and their publishing house "Les éditions des femmes." They reflected on, analyzed and supported women's difference (see "la différence internée"). They considered that women's oppression was largely the denial of this difference; therefore, by affirming it, they could liberate themselves from oppression.

The other current, which included Monique Wittig and certain other editors of *Questions féministes*, elaborated a radical lesbian variety of materialist feminism. In 1975, Christine Delphy and the other materialist feminist theorists had used marxist methodology to argue that just as the working class is defined by its exploitative relationship to the means of production, so the class of women is defined by its exploitative relationship to the means of reproduction. It follows that the end of women's oppression would implicate the disappearance of women as such; this process would be analogous to the eventual withering away of the proletariat and its dictatorship, which V.I. Lenin discusses in chapter 5 of *The*

---

volumes of *Questions féministes* and *Feminist Issues*; *Feminist Studies* 1, 2 (Summer 1981); Ellisa Gelfand and Virginia Thorndike Hules, *French Feminist Criticism*; *Signs* 3, 4 (Summer 1978); *Sub-stance* 13 (1976), 27; *The Women's Review of Books* 3, 6 (March 1986).

7 We don't identify ourselves as women.

8 In discussion at the Association for Canadian Studies, "Theoretical Discourse in the Canadian Intellectual Community," Gray Rocks, Québec, September 24-27, 1992.

State and Revolution. Materialist feminist analysis structurally implicates the heterosexual family as the social institution that reproduces the oppression of women in the so-called private domain. To liberate women therefore implies the de-naturalization and rupture of the heterosexual contract and the end of the existence of women as an exploited class. The *Questions féministes* group supported lesbian feminism and the struggles of all women, but sometimes rejected the word "woman," as, for example, in "Variations on Some Common Themes," where Nicole-Claude Mathieu wrote: "The word *woman*, I cannot and never could bear it. . . . With [this word] they 'have had us' as THEY SAY" (14). In pursuit of such sentiments, a radical lesbian tendency, which included Wittig, split from the journal in 1979, effectively abandoning the action-oriented materialist feminism that Christine Delphy and Emmanuèle Lesseps continued to elaborate. By refusing to self-identify as women and by targeting heterosexual women as traitors, the French radical lesbians undermined the basis for solidarity in the women's movement. History has made their error appear quite clearly. *Psych et Po*, on the other hand, characterized by homophobia, anti-activism and bona fide essentialism, were at least equally destructive. They refused the words "lesbian" and "feminist," reiterating always the word "woman."

The philosophical framework of the debate can be traced to Simone de Beauvoir's 1949 assertion that one is not born a woman (2, 13). In distinguishing between nature and gender, de Beauvoir made possible a feminist critique of the social construction of woman. Wittig elaborates this position in her text "On ne naît pas femme": "quand on analyse l'oppression des femmes avec des concepts matérialistes et féministes, on détruit ce faisant l'idée que les femmes sont un groupe naturel"[9] (75). In this article, Wittig softens an argument she had made just months before, in "La pensée straight," that lesbians are not women; perhaps she already saw evidence of the negative political impact the slogan was to have on the French feminist movement. In any case, the analysis itself imposes the question: if woman is a social construction, and one which we reject, then on what basis can we come together as a movement? The issue erupted violently at the feminist conference held in New York, in September of 1979, to honour the thirtieth anniversary of the publication of Simone de Beauvoir's *The Second Sex* (1949). Michèle Le Doeuff tells

---

9 A materialist feminist approach to women's oppression destroys the idea that women are a "natural group" (47).

us that Hélène Cixous, speaking for *Psych et Po*, repudiated de Beauvoir's key theoretical distinction precisely because it defines the category of women around the fact of oppression (106). Cixous announced, "nous en France nous ne nous appelons plus féministes parce que nous avons abandonné ce point de vue négatif" and "nous en France nous ne nous appelons plus lesbiennes, parce que c'est un mot négatif et péjoratif"[10] (106). At this, Monique Wittig is supposed to have stood up and directly challenged Cixous in an explosive confrontation: "Ceci est un scandale, qui ça, 'nous en France,' qui ça?"[11] (106). Dialogue collapsed.

Brossard intervenes in this debate in two texts in particular, "De radical à intégrales" (1982) and *Picture Theory* (1982). Ignoring all conflicts of personalities and power, she addresses the substantive and philosophical issues. The impact of her intervention is a positive one: to reinstate all three words, "femme," "féministe" and "lesbienne," and make them available for feminist thought.

"De radical à intégrales" was first presented at "L'émergence d'une culture au féminin," a conference held at the University of Montreal in 1982. The title of the essay epigrammatically narrates a movement from the masculine singular "radical" to the feminine plural "intégrales." "Radical" signifies, among other things, the radical feminist who gets to the root of women's oppression and eventually becomes part of a collectivity of women who are whole people, no longer divided against themselves. This utopian direction is dialectically represented as a process rather than an either/or choice. Brossard thus responds to *Psych et Po*'s 1979 slogan, "Nous nous sommes libérées de l'oppression"[12] (Le Doeuff, 106), which implies that women can just choose to be "intégrales." In "De radical à intégrales," Brossard indicates some of the obstacles to such choice, noting that dominant values are able to normalize meaning and thus control eccentricity or transgression (88; see also Chamberlain, 111).

Brossard represents patriarchal control as a circle, signifying the closure of binary oppositions such as inside/outside, centre/margin and sense/nonsense (101). As Cixous had observed in *La jeune née* (1975), the feminine traditionally aligns with the negative term: she is outside,

---

10 We in France no longer call ourselves feminists because we have abandoned this negative point of view. We in France no longer call ourselves lesbian because it is a negative and pejorative word" (my translation).

11 This is a scandal! Who is this "we in France"? Who is this? (my translation).

12 We have freed ourselves from oppression (my translation).

she is nonsense. Therefore, Brossard's initial proposition is a pun—women must make sense. She writes, "affirmer l'émergence d'une culture au féminin dans le contexte des millénaires et au présent d'une civilisation patriarcale est un projet que je ne saurais envisager autrement qu'autour d'une seule expression: *faire sens*"[13] (88). Her double use of "sens" as both sensation and meaning is conceptually carried over into the idea of an embodied feminist practice of building culture in the feminine (*au féminin*) by making sense. Making sense implicates language and writing. For writing that makes sense, Brossard uses the expression "écriture au féminin," reminiscient of, but distinct from, Cixous's "écriture feminine." The meaning of the expression "au féminin" is explored more fully in chapter 2 and again in chapter 12.

The question, then, becomes how to make sense (*faire sens*) of the problematic word "woman." Brossard first confirms the French critique, demonstrating that "woman" is indeed a word with roots deep in patriarchal soil. Acknowledging both *Psych et Po* and *Questions féministes* by citing Jacques Lacan *and* Simone de Beauvoir, she moves beyond the binary logic of the split by agreeing with and then rejecting both authorities:

> Entre la phrase de Simone de Beauvoir "On ne naît pas femme: on le devient" et celle de Jacques*: "La femme n'existe pas," l'effet sémantique du mot femme nous permet de penser que dans un cas comme dans l'autre, parler de *la* femme ne saurait être adéquat qu'en un lieu dit de fiction. . . . Pourtant, si le contenu de ces deux affirmations semble concorder, "la femme est une fiction," il en va tout autrement de ce qui les a produites. Alors que l'énoncé de Simone de Beauvoir est le fruit d'une recherche qui aboutit au douloureux constat de la non-existence de l'être femme, l'énoncé de Jacques est la répétition d'une formule politique ayant fait ses preuves, soit la fortune des maîtres.
>
> Femme, à sens unique, serait donc un mot sans autre racine que patriarcale. Or, à la racine des mots, il y a ce que nous croyons être.[14] (89)
> * Lacan

---

13 To attest to the emergence of . . . a female culture in the context of millennia and the present patriarchal civilization, is a project I can only envision around a single expression: *to make sense* (103).

14 Between Simone de Beauvoir's expression, "One is not born a woman, one becomes one" and Jacques' [Jacques Lacan, French psychoanalyst and theoretician] "Woman does not exist," the semantic effect of the word *woman* allows us to think that, one

Brossard examines three statements a woman might make concerning her rapport with the word "woman": "une femme est un homme, une femme est une femme, une femme, c'est moi"[15] (92-93). The synonymous statement, "une femme est un homme," invokes the masculine generic. While making it possible for a woman to participate in society, this statement avoids recognition that she is not a man. In choosing this path, she internalizes a contradiction. The polysemic solution, "une femme, c'est moi," expresses a strictly individual attitude. This option too refers back to a masculine generic that provides the epistemological ground for the subjectivity and being of a woman who refuses to identify as a woman. The third possibility, "une femme est une femme," is a tautology tending towards a biological or essentialist definition of "woman." All three of these statements converge in what Brossard, elaborating the polyvalence of "sens," and possibly also thinking of Luce Irigaray, whose *Ce sexe qui n'en est pas un* was published in 1977, refers to as "sens unique," or one-way meaning (93). She asks, "Qui donc étant femme voudrait prendre le risque d'être femme, c'est-à-dire une fiction dont elle ne serait pas à l'origine"[16] (94). It would seem that "woman" is a word that cannot be used.

This is the moment of Brossard's most elegant play. Neither embracing nor rejecting the word "woman," she focuses on the non-sense created by the tautology, "une femme est une femme." The redundancy and the lack of meaning that characterize this expression make it susceptible to the interventions of radical feminist consciousness: in defiance of patriarchal logic, some women claim full humanity as women in solidarity with the common cause of women who are denied full humanity. "On les appelle féministes radicales et leur humanité se trouve justement là, dans la conquête qu'elles font mot à mot, corps à corps, de *l'être*

---

way or the other, to speak of *woman* is something which is appropriate only in a so-called fictional environment or, to return to the etymological sense of the word *fiction*, in a realm of pretence and deceit. If the content of these two affirmations seems to be in agreement, "woman is a fiction," those who produced them certainly are not. While Simone de Beauvoir's statement is the product of a search ending in the painful recognition of the non-existence of woman as being, Jacques' statement is the repetition of a proven political formula; men's good fortune proves it.

Woman, in the one-way sense, would thus be a word having only a patriarchal root. For there, at the root of words, lies what we believe exists (104).

15 a woman is a man, a woman is a woman, a woman is what I am (107).

16 What woman would want to take the risk of being a woman, a fiction she did not originate? (109).

femme"[17] (95). Furthermore, in intervening around the word "woman," radical feminists "ont alors mis le doigt sur le bouton qui donne accès à la magie des mots"[18] (95).

"The magic of words" is a metaphor for the general excitement of "sens," which is produced by women's collective divergence from "le sens unique." "Le sens unique oscille sous un déferlement continue de mots allant dans toutes les directions"[19] (96). The oscillation of meaning is preparatory to a critical development that Brossard names "l'éclat du sens"[20] (95). This "éclat" shatters the masculine generic and breaks open the circle of femininity. Breaking with Aristotelian logic at the line of demarcation where women are named as a gender or class, the non-sense of "une femme est une femme" creates a paradoxical semantic vacancy, a free zone full of potential for actual human beings who are women. In *Picture Theory*, this vacancy, or "vacance," is represented as an island vacation.

In Brossard's thought, then, the effort to make sense of the word "woman" leads to a strategy of feminist semantics which is philosophically and politically distinct from the orientation, shared by both French tendencies, towards lexical purification by elimination. Semantic deviation is at the heart of Brossard's feminist theory. Like *Psych et Po*, she will criticize the idea that radical feminist consciousness is created by a shared focus on women's oppression; for example, in "Mémoire: hologramme du désir," she argues that a collective deviation away from "le sens unique" and towards meaningful experience is what characterizes radical feminist consciousness.

Brossard writes that an imaginary territory in which women's energies can begin to take form "serait . . . constitué de la subjectivité féminine traversée par une conscience féministe"[21] (98). The notion of a field traversed by another energy brings into play an intertext reaching to Wittig, on one hand, and to the holographic language of the human brain, on the other. In a widely admired passage in *Les guérillères*, Wittig wrote of the

---

17 We call them radical feminists and their humanity is found precisely there, in the conquest they make, word by word, body to body, of the being, *woman* (109).

18 women who are radical feminists put their finger on the button which gives access to the magic of words (109).

19 "One-way thinking" falters under a continuous onslaught of words going off in all directions (111).

20 The explosion of sense (110).

21 This territory would thus be constituted by female subjectivity traversed by a feminist consciousness (113).

impact of patriarchal language on reality: "il n'y a pas de réalité avant que les mots les règles les règlements lui aient donné forme"[22] (192). Women, she thought, must work on every word: "le vocabulaire de toutes les langues est à examiner, à modifier, à bouleverser de fond en comble, que chaque mot doit être passé au crible"[23] (192). A "crible" is a "screen" in the sense of a sieve or a sorter. In *Picture Theory*, Brossard translates Wittig's "crible" into English, the idiom of Hollywood, so that it appears exclusively as "screen." This polyvalent screen is critical to the production of the hologram, created by recording, on a screen, the interference patterns of two interacting wave fronts (see Caulfield). Neuropsychologist Karl Pribram writes that the process of hologram formation resembles the neuropsychological process through which we experience changes in consciousness and brain modification through experience, i.e., memory. The technology of hologram production parallels the mechanisms necessary for semantic deviation which liberates "the magic of words."

Although *Picture Theory* often seems to be "listening" to Wittig, it would be a mistake to think that Brossard took sides in the French feminist conflict. *Psych et Po* is also integrated into the hologram, if in no other way than by Brossard's insistence on her right to use the word "femme." A more subtle integration is suggested by the dreamy accent which falls on particular words and phrases, suggesting the style and the characteristic preoccupations of *des femmes en mouvements*. For example, in a text from *des femmes* titled "Pour la première fois, peut-être, en vacances," we read of the vacationing women: "c'est toujours à table, qu'éclatent les plus beaux fou-rires"[24] (42-43). In *Picture Theory*, the motif of the vacationing women around the table is a basic element of the narrative grammar. The word *travesti* occurs in *Picture Theory* (97) and in *Le quotidien des femmes* (lundi 3 mars 1975, n.p.); the phrase, *pour la première fois*, in *Picture Theory* (82), and in "Pour la première fois, peut-être, en vacances"; the theme of torture in *Picture Theory* (39) and in *Le quotidien des femmes* (*mai* 1978). *Picture Theory* signifies a "synthèse" (92) of Western culture with feminist consciousness, and *Psych et Po* are not left out. Rather, the book incorporates the opposing

---

22 there is no reality before it has been given shape by words rules regulations (134).
23 the vocabulary of every language is to be examined, modified, turned upside down . . . every word must be screened (134).
24 It is always around the table that the most beautiful, the wildest laughter, breaks out. (My translation.)

parties into the picture/hologram of "la femme intégrale" who can no longer be divided against herself.

It is difficult to evaluate the pragmatic effect that Brossard's texts could have had, but, in any case, it does not seem that either *Picture Theory* or the more accessible "De radical à intégrales" was fully read either in the United States or in France. A truncated version of French feminism has maintained international credibility, notwithstanding the fact that it has been historicized within a homophobic framework which erases or minimizes the contributions of materialist feminism and which omits any mention at all of radical lesbians. Toril Moi, for example, excludes Wittig as a feminist theorist on the grounds that hers is lesbian theory (86). Moi does not acknowledge that the lesbian strategy articulated by Monique Wittig is developed unequivocally within the context of the materialist feminist theory of the oppression of all women. Wittig is included in the 1991 collection of interviews edited by Alice Jardine and Anne Menke, *Shifting Scenes: Interviews on Women, Writing, and Politics in Post-68 France*; however, that collection reproduces the split in French feminism in the form of a blank which appears on the page when Wittig "[chooses] not to answer" the question "Is it valid/of value to write as a woman, and is it part of your writing practice today?" (193). A footnote directs us to Wittig's "The Straight Mind," the essay in which she distinguishes between lesbians and women. In this way, the editors censor the materialist feminist theory which proposed lesbianism as a strategy to resist women's exploitation. Whether one is in agreement with the theory or not, to censor it is to destroy the possibilities of feminist thought.

The erasure of key words and concepts such as "woman," "lesbian" and "feminist" from a discourse as influential as that of French feminism could only have had negative effects. On the political front, there is no doubt that whenever lesbianism and feminism have gone their separate ways, both have suffered and the women's movement has lost many— perhaps the majority—of its most hardworking and serious activists. This fact alone can largely explain the weakness of the women's movement in France. But Brossard's philosophy is more profound than any purely strategic consideration could ever be. She intervenes against mental censorship or authoritarian intervention into "la pensée." In "De radical à intégrales," she theorizes an end to women's marginality in Western culture, and in *Picture Theory* she constructs a virtual reality on the basis of this theory. Rewriting the Dantesque tradition of the spirit's journey towards the rose of paradise, Brossard universalizes a lesbian perspective, as Wittig argues we must. Unlike Wittig, however, Brossard maintains that lesbians are women, for example when M.V., the narrator of *Picture Theory*, affirms in these terms her profound sexual, intellectual and spiritual rapport with her lover: "j'étais dans l'expression de l'utopie une femme touchée par l'apparence d'une rose"[25] (88).

"Woman" and "lesbian" are words full of consequences, to paraphrase *L'amèr* (53), and as such they constitute an important *topos* for the renewal of feminist theory. On the other hand, if Canadian feminist theory has been renewed since the early 1980s, it has not been in response to the debate over lesbianism, which remains outstanding, nor has it been in relation to French feminist theory. Our catalysts for change have been the struggles and the ideas activated around "race," "marginality," "difference." It is in the context of a Canadian feminist response to racism that Daphne Marlatt's feminist *praxis* has been most audacious.

In her texts of the mid-1980s such as *Touch to My Tongue* (1984) and *Double Negative* (with Betsy Warland, 1988), Marlatt welcomes French feminist theory.[26] Julia Kristeva's *Desire in Language*, for example, is cited in "Musing with Mothertongue" to explore women's gendered rapport with language. Marlatt's feminist readings supplement her earlier inflections of Black Mountain, Francis Ponge, Malaysia and collaborative writing. During this period, she also learns from the anti-racism activists within the women's movement. As Lorna Weir notes, the 1980s produced in Canada "a leadership layer of feminists of colour" who provoked "a sustained, intra-feminist concern with the race politics of the Canadian women's movement" (20). Among feminist readers internationally, the furor provoked by texts such as Moraga and Anzaldúa's *This Bridge Called My Back* (1981) and Beck's *Nice Jewish Girls* (1982) nourished widespread awareness that "an effective lesbian politics will have to be based on diversity and multiplicity, not on a sameness that melts all women down into one mold" (Zimmerman, 676). The feminist utopianism of the late 1970s, with which Brossard and Wittig were associated, was criticized during these years for its idealist vision of a "lesbian nation" in the place of sustained struggle to "transform the social and political structures of a capitalist patriarchy" (Zimmerman, 675). While Marlatt tends to recuperate some of the early lesbian idealism, for example, when she talks about the importance of living in lesbian community,

---

25 i was a woman touched by the appearance of a rose in Utopia's expression (64).
26 See "When We Change Language . . ." for Marlatt's own reflections on her feminist influences.

she also expresses her hope that "there will be other women who join us
so that the dialogue can grow" (Wright, 5). Her political work demonstrates that this hope is more than a pious wish.

In 1988, as the Ruth Wynn Woodward Chair of Women's Studies at
Simon Fraser University, Marlatt organized a feminist conference which
ambitiously attempted to generate a discourse linked to real communities, on one hand, and engaged with the three explosive *topoi* of
"woman," "lesbian" and "race," on the other. Marlatt envisioned the
conference as

> communities-(in the plural)-focused. Limited in size, yet aspiring to
> showcase the writing and thought of women who are marginalized in
> different ways, it drew on the three largest groups of marginalized
> women in British Columbia . . . Native Indian, Asian-Canadian and
> lesbian communities. . . . It was designed to be a celebration of the
> work by these writers—work which i felt to be ground-breaking in
> different but related ways—and a space for dialogue between them
> and their audiences. (*Telling It* 12)

The conference was oxymoronic; created to recognize diversity and difference among women while bringing them together, it would follow up
on important discussions of racism and cultural appropriation which took
place at the Third International Feminist Book Fair in Montreal in 1987,
and it would also challenge the invisibility of lesbians within the women's
movement. This was critical, since, as Marlatt wrote,

> discussion . . . seemed long overdue about difference on several
> crucial rift-lines, not the least of which are the rifts of race and sex-
> ual orientation. . . . Bringing women together in the same room
> implied a hope that our differences were not completely unbridge-
> able, that women with dissimilar, even unequal experiences of
> oppression, might be able to speak openly and hear each other other
> openly, might even (and this was a wilder hope) find some sense of
> shared ground to enable us to help each other in our struggle
> against the forces of a society that continues to marginalize us.
> (*Telling It* 12-13)

Remarkably, the conference succeeded in "carry[ing] the dialogue one
step further" (17), as she hoped it would, through *Telling It: Women and
Language Across Cultures*, the memoir and proceedings edited by Marlatt
with Sky Lee, Lee Maracle and Betsy Warland.

The book testifies to the humanity of the editors and other conference
participants who struggled to speak honestly to each other in a context of

feminist solidarity without hiding or glossing over racism and homophobia. Lee Maracle, in "Ramparts Hanging in the Air," makes it clear that
nothing less was (and is) demanded; in any case, we have only just
begun. We cannot yet answer the question: how do we, or should we, dis-
entangle the interconnected layers of sexism, racism and homophobia in
order to fight effectively against gender oppression which exists in so
many different forms and in virtually all human cultures? For this much
seems clear: that although various languages and cultures produce gender differently, something like "patriarchy" is a cross-cultural phenomenon. Audre Lorde put it like this: "the oppression of women knows
no ethnic nor racial boundaries . . . but that does not mean it is identical
within those boundaries. . . . [T]o imply . . . that all women suffer the
same oppression simply because they are women, is to lose sight of the
many varied tools of patriarchy" (101).

To argue in these terms requires a working definition of "patriarchy."
In my study, patriarchy is defined structurally as a semiotic/social/cul-
tural typology that categorizes people according to a binary gender opposition itself aligned with other cultural oppositions and in which the male
term is privileged. Of course other definitions of patriarchy are possible;
a compelling historical definition of European patriarchy is suggested by
the archaeological record, and in particular by the work of Marija
Gimbutas. Historical and structuralist definitions of patriarchy are both
congruent with the feminist conviction that patriarchy, like racism, is a
complex but identifiable historical phenomenon that can be changed.

It is not necessary to discard or reinvent feminism in order to avoid
gender essentialism. Many feminists have developed personal analyses of
gender not as biological or metaphysical essence but as the complex sum
of signifying processes suffusing, as Judith Lorber and Susan A. Farrell,
the editors of *The Social Construction of Gender* (1991) write, "all
aspects of our lives" (9). It is broadly understood, as well, that language—all languages—viewed as discourse, grammar or narrative, are
key producers of gender, and that the writing woman, whatever her race
or sexual orientation, is also constituted by a milieu in which gender is
encoded among the multiple exchanges that govern her psyche, physiol-
ogy and language. Insofar as the gender system in which she lives is a
patriarchal one, she will find herself positioned as symbolically less than
fully human, and her response will be inscribed in some way in her writing. Many feminist writers have theorized writing and gender without
posing gender as a biological or metaphysical essence. Hélène Cixous

does it herself when she theorizes "une ecriture marquée" (*RM* 42)[27] (1981, 249). In her authoritative 1984 study, *Alice Doesn't: Feminism, Semiotics, Cinema*, Teresa de Lauretis locates gender unequivocally within a semiotic field at the same time that she uncovers and critiques the formal complicity between basic European narrative structures and m/f gender. Daphne Marlatt's *How Hug a Stone* and Nicole Brossard's *Picture Theory* were written in full awareness of feminist writing theory. Both texts, to a certain extent, begin but do not end, just there.

---

27   a marked writing (249).

CHAPTER 2

Theories of the (Masculine) Generic

> Patriarchal Poetry is the same as Patriotic poetry
> is the same as patriarchal poetry is the same as
> Patriotic poetry is the same as patriarchal poetry
> is the same.
> Patriarchal poetry is the same.
> — Gertrude Stein, *Bee Time Vine and*
> *Other Pieces*

WRITING IN THE FEMININE can be accurately defined as writing that encodes a feminine generic. Unfortunately, the usefulness of this definition is limited in that it requires answers to two questions: what is the meaning of *feminine*, and what is the meaning of *generic*? It has become important to specify that *feminine*, in this formula, does not signify the "always already other" of patriarchal discourse, nor the passivity, hysteria or lace often associated with the word. Rather, *feminine* here refers to the perspective of human beings located by culture on the female side of the gender divide; it is a question of language generated by women. Generic, too, is a word that means different things to different people; we can speak of generic fiction, generic drugs and generics in computer programming. I am using the term in its grammatical sense, referring to the principle of the masculine generic whereby masculine pronouns and nouns take precedence over their feminine counterparts which they theoretically include. It has been widely observed that the supposed universality of the grammatical masculine generic extends far beyond sentence grammar to govern gender structures in discourses of all kinds. This sense of the term generic is the starting point for a broader analysis of the rapport between language and privilege outlined in this chapter.

Some readers might feel that since *How Hug a Stone* and *Picture Theory* explore the generic in relation to gender, and not in terms of other forms of social privilege, that I digress when I discuss the generic in

23

terms of culture, "race" and (dis)ability. In response to this anticipated perception, I would say that it is impossible to understand the generic if it is conceived strictly in terms of gender. Generic theory is a good example of the ways that feminist theory can expand into interdisciplinary discourses and domains.

Joanna Russ's "What Can a Heroine Do? Or Why Women Can't Write" (1972) is an early and astute commentary on the difficulty of writing in the feminine, although she does not use the term. Russ switches the gender-assignment in a variety of popular plots, revealing them to be unusable from the perspective of a feminist writer. Today, the plots she generates seem less outrageous: "a young girl in Minnesota finds her womanhood by killing a bear" (3), for example, will encounter readerly resistance more likely for environmental reasons than because of gender. Taken together, however, they still demonstrate that we can not create a feminine generic by renaming our characters or changing the words *he* and *man* to read *she* and *woman*, although that strategy is sometimes useful and amusing. The creation of a feminine generic is more complex.

How *do* we create a feminine generic, and what is formally innovative about a text written in the feminine? Before we can answer these questions, we must look again at the structures of the grammatical generic. Although theories of the (masculine) generic have received quite a bit of attention since the late 1960s, it is my contention that we have not finished learning about them yet.

Louky Bersianik, Benoîte Groult, Deborah Cameron and Denis Baron are among the many writers who have analyzed the ways in which both English and French are sexist, privileging the male over the female and producing binary, patriarchal gender as our daily fare. Breakthroughs in feminist linguistics have revised traditional views that saw linguistic gender as "fictitious[1] or "natural"[2] but, in either case, unproblematic. Today

---

1 Du point de vue de sens, le genre constitue . . . un "sexe fictif" (Chevalier et al., 164). From the point of view of meaning, gender constitutes a fictitious sex. (My translation.)

2 Thomas Wilson, writing in the sixteenth century, argues that gender in English should reflect both the division of animals into male and female and the natural superiority of the male: "Some will set the carte before the horse, as thus. My mother and my father are both at home, euen as thoughe the good man of the house ware no breaches, or that the graye Mare were the better Horse. And what thoughe it often so happenenth (Got wotte the more pitye) yet in speakinge at the leaste, let vs kepe a natural order, and set the man before the woman for maners sake" (189; cited in Baron, 3).

it is recognized that gender systems in language articulate semantic typologies of reality and are, therefore, enormously influential. As Greville Corbett concludes in his 1991 study, "the relations between language gender, sex and the perception of attributes are much more complex than is usually assumed" (96).

By the early 1980s, feminist linguistics had mounted a vigorous attack on lexical assymetry: the number and virulence of negative words for women, the lack of honourable job titles for women and the suppression or distortion of gynocentric power words such as *clitoris* and *mistress*. The apparent congruence between lexical asymmetry and the effects of the masculine generic (both excluding women from the full range of the human) meant that in a wide variety of creative and scholarly texts, the masculine universal, or generic, was identified as a key target of feminist linguistic reform. Countless handbooks, directed to students, government employees and business people, proposed new job titles and explained how to avoid the extremes of sexist language which follow from the use of *he* and *man* to represent the human race.[3] The widespread response to the feminist theory of the masculine generic and to the feminist campaign for more adequate job titles demonstrates that, to a significant extent, these analyses were successful and correct. As a result of them, language practices have evolved.

In the early years of the feminist campaign for linguistic reform, the structures of the masculine generic were the object of real debate. One key article of the period is Maria Black and Rosalind Coward's "Linguistic, Social and Sexual Relations: A Review of Dale Spender's *Man Made Language*" (1981), in which the authors reorganize the terms of the debate over the masculine generic. Dale Spender, following Julia (Penelope) Stanley, had theorized a "negative semantic space" accruing to women in language, and in a theoretical move which was congruent with the notion of the phallus as a symbolically positive element, Spender had formalized gender opposition in language as "plus or minus male" (19-20). Black and Coward, and, shortly afterwards, Monique Wittig (in "The Mark of Gender"), argued convincingly that, on the contrary, the correct paradigm for gender opposition in language is the traditional one of [+−female], because it is a question of a standard, binary, linguistic opposition between a marked and an unmarked term. The unmarked term

---

3 See Miller and Smith (1980), Katz (1981), Dumond (1984), Martin and Dupuis (1985), The Province of British Columbia (1991, 1992), Labrosse (1996).

is the default, corresponding to the generic, or universal; the female is the marked term. They clarified that the female is always marked for gender, and only male human subjects have access to the unmarked generic.

Black and Coward also make the critical point that generic function is a discursive function; however, the discursivity of the generic remains less well understood, even today. Many people recognize the masculine generic in a sentence such as "man's vital interests are food, shelter, and access to females," but fail to see it in an expression such as "my neighbour's wife." The mechanism of the generic in fact extends far beyond the use of "he" and "man." The point can be elaborated in relation to the following passages, cited in Cameron (85):

> 1. The lack of vitality is aggravated by the fact that there are so few able-bodied young adults about. They have all gone off to work or look for work, leaving behind the old, the disabled, the women and the children (*The Sunday Times*).
> 2. A coloured South African who was subjected to racial abuse by his neighbours went berserk with a machete and killed his next-door neighbour's wife, Birmingham Crown Court heard yesterday (*The Guardian*).

In the first passage, the functioning of the generic determines that women are not adults. In the second passage, the generic operates twice, once to establish that the generic human is white, thus "a coloured South African," and once to establish that the generic neighbour is male.

A related point, also often overlooked, is the extent to which the generic governs popular, social and legal modes of address. Members of non-generic groups may be quite far along in their reception of a discourse before they discover, perhaps through the generic action of a quite "insignificant" detail, that they are not being addressed. How many proverbial expressions ("wine, women and song") and folksongs ("Yankee Doodle Dandy") exclude women? How many philosophical, political and educational texts address themselves to the generic white or European man? Failure to provide access for people with disabilities characterizes the generic address of much civic architecture. Family rates are for heterosexual couples and children. In all of these examples, the generic is a cultural mechanism which defaults to the "normal," or privileged, term along the axes of gender, race, sexual orientation, (dis)ability and class; it is often independent of grammar, and never limited to gender.

Political discourses on family and disability are part of the public domain, but their modelling in terms of a generic function is not. To identify the operation of a generic in the place of, say, discrimination, sexism or ill will is to move away from a confrontation of essences into a postmodern field of interactive possibility, because the generic in itself is a mechanism, a semiotic technology, which is context-dependent, subject to manipulation and relatively responsive to social pressure. As an analytical paradigm, the generic has the advantage of accuracy; for example, when Anne Cranny-Francis, in her fine study of feminist generic fiction, wonders if "audience is an implicitly (male) gendered concept" (22), we could use a generic model to respond to her question in terms of specific audiences and as a result of specific elements in an artwork's mode of address. A generic model can identify and theoretically, at a future stage of analysis, neutralize a number of common mechanisms for the reproduction of privilege.

Unfortunately, the feminist literature on gender and the generic initially failed to recognize privilege in combination with race, class, sexual orientation and ability. In the texts of the 1960s and 1970s, sexism is denounced almost exclusively from the limited perspective of white, able-bodied, middle-class women, giving rise to faulty and incomplete analyses and political programs badly in need of input from those whose perspectives had been marginalized or excluded.[4]

Writers of colour have exposed the extent to which white supremacy is deeply encoded in language. In a landmark 1989 text, "The Absence of Writing or How I Almost Became a Spy" (*She Tries Her Tongue*), Marlene Nourbese Philip describes the painful relationship between the English language and an African-Caribbean writer working in English. Historically, faced with "the almost complete destruction and obliteration of the African languages," and the "accompanying act of renaming by the European" (15), the African was forced to use English, a language "that even then had affirmed negative i-mages about her, and one which was but a reflection of the European ethnocentric world view" (16). English was radically changed in the process:

---

4 Thanks to Joan Meister and the other builders of the DisAbled Women's Network (DAWN CANADA) for educating us to recognize language which discriminates against people with disabilities.

> In the vortex of New World Slavery, the African forged new and dif-
> ferent words, developed strategies to impress her experience on the
> language. The formal standard language was subverted, turned
> upside down, inside out, and even sometimes erased. Nouns
> became strangers to verbs and vice versa; tonal accentuation took
> the place of several words at a time; rhythms held sway. Many of
> these "techniques" are rooted in African languages; their collective
> impact on the English language would result in the latter being, at
> times, unrecognizable as English. Bad English. Broken English.
> Patois. (17)

The evolution of Caribbean demotic English has meant that contemporary African-Caribbean writers must negotiate a complex route between
the demotic and standard varieties of this language that "was used to
brutalize and diminish Africans so that they would come to a profound
belief in their own lack of humanity" (19). Nourbese Philip argues that a
language which thus dehumanizes its subjects must itself be

> profoundly affected. . . . The challenge, therefore, facing the African
> Caribbean writer who is at all sensitive to language and to the
> issues that language generates, is to use the language in such a way
> that the historical realities are not erased or obliterated, so that
> English is revealed as the tainted tongue it truly is. Only in so
> doing will English be redeemed. (19)

Nourbese Philip's condemnation of English as tainted by racism, colonialism and slavery parallels the feminist linguistic discoveries of the
1960s and 1970s, underlining the fact that both sexism and racism deny
the humanity of some of us in order to increase the privilege of others.
She herself explores the conflation of sexist and racist dehumanization in
her 1989 fiction theory, "Whose Idea Was It Anyway?" Linking the origins of slavery to both sexism and Christianity, the text offers a chilling
insight into the failed imagination of a man who cannot see the humanity
of his lover although she holds their child in her arms. Feminist strategies for accessing full humanity through subjectivity in language have
parallels throughout Caribbean literature, where "the issue of identity
and the quest for wholeness [is] central . . . and a continuing preoccupation of both male and female writers" (Mordecai and Wilson, xv). For the
Caribbean writer, Nourbese Philip proposes a complex articulation of
reality by writing both *in* and *against* the grain of the language, a strategy
which resembles that of feminist writer Louise Cotnoir, for example, who

writes from Québec of women's coming to writing: "s'écrire avec, dans et contre le langage"[5] (1984).

In "Obscuring the Importance of Race: The Implications of Making Comparisons between Racism and Sexism (or Other -isms)" (1995), Trina Grillo and Stephanie M. Wildman argue that from an anti-racism perspective, analogies with sexism are neither compelling nor useful, but, in fact, pernicious, because they obscure the importance of white supremacy. If we "add racism" but stay within the general perspectives of (generic?) feminist theory, the masculine generic is amended to read the masculine, white, able-bodied, bourgeois, heterosexual, and etc. generic—and the urgency of anti-racist theory and practice is lost. While acknowledging the justice of Grillo and Wildman's argument, I think that we (human beings) cannot afford to dispense with the analogy between racism and sexism, and that feminism needs the analogy and the work that has been done concerning racism in language in order to move ahead. With respect to generic theory, analogies between racist and sexist functions are crucial. The encounter with anti-racism produces a potent effect in feminist linguistics and further exposes the mechanisms of the generic.

The critical race theory of Richard Delgado and others has identified, in a wide variety of contexts, the dominance of a white generic in American legal discourse. Generic theory also surfaces in the legal struggle to change established patterns of precedent-determined and default-driven decision making in the Canadian legal system, particularly with reference to the administration of justice in Canada's First Nations communities (see Cayley, 70-89). A comparison of these legal and literary analyses allows us to identify the attributes most often associated with generic functions:

1. the normally binary structure exhibited by generic typologies;
2. the dependence of such typologies on "common-sense" definitions;
3. the invisibility of generic processes from a generic perspective; and
4. the context-dependence of generic attribution.

Along with the overarching issue of access to universal attributes, these four tendencies are generally apparent when generic mechanisms are analyzed.

Unexamined generic function tends to rely on either/or binary typologies such as male/female, white/black or normal/aberrant, in which the

---

5 To write oneself with, in and against the language. (My translation.)

first term is privileged over the second, and the operation of the generic often entails the rigid maintenance of such binary structures. In practice, this translates into a social intolerance for intermediate terms and non-binary typologies, so that actual and variegated typologies of sex and physical features are suppressed. Miscegenation, hermaphroditism and gender variance of any kind (homosexuality, gender performance, trans-gendering) contest the rigid determination of deeply structuring and culturally embedded binary oppositions governing gender and race. In "White by Law" (1995), Ian F. Handy López elaborates the legal intolerance for what he calls "in-between constructions of race" in American law. To this intolerance, we can compare the legal, social and medical intolerance that exists for hermaphroditism and other queer gender identities.

Common sense governs the reproduction and functioning of generic typologies. Handy López also points out that whiteness is legally constructed using "common knowledge" (547) and on the basis of differentiation from what is "non-white" ("white" is what is *not* constructed as "non-white"; "white" is the unmarked term, the default and the generic within European-North American jurisprudence). The analogy with sexism is sound: as Cranny-Francis and others have argued, "common knowledge" is the dominant determinant in social constructions of gender, and in the regulation of the masculine as the generic and universal term in a wide variety of discourses (Cranny-Francis, 10). The disruption, the denaturalization of ordinary, common-sense sexist and racist discourse is a key political task.

The third tendency relates to a specific privilege enjoyed by the unmarked or generic term in such a binary opposition: the privilege to ignore the content of the opposition. The point is made powerfully and practically in both feminist and critical race theory. The privilege to ignore race and/or gender is a (normally unconscious) side effect of basic generic function as it operates in relation to gender and race. From the perspective of the generic term, generic functions are invisible.

Perhaps most important is the fact that the content or coding of the generic term itself is not absolute or "essential," but is context dependent. In the same way that languages exist in relation to speech communities, generic codings exist in relation to the cultural formations that practise them. Ontologically, a generic is the mental representation that comes to mind, unless otherwise specified, for most people in a given cultural formation. Because it is possible to specify otherwise, it is also possible to change the default cultural "settings": for example, at a congress of the Disabled Peoples International, the generic is a person with a disability. The context dependence of the generic has been insufficiently recognized, in spite of the fact that most people experience this context dependency from time to time.

Generic function in itself is neither good nor bad; it has no moral or ethical content. Work in artificial intelligence and language production shows that some kind of generic or default is a necessary mechanism for most communication (see Philip Johnson-Laird). It is both possible and desirable that we develop a clearer understanding of the generic as a semiotic mechanism. Given the considerable force of generic function in structuring all kinds of discourses, the fact that generic content is programmable and context dependent has significant political, legal and social implications, and opens up a variety of research avenues. The question, furthermore, leads to another which is less well understood— that of the typologies or collections of types—archetypes, stereotypes, character types, sexual personae, legal categories of person, citizen, immigrant, refugee, etc.—which inhabit our language and from which choices, generic or otherwise, are made. Like generic functions, functional typologies exercise a powerful and largely unconscious influence in a wide variety of decision-making contexts. They are related to the function of the generic, default or universal, in that typologies are the matrix, context, frame or field within which choices are made.

Black and Coward make an important point about the masculine/feminine gender typology:

> Women are . . . *defined* [by] specifically feminine, and frequently sexual, categories: whore, slag, mother, virgin, housewife. . . . The curious feature is exactly the excess of (sexual) definitions and categories for women. A similar profusion is not found for men, whose differentiation from one another comes not through sexual attributes and status, but primarily through occupation, or attributes of general humanity, eg., decent, kind, honest, strong. (83)

The redundancy of sexual definition adhering to feminine types is tautological—the female types are the types marked for sex, just as racial types are marked for race. This points to the complicity of the principle of the (white, masculine) generic in the construction of the asymmetrical, racist, sexist human typologies which are distributed throughout Western culture and upon which people necessarily draw when they construct mental representations.

This study uses generic theory as a starting point for the analysis both of narrative structures and human types. A long fictional narrative is, among other things, a powerful contextualizer which is able to reprogram the generic content of the character-types inhabiting the fictional world. Narrative itself is the context for a traditional set of types which are determined by their place in conventional quest narrative. These are governed normally by the generic, but are susceptible to disruption, mixed messages and conflictual readings when manipulated with human equality in mind. Writing that provokes contested readings of traditional formulae will disclose the extent to which criticism is also entangled in the reproduction of the status quo, however much it may have striven for objectivity. First, however, we must look at some of the features of narratology, and at the questions posed by both Marlatt and Brossard concerning narrative structures.

CHAPTER 3

Narrative, Gnosis, Cognition, Knowing: Em[+female]bodied[1] Narrative and the Reinvention of the World

A plot is a clearing in the trees.
—Barbara Einzig, The New Poetics Colloquium,
Vancouver, 1985

LANGUAGE AT EVERY LEVEL, from the smallest semantic unit, or seme, to the elaborate achievements of scientific and philosophical discourse, is constitutive of human thought. In the last twenty years, scholars have focused increasingly on the link between cognition and the naturalized linguistic organization we call narrative. An ancient and foundational link between narrative and knowledge is suggested by the etymology of the word "narrative," from the Proto-Indo-European root *gna-*, meaning "to know." Narrative is our quintessential means of organizing, readily transmitting and preserving knowledge, and this may be particularly true of the everyday kind of knowledge that Jerome Bruner calls folk psychology or ethnosociology ("The Narrative Construction of Reality," 21). Clearly narrative must be of special interest to feminism, which takes as its object a domain as subject to popular expertise as is gender. My study deploys both feminist and classical narratology to read Marlatt and Brossard in the light of narrative's role as an "instrument of mind," which both represents and constitutes "reality" (4).

Narratology is an orderly and systematic method of mapping a narrative text, even a large or complex one. Narrative itself is a powerful means of winding together disparate textual elements so organically that efforts to isolate a part will often provoke the appearance of the entire story, revealing the hermeneutic circle that characterizes the relationship between the parts and the whole of any narrative. A narratological reading, on the other hand, is able to reorganize narrative textual space into

---

1 The sign [+female] in this expression indicates the silent gender coding of an operative generic.

discrete zones, themselves composed of typical parts that can be isolated. In this way, narratology constructs frameworks that are useful in the study and comparison of literary texts. Yet, as we shall see, classical narratology cannot be used uncritically, and, surprisingly, proves incapable of accounting for the parent-child relationships integral to *How Hug a Stone*.

The classical narratology I am referring to emerged in the Soviet Union during the heady years after the revolution, when Russian formalist scholars Victor Shlovsky, Boris Tomashevsky and Vladímir Propp collaborated in the structuralist and, as they thought of it, the scientific analysis of the Russian fairy tale. Vladímir Propp's *Morphology of the Folktale* was completed in 1928, but because of Stalinist persecution was not translated or widely read until 1958, when it inspired significant scholarly response from Claude Lévi-Strauss, Claude Brémond, A.J. Greimas and others. Alan Dundes, in the Introduction to the revised English translation of Propp's *Morphology* (1968), reviews the history of the book's reception by European and American scholars who were themselves caught up in the structuralist revision of the human sciences.

As Dundes points out, the earliest narratology was inductive and linear, following "the chronological order of . . . elements in the text as reported from an informant. Thus if a tale consists of elements A to Z, the structure of the tale is delineated in terms of this same sequence" (xi). Propp identifies thirty-one narrative events such as "the hero, unrecognized, arrives home or in another country," "a false hero presents unfounded claims" and "a difficult task is proposed to the hero." These combine to form specific narratives, and are numbered according to their typical order of occurrence. Borrowing the notion of syntax from linguistics as Propp had borrowed the notion of morphology, Lévi-Strauss named this method "syntagmatic" (xi). European structuralist readings, especially those of Lévi-Strauss, Greimas and Brémond, responded to Propp's work by shifting it towards the paradigmatic and deductive methodology inspired by Saussure, and explored by Lévi-Strauss in his "Structural Study of Myth" (1955). Lévi-Strauss himself considered linear sequential structure to be "apparent or manifest content, whereas the paradigmatic or schematic structure is the more important latent content" (xii). The syntagmatic method has left as its permanent heritage the notion of narrative syntax and a typology of recurring narrative functions. The latent, paradigmatic content, as it turns out, appears to have included binary masculine/feminine (m/f) gender.

Roland Barthes's landmark article "Introduction à l'analyse structurale des récits" (1966) redefined narratology as that branch of linguistics able to treat units of language larger than the sentence: "le discours [avec] ses unités, ses règles, sa 'grammaire' "[2] (3). Barthes went on to posit a homological relation between narrative and sentence structure: "le discours serait un grande 'phrase' (dont les unités ne sauraient être nécessairement des phrases), tout comme la phrase, moyennant certaines spécifications, est un petit 'discours' "[3] (3). The homology with the sentence is a recurring element of narratology. Barthes uses it in arguing that just as linguistics reads a sentence at the descriptive levels of phoneme, morpheme and syntax, so narratology reads narrative at various descriptive levels, defining in this way the basic units, rules and grammar of narrative discourse.

The complex relationship between gender, narrative and narratology has often been unacknowledged by the narratologists themselves, even when it seems to be, in part, their construction. For example, in their search for narrative grammar, scholars interpreted narrative events at increasingly abstract levels. While Propp identifies thirty-two narrative functions, Greimas suggests eight, and the paradigmatic method ultimately proposes two: the two terms of a binary structure which represent the idea of an event at its most abstract. The structuralists could have described such a structure in non-gendered terms such as energy/inertia or animate/inanimate, but they did not. Dundes comments, "The hypothetical paradigmatic matrix is typically one in which polar oppositions such as life/death, male/female are mediated" (xii). In "The Origin of Plot in the Light of Typology" (1979), semiotician Jurij Lotman also interprets narrative structure paradigmatically only to discover the familiar form of binary m/f gender:

> The elementary sequence of events in myth can be reduced to a chain: entry into a closed space—emergence from it (this chain is open at both ends and can be endlessly multiplied). Inasmuch as closed space can be interpreted as "a cave," "the grave," "a house," "woman" (and, correspondingly, be allotted the features of darkness, warmth, dampness) (Ivanov and Toporov, 1965), entry into it is interpreted on various levels as "death," "conception," "return home," and so on; moreover all these acts are thought of as mutually identical. (168)

---

2 discourse [with] its units, its rules, its "grammar" (83).

3 a discourse is a long "sentence" (the units of which are not necessarily sentences), just as a sentence, allowing for certain specifications, is a short "discourse" (83).

Lotman's plot typology, implicating both a theoretical model for the origin of culture and a structuralist analysis of plot types, has been extremely suggestive for feminist theory.

The structuralists' formulation of the mythical structure of narrative as a dynamic model rather than as a sequence of functions led them, as Dundes notes, to "an *a priori* principle of opposition" (xi); from a contemporary perspective it appears that they uncritically imported binary structures such as m/f gender into their analyses. Binary gender, however, was already there. Dundes points out that Propp's first function, "One of the members of a family is absent from home," and the thirty-first or last, "The hero is married and ascends the throne," together indicate the reformation of an "old nuclear family" (xiii) and the foundation of a new one: "fairy tale structure has something to do with marriage" (xiii). Feminist theory reads this point to mean that binary gender is foundational to Indo-European stories—whether the prince seeks a princess or the farmer takes a wife, he is the subject and she the object in these tales.

Feminist narratology must be aware of its agenda for social change, but classical narratology aspired to be a neutral, analytical tool, and it is in that spirit that the method is codified by Mieke Bal, in *Narratology: Introduction to the Theory of Narrative* (1985). My study follows Bal's methodology throughout, except where it is supplemented or contested by feminist narrative theory. If narratology can at times provide a critical prism that permits us to read the narrative traces of European patriarchy, it is not in one giant debunking but in a series of context-dependent readings. Patriarchal m/f gender is produced as meaning in countless ways in myriad contexts, and its deconstruction and displacement is equally dispersed. In this sense, narratology is an invaluable aid in mapping a seemingly endless terrain and managing a theoretically endless interpretive task.

By the early 1980s, as Jonathan Culler has noted, researchers working in a variety of traditions and languages had defined the units of narrative grammar differently and assigned terms that are not globally consistent (169-70). Bal's book clarifies terms and definitions for the parts of narrative, and describes narratological method in a logical way without neglecting the rich history of certain aspects of narrative theory. She describes narrative texts on the three levels of FABULA, STORY and TEXT. For the critical distinction between the story as a series of events and the story as reported in the narrative, Bal suggests "fabula" and "story," where Culler would speak of "story" and "discourse." In her use of these terms, Bal follows Tomashevsky, who, in 1925, carefully distinguished between fabula and story (*sjuzet*).

Fabula is the narratological term for the underlying sequence of events conceived abstractly and arranged in chronological order: the deep narrative structure at its most abstract. Narrative event or events are the primary components of any fabula, and since an event must happen to someone somewhere, event implicates actor(s), time and location. Defined by Bal as "a transition from one state to another state, caused or experienced by actors" (*N* 13), event—and thus, transformation—is the essence of fabula.

In order to determine fabula events, a reader can generate a one-sentence summary of the narrative or ask other readers to write short summaries and then select what they have in common. This intuitive approach is based on the resemblance between sentence and fabula structure. Narrative grammar is imagined as homologous to sentence grammar, with its nominative subject and verbal predicate governed by grammatical rules of combination. Bal summarizes narratological theory on this point, citing Gérard Genette, who describes narrative as "le développement, aussi monstrueux qu'on voudra,"(75)[4] of the verb. Here is Genette:

> *Je marche, Pierre est venu*, sont pour moi des formes minimales de récit, et inversement *l'Odyssée* ou la *Recherche* ne font d'une certaine manière qu'amplifier (au sens rhétorique) des énoncés tels qu'*Ulysse rentre à Ithaque ou Marcel devient écrivain*. Ceci nous autorise peut-être a organiser, ou du moins à formuler les problèmes d'analyse du discours narratif selon des catégories empruntées à la grammaire du verbe.[5] (75)

Bal clarifies this point: "the correspondence . . . between the sentence and the fabula rests upon a common *logical* basis . . . logical principles of construction familiar to us from sentence analysis" (*N* 11-12). Sentence logic refers us to the familiar world of subjects and objects, actions and people or things acting or acted upon.

---

4 the development—monstrous, if you will (30).

5 *I walk, Pierre has come* are for me minimal forms of narrative, and inversely the *Odyssey* or the *Recherche* is only, in a certain way, an amplification (in the rhetorical sense) of statements such as *Ulysses comes home to Ithaca* or *Marcel becomes a writer*. This perhaps authorizes us to organize, or at any rate to formulate, the problems of analyzing narrative discourse according to categories borrowed from the grammar of verbs (30).

In the narrative sentence a SUBJECT ACTANT corresponds to the sentence subject, or noun, and the OBJECT ACTANT, or goal, corresponds to the sentence object. The subject's movement towards the object is helped or hindered by an OBSTACLE ACTANT and a HELPER ACTANT, and the whole is framed by a POWER ACTANT and RECEIVER ACTANT, who contextualize the narrative. These three binary pairs, subject/object, helper/obstacle and power/receiver, compose the six terms of narrative grammar. Formulated as a paradigmatic narrative sentence in which a subject seeks an object, they form the fabula structure of the QUEST.

Quest structure is the normal fabula structure of the fairy tale, romance, *Bildungsroman*, love story, tale of adventure or detective thriller; the quest occurs as well in non-fiction, biography, autobiography and even in how-to books which cast the reader as the subject-hero and the desired set of skills as the goal. Perhaps because of its ubiquity, or perhaps on the premise that human behaviour is essentially goal oriented, scholars claimed universal validity for the narrative grammar of the quest (*N* 26). However, it is important to remember that the fairy-tale fabula, described by the Russian formalists and refined by Brémond and Greimas, was the initial model for this grammar. As a narrative grammar, the quest is historically and structurally related to the fairy-tale fabulas which were the objects of Vladímir Propp's early narratology and which, as Dundes noted, have something to do with (patriarchal) marriage.

The second register of narratological analysis is that of story. Major contributions to the analysis of story have been made by Wayne Booth (1983) and Gérard Genette (1980). Story is the particular presentation of fabula in a given narrative; it includes characterization and plot. At the story level, events are arranged for story tension based on psychological development, flashbacks, foreshadowings and so on. At the story level, a fabula is endowed with symbolic and cultural specificity. Insofar as fabula events are temporally reordered, we can speak of an artistic tension between story time and fabula time. Story is also the register of FOCALIZATION. Focalization is the term by which narratology designates the sensory, emotional or mental focus of a narrative; a narrative fabula is focalized through the experience of one or more characters through whom the reader experiences the fabula events. The focalizer may or may not be the narrator, and may or may not be the subject or protagonist of the fabula events. Focalization varies in intensity and completeness.

Bal's narratology differs from Tomashevsky's in the addition of the third descriptive level, that of the text. Text is the level of locution, or words narrated by a narrator. It is also the dominant register of intertextuality. Here Bal's definition of narrative differs also from that of Barthes, who defines narrative as semiotic but not necessarily linguistic, leaving open the possibility of narratological analysis of visual materials such as painting, stained glass and mime (*IASR* 1). In Bal's narratology, narrative is defined by the presence of the three levels of fabula, story and text, and thus by the presence of a narrative agent. In specifying that narrative requires a narrator who is the linguistic subject of the language of the text, Bal points to the narrative construction of subjectivity through the deictic presence of a narrator (*N* 119). This proves to be a particularly interesting point for feminist narratology.

Today, when claims to objectivity are displaced everywhere by studies of situated knowledge, it is clear that narratology has at times mistaken its own cultural codes for the universal. The biases of European patriarchy are wound into narratology's theory that the quest is a universal narrative structure, and its discovery that at the most abstract level of story, women are matrices and objects rather than subjects. Such mistakes, particularly when combined with the growing recognition of narrative's cognitive and social role in the construction and maintenance of a human universe, have made the tasks of a self-reflexive, feminist and anti-racist narratology particularly critical.

Feminist narrative theory is itself diverse, and susceptible to further theoretical elaboration. The theory of the generic, for example, has a narrative application: the white, masculine generic which functions at the sentence level also governs representations of the narrative subject, as Susan Wolfe's 1980 study of the association between Indo-European action words and the semantic feature [+male] shows. Who doubts that the traditional subject of European action narratives has for many years been a white, able-bodied, heterosexual man? Who doubts the complicity between this deeply naturalized figure and equally naturalized common-sense constructions of superiority according to gender or race? The structural force of the white, masculine generic and the enormous power of narrative to organize reality here combine.

Rachel Blau DuPlessis, in *Writing beyond the Ending* (1985), makes an important contribution to the evolution of feminist narrative theory. She notes that, until the twentieth century, female characters in novels typically ended up married or dead. The novel both reflected and reinforced the reality that successful social integration for women was achieved through marriage. "Once upon a time, the end, the rightful end,

of women in novels was social—successful courtship, marriage—or judg-
mental of her sexual and social failure—death. These are both resolu-
tions of romance" (1). A romantic death such as that of Beth in *Little
Women* is a reasonable alternative to the poverty, dependency or prostitution that confronted many unmarried women. Blau DuPlessis documents
"the project of twentieth-century women writers to solve the contradiction between love and quest and to replace the alternate endings in marriage and death . . . [with] a different set of choices" (4). She relates this
project to the impact of the women's movement in the nineteenth and
twentieth centuries.

Blau DuPlessis represents narrative in Althusserian terms, as a systematic representation through which individuals structure their relationship to cultural values and institutions:

> Narrative . . . is a . . . a special expression of ideology: representa-
> tions by which we construct and accept values and institutions. . . .
> [R]omance plots of various kinds and the fate of female characters
> express attitudes at least toward family, sexuality, and gender. The
> attempt to call into question political and legal forms related to
> women and gender, characteristic of women's emancipation in the
> late nineteenth and twentieth centuries, is accompanied by this
> attempt by women writers to call narrative forms into question. The
> invention of strategies that sever the narrative from formerly con-
> ventional structures of fiction and consciousness about women is
> what I call "writing beyond the ending." (x)

Writing beyond the ending is Blau DuPlessis's metaphor for narratives
that represent new possibilities for women. Virginia Woolf's denunciation
(in "Women and Fiction") of male values in fiction reverberates throughout the book; Blau DuPlessis argues, with Woolf, that writing from a
woman's point of view inevitably involves breaking with traditional values: "trying to make fiction talk about women and their concerns, especially when a woman is the speaking subject, may necessarily lead to a
critical transformation of narrative structures" (56). The changes that she
documents in the novel include the reinterpretation or revision of classical myths, the self-conscious critique of the plot ending in death or marriage and the development of a collective protagonist.

Writing beyond the Ending is an important analysis of twentieth-century women writers' refusal to be complicit with social oppression as codified and reflected in the conventions of romance. However, since Blau
DuPlessis does not make the structuralist distinction between fabula and
story, she conflates to some extent the conventions of the romantic plot

and narrative structure per se. Fabula, or deep narrative structure, is subject to the law of the generic, whereby female characters historically dominate as objects (rewards—the hero marries her), helpers (the fairy godmother) and opponents (the wicked stepmother/witch), and rarely as subjects. In narratological terms, what Blau DuPlessis is suggesting is not that women writers altered narrative structures but that they gave us female narrative subjects who achieved objects such as jobs and rooms of their own. While this is a notable achievement, it leaves the dominant quest narrative structure intact. Structuralist feminist narratology indicates that abstract quest narrative structures codify patriarchal gender: a generically feminine matrix is traversed by a generically masculine hero. This quest structure reproduces m/f gender regardless of whether or not a female character occupies the subject position.

A breakthrough in feminist narrative analysis was made in the early 1980s, when Teresa de Lauretis, reading Jurij Lotman, argued that desire in conventional quest narrative is none other than the Oedipal desire of a male subject who must overcome a generically female obstacle or narrative matrix in order to achieve masculine identity. In *Alice Doesn't*, de Lauretis uses semiotic and Freudian theory to contend that all quest narratives are governed by an Oedipal desire. She reminds us that Freud interpreted the Oedipal narrative to be productive of human subjectivity; everybody passes through it and is thereby produced as a member of society, male or not-male. The Oedipal story is in this sense a paradigm for European patriarchy. The hero, the little boy, quests for and achieves (or fails to achieve) manhood. For the little girl, the same mechanism "works to construct *her* as a 'personified obstacle'" (133). This is the Oedipal logic that de Lauretis discovers to be equally apparent in Lotman's "elementary sequence of events." As I have noted, Lotman's elementary sequence of events consists of entry into a closed space and emergence from it, where the closed space is allotted the archetypal features of darkness, warmth and dampness, and interpreted to mean a cave, grave, house, womb or *woman* (Lotman, 168). De Lauretis argues that if Lotman is correct, then binary m/f gender truly lies at the heart of Western culture, as Lévi-Strauss's work on the incest prohibition also maintains. Lotman's work suggests that the Oedipal narrative is not alone in constructing girls as obstacles instead of human subjects; rather, *all* quest narratives construct girls in this way because the structure requires a generically female matrix. Worse, since narratology interprets the quest as universal, this situation is understood to be "natural" and "real":

male subjectivity is formed in relation to a female matrix, and the process takes place within an ontological hierarchy of male and female which is both metaphysical and essential, existing beyond the realm of human intervention. Of course, feminism rejects this idea, but its existence as a kind of naturalized substratum observable in Western narrative structure does explain why many women and girls find themselves alienated from the building blocks of their own cultures.

In a key passage, de Lauretis teases out the implications: the hero/obstacle opposition is one of the binary oppositions structuring Western culture; in our patriarchal culture, the inherent logic of narrative is patriarchal.

> [T]he hero must be male, regardless of the gender of the text-image, because the obstacle, whatever its personification, is morphologically female and indeed, simply, the womb. The implication here is not inconsequential. For if the work of the mythical structuration is to establish distinctions, the primary distinction on which all others depend is not, say, life and death, but rather sexual difference. In other words, the picture of the world produced in mythical thought since the very beginning of culture would rest, first and foremost, on what we call biology. Opposite pairs, such as inside/outside, the raw/the cooked, or life/death appear to be merely derivatives of the fundamental opposition between boundary and passage; and if passage may be in either direction, from inside to outside or vice versa, from life to death or vice versa, nonetheless all these terms are predicated on the *single* figure of the hero who crosses the boundary and penetrates the other space. In so doing the hero, the mythical subject, is constructed as human being and as male; he is the active principle of culture, the establisher of distinctions, the creator of differences. Female is what is not susceptible to transformation, to life or death; she (it) is an element of plot-space, a topos, a resistance, matrix and matter. (118-19)

The hero/obstacle opposition is basic to the larger cultural system of structuring oppositions such as inside/outside, raw/cooked and life/death, which systematically define "woman." The plot positions, and not simply the characters who occupy those positions, are always already gendered, which means that a female character in the hero's role might be read as hermaphroditic, masculine-feminine, unnatural or androgynous: binary semiosis in conflict. She will not emerge as a female hero without the oxymoron being felt; she will not call up our cultural generic mental representation of "woman."

De Lauretis reworks Lévi-Strauss's contention that the incest prohibition, which he interpreted as the exchange of women, is the principle found at the origin of human culture. "If narrative is governed by an Oedipal logic, it is because it is situated within the system of exchange instituted by the incest prohibition, where woman functions as both a sign (representation) and a value (object) for that exchange" (140). By crossing a frontier and penetrating what was other, the narrative subject is constructed as a human being and male (119).

> The story of femininity, Freud's question [what do women want?], and the riddle of the Sphinx all have a single answer, one and the same meaning, one term of reference and address: man, Oedipus, the human male person. And so her story, like any other story, is a question of his desire: as is the teleology that Freud imputes to Nature, that primordial "obstacle" of civilized man. (133)

In deconstructing the gendered form of narrative which is our Indo-European inheritance, we may better understand the fate of our classical female heroes. In spite of their courage and daring, Eve, Guenevere, Clytemnestra and Medea are represented not as transgressive heroes but as obstacles through which a male hero must pass. Orestes overcomes his mother, Theseus leaves Medea, Everyman must resist the temptation of Eve. Arthur turns a deaf ear to his Queen, who is, furthermore, an obstacle in Lancelot's quest for the Grail. Such stories encode the foundation of patriarchy. It is no accident that Clytemnestra's defeat signals the end of mother-right and the triumph of the patriarchal state. The sign of the woman appears in its classical, fixed position and the male hero progresses to the end of the story.

In the end, de Lauretis comes to the modest conclusion that the "story must be told differently" (156). And stories *are* being told differently, and probably always have been somewhere in the world. My own study demonstrates how profoundly both Marlatt and Brossard contest traditional Western narrative structures. Prehistorical stories were likely structured differently, particularly if non-patriarchal Old European traditions played the foundational role that the archaeological record suggests (see Gimbutas). Lotman's own theory of the origins of narrative provides feminism with a good argument that narrative structures once had a very different, and to us, mysterious, relationship to meaning.

Lotman's discovery of complicity between m/f gender and narrative quest grammar occurs in the context of his theoretical distinction between two proto-plot-types. The first is a non-teleological chronicling of events that are excessive in that they exist outside the integrating framework of a life, season or day; this plot would be a list of miracles, disasters and inexplicable, anomalous events. News, scandals and miracles originate with this type of plot. The more important, mythological type of plot reproduces the cyclical flux of patterned reality exemplified by the rise and fall of days, seasons and life-cycles. This cyclical, mythical plot-type is anterior to true plot, because it does not rest upon opposition between discrete events, but on "the establishment of iso- and homomorphisms and the reduction of the diversity and variety of the world to invariant images" (162). Absolute equivalence is established between parallel events organized topologically:

> such cycles as the day, the year, the cyclical chain of life and death of man [sic] or god, are considered as mutually homomorphous. Thus, although night, winter and death are in some respects dissimilar, their close identification is not a metaphor as the consciousness of today would interpret it. They are one and the same thing (or rather, transformations of one and the same thing). (162)

This mythological mechanism was a way of making sense of the world; Lotman argues that it lies at the origin of human science, categorization, regulation, order and religion. Linear-temporal categories such as beginning and end are not pertinent to this type of mythological text, which interprets life as a recurrent, self-repeating cycle that can be told starting from any point.

Neither of these narrative prototypes displays the supposedly inherent narrative features of binary opposition, goal orientation and teleology. Quest grammar is clearly inapplicable to a series of isomorphic cycles or a list of inexplicable phenomena. While Lotman's mythical type of proto-narrative would have the explanatory power that we associate with narrative, explaining a day, for example, in terms of a year, and a lifetime in terms of a day, it would lack the diachronicity thought to be essential to narrative. The list plot-type lacks explanatory power.

According to Lotman's theory, the birth of modern narrative is an evolutionary landmark marking the beginnings of human culture and taking place at a hypothetical moment existing only in theory. In this view, the mythological, cyclical plot ideal, operating as a moulding force on linear representation of events, results in a manifest plot which has the characteristics of a sentence. This proposes that the Indo-European narrative sentence—the quest—evolved in the context of an isomorphism established between a myth-making cultural mechanism, the narrative structure it engenders, a sentence and a model of the world (173). But, like Lévi-Strauss, Lotman mistakes the origins of Western patriarchy for the origins of human culture per se.

Instead of considering Lotman's plot-types in a chronological framework, we can read them as prototypes for non-binary narrative structures to be explored in relation to contemporary literature. The quest narrative sentence which is their hybrid can then be interpreted as a dominant and successful, but not essential or universal, plot-type. Lotman's model, however, would essentialize gender from the beginning, since the non-particular status that he accords to his elementary sequence of events, and its character as an underlying or structural meaning, is based on a prior privileging of birth as an ur-narrative: the not-yet-human crosses the birth passage and enters the world as a human. Birth, or, more particularly, a certain interpretation of birth, is the passage on which all subsequent rites of passage and initiation are modelled. In this interpretation, woman is not only *not* constructed as mythical subject and human, but is specifically that which remains unmoved, stationary and resistant. She is the other, against which the human subject is defined, the mighty matrix mother hinted at in the etymology from *mater-*, the Proto-Indo-European root of matrix, matter, material and metropolis. The crossing from the womb into the world is the rite of passage into culture. Why are not women thereby constructed as mythical subjects and female? Only because binary patriarchal logic forbids it. The truth of the matter, of course, is that women are born as well.

There is nothing essentially gendered about the crossing of a line, but the binary oppositions naturalized by our culture and by our stories make it seem so. The function of the narrative generic makes it look as if narrative is in league with nature to produce women as passive and men as heroes. The generic as it operates within narrative grammar dictates that a hero overcoming obstacles and achieving goals, unless otherwise marked, is male, white, able-bodied, heterosexual; concomitantly, one of the ways that European culture defines a man is as a generically white, able-bodied, heterosexual hero who overcomes obstacles and achieves goals. Obstacles and goals, unless otherwise marked, are defined as marginal, inhuman, deviant or monstrous; and one of the ways that "female" is defined and socially produced is as an obstacle and/or a goal.

My study follows de Lauretis in interpreting the quest structure itself as a dominant cultural mechanism for the semiotic reproduction of m/f gender, a hierarchical and teleological structure that subordinates other fabula

elements to the *telos* of the generic hero's desire. This is the most fundamental reason why the quest, as our culturally generic narrative sentence,
is such a problematic vehicle for feminist narrative—because telling the
heroic story from woman's point of view is more than a simple reversal, and
a woman slipping to the other side of the [+male]hero/[+female]obstacle
opposition is read as [+male] when the opposition is allowed to remain
intact.

Daphne Marlatt and Nicole Brossard each find ways to deconstruct
the [+male]hero/[+female]obstacle opposition. Feminist poets and
scholars formed within the modern and postmodern poetic traditions, dis-
affected from the sexism of those traditions and the worlds they imagine
and project, both poets were well prepared, by the early 1980s, to
reimagine the narrative *gnosis* which was their inheritance. Both recognize and specify the double bind that the generically female narrative
matrix imposes on women who write.

Brossard develops her theory of gender and narrative in two texts in
particular, *L'amèr* and *Picture Theory*. Louise Dupré points out that
L'amèr, in spite of its difficulty, was widely read and successful when it
first appeared in 1977, precisely because of its timely political protest
against motherhood as defined by a patriarchal system that has no place
for women as fully human subjects in the symbolic field (1988, 7). In
L'amèr, Brossard's writing persona deconstructs narrative grammar in
order to free herself from the belly of the whale:

> S'il n'était lesbien, ce texte n'aurait point de sens. Tout à la fois
> matrice, matière et production. Rapport à. Il constitue le seul relais
> plausible pour me sortir du ventre de ma mère patriarcale. Dis-
> tancer d'elle suffisamment mon regard pour la voir apparaître
> autrement que fragmentée dans ses parties métaphoriques. Tra-
> verser le symbole alors que j'écris. Une pratique de décondition-
> nement qui m'amène à reconnaître ma propre légitimité. Ce par
> quoi toute femme tente d'exister: de plus être illégitime.
>
> La légalité pour une femme serait de n'être pas née d'un ventre
> de femme. C'est ce qui les perd toutes deux.[6] (*L'amèr*, 22)

---

6 If it weren't lesbian, this text would make no sense at all. Matrix, matter and production,
all at once. In relation to. It constitutes the only plausible system to get me out of the
belly of my patriarchal mother. And of distancing my eye from her enough so as to see
her in a different way, not fragmented into her metaphoric parts. Crossing through the
symbol while I am writing. An exercise in deconditioning that leads me to acknowledge
my own legitimacy. The means by which every woman tries to exist: to be illegitimate no
more.

In this angrily rewritten birth ur-narrative, the text itself is a lesbian matrix/mother which enables the writer to access full subjectivity, freeing herself from the patriarchal matrix through a rigorous deconditioning. The lesbian matrix is also the means through which Brossard is able to dislodge the patriarchal generic and its symbols. *L'amèr* thus makes possible the generically female world of *Picture Theory*, which positions itself clearly with respect to traditional narrative grammar by announcing its own creation to be "depuis la mort du héros à double sens patriarcal"[7] (41).

In *How Hug a Stone*, Marlatt thematizes the closure that quest narrative structure enacts on women and girls. She cannily describes the archetypal matrix mother:

> although there are stories about her, versions of history that are versions of her, & though she comes in many guises she is not a person, she is what we come through to & what we come out of, ground & source. the space after the colon, the pause (between the words) of all possible relation. (73)

While acknowledging the mother as matrix, Marlatt disrupts the default operation of binary gender by ensuring that her subjective "we," which comes through the mother, unambiguously includes both women and men. Marlatt constructs a powerfully inclusive human generic in her text.

Her analysis of traditional narrative form is carried further in the ironic representation of Kit's boyish antics as masculine heroics, represented in "on the train," "boy with tape recorder stalking horses in a field of cows:" and "Avebury *awi-spek*, winged from buried (egg." As a child, Kit is unaware of the long cycles of patriarchal history that frame his play in a context immeasurably more powerful than he: "—& small, toy pistol in one hand, cupped, & sheltered by the pelvic thrust of rock, jumps, gotcha mom!" (74). In "Always having to fight Wild Animals" (36), Kit's juvenile behaviour reflects the origins of human culture, now linked to war games which threaten rather than promote human survival: "Nott planning to plug the Faroe gap with *nuclear-powered killer submarines & radar-equipped reconnaissance aircraft*. (getting rid of us)" (48).

Decrying the power of scripts that "write our parts" (73), the narrator meditates on the possibilities of freedom from narrative's determining force.

Legality for a woman: not to be born from the womb of woman. That is what ruins them both (16).

7 since the death of the hero double(d) patriarchal (21).

to be free, have scope, do what you like, go at large, feel at home,
stand on your rights

to feel at home, even on unfamiliar ground, stand on your own (two
feet, two eyes, ears, nose, ten tactile fingers goes where the wind
goes . . .

                    be unnamed, walk
unwritten, de-scripted, un-described. or else compose, make it
say itself, make it up. (35)

Does naming stand in the way of freedom? Is being de-scripted the
same as being unwritten and un-described? Etymologically, to lose
something is to set it free by loosening or uncutting a bond: Proto-
Indo-European *leu-*, "to loosen or cut apart"; cognate to Greek *leuin*,
to loosen, release, untie. If narrative is that paradoxical bond, then to
be without a story is both to be lost and to be set free. The goal is to be
a subject of language, the poem concludes, without sacrificing freedom. She imagines life on the other side of the binary divide.

    In the fear and danger that circulate around the scripts' closure, the
narrator senses her mother's despair and recent death: "where was
she? Tino, my mother, small in a henge of emotion, removed somewhere. no stars to plot this course, only foreboding & hope against her
father's words, against the script. learning how to fly" (45). The henge,
built in relation to more ancient stars, cannot guide. Edrys is associated with the birds of the arché-mother, but like that stone goddess,
she cannot fly. She "had her wings clipped growing up" (67), and the
patriarchal script is what clipped them.

    "Stories can kill" (51)—but more often they simply frame, and
thereby limit, our apprehension of the real. The movie begins, so
"they" pull the blinds, shutting out what doesn't fit into the plot: the
"crazy paving" that is the surface of the earth and the reality of flying.
In rebellion, the narrator articulates their flying—not the Apollonian
version of it, but "with our shit, leftovers, earthladen sacs, thanks to
23,000 gallons of fossil fuel" (15). Unable to do without narrative, the
narrator chooses to invent: "so as not to be lost, invent: one clear act
in all that jazz. (in flight? & if the plane goes down?)" (15). She is
"wanting to make us new again: to speak what isn't spoken, even with
the old words" (73). The desire for a new story about women is the
utopian emotion of *How Hug a Stone*.

Brossard and Marlatt both respond implicitly to Jean François Lyotard's *La condition postmoderne: rapport sur la savoir*, prepared for the government of Québec in 1979. As is well known, Lyotard argues that Western civilizations have traditionally explained life's meaning using two basic narrative forms, or *metanarratives*. The first of these, the liberation of the people, embraces classical heroic ethics, transcendental religions and marxism in all its forms. The second, the perfection of human knowledge, characterizes humanist scholarship and the discourses of science, business and technology. Narratives have always been an important medium of subjective interpellation into ideological systems, but, Lyotard argues, in this postmodern era, our culture's metanarratives are in crisis and have lost their explanatory power.

According to Lyotard, the narrative function has lost "le grand héros, les grands périls, les grands périples et le grand but[8] (7-8). The slippage between Lyotard's *great* hero and Brossard's *patriarchal* hero is a critical one. Brossard's postmodernity conflicts with Lyotard's insofar as the French philosopher fails to take issue with privilege. Lyotard argues that in traditional cultures, conditions for the transmission of narrative knowledge both create and presuppose community:

> la tradition des récits est en même temps celles [*sic*] de critères qui définissent une triple compétence, savoir-dire, savoir-entendre, savoir-faire, où se jouent les rapports de la communauté avec elle-même et avec son environnement. Ce qui se transmet . . . c'est le groupe de règles pragmatiques qui constitue le lien social.[9] (40)

Until recently, narrative has codified and made memorable essential lessons for a subject's integration into established institutions: what to know, what to say and what to listen for (20-21). But who has the privilege to integrate? What are these institutions, and whom do they serve? In the contemporary world, the rules that constitute the social bond have been problematized in a hundred ways by all of those who are excluded by them, and not least by women. Narrative may be "the quintessential form of customary knowledge," as Lyotard argues (38), but the customary is in the process of change. If the master narratives of Western civilization—the liberation of the people and the life of the spirit—have lost

---

8 its great hero, its great dangers, its great voyages, its great goal. (xxiv).

9 a narrative tradition is also the tradition of the criteria defining a threefold competence—'know-how,' 'knowing how to speak,' and 'knowing how to hear'—through which the community's relationship to itself and its environment is played out. What is transmitted . . . is the set of pragmatic rules that constitute the social bond (21).

their power to legitimate knowledge, the oppressed are not, by that account, left without vision. The *masters'* narratives are in crisis; "the people" and "the spirit" can recover their legitimizing functions. Brossard clarifies to whom the problem belongs: "En cris(e) sinistre et sanglant patriarcat"[10] (*PT* 112).

Since narrative is the exemplary form of customary knowledge, and since patriarchal gender is profoundly customary, feminist writers such as Brossard and Marlatt will always have a stake in the process through which the crisis in metanarrative is resolved. Feminist literature addresses itself to the outcome directly because of feminism's commitment to liberation. The non-feminist postmodern writer, faced with the collapse of metanarrative and the ongoing deconstruction of Western metaphysics, may have become, as Frank Davey suggests, an eclectic materialist who raids the ruins of Western metaphysics for materials to generate meaning and serenity (*From There to Here* 264). In this circumstance, feminist writers may find themselves in an advantageous position, less threatened by the laying waste of the customary and more practised at salvaging what remains. While Lyotard argues that incredulity towards metanarratives in science as elsewhere marks the end of the modern age, Marlatt and Brossard incorporate their gleanings in "an absolutely other book": "*C'était absolument dans un autre livre* qu'elle saurait retracer le moment venu, les lignes d'une forme humaine parfaitement lisible"[11] (*PT* 41). Displacing the stubborn cultural generic, both *How Hug a Stone* and *Picture Theory* (meta-)narrate spiritual liberation as em[+female]bodied, contested, *new*.

---

10 In cr(y)sis, sinister and bloody patriarchy (84).
11 *It was absolutely in another book* that she would know how to retrace when the moment came, the lines of a perfectly readable human form (21).

PART TWO

A Narratological Reading of
How Hug a Stone

CHAPTER 4

Fabula: Beyond Quest Teleology

> It is difficult to imagine that access to the possi-
> bility of a road map is not at the same time
> access to writing.
> — Jacques Derrida, *Of Grammatology*

NARRATOLOGICAL ANALYSIS often begins by establishing fabula events, perhaps rephrasing the narrative as a sentence. Using this procedure, we could describe *How Hug a Stone* as follows: the narrator and her son travel in England for a month with the intention of better understanding the narrator's mother. As a working model of the fabula, such a summary corresponds to the narrator's intentions, which are articulated in the poem "Introduction":

> June 14, 1981. we fly to England for a month of visiting my mother's side of the family, my mother now dead, her mother still alive. my son wants to meet his great-grandmother & i want to see her again, this writer of faithful letters that have crossed the Atlantic & Canada for 30 years. letters that reflect what we tell her but never say much about her own life. letters that remember me when i was small, tugging me back to a mother who was once my age.

> now my son & i fly across, two living letters in reply, two single i's with Canadian accents, one 39, one 12. my Canadian-born son, who barely knew & didn't understand his English grandmother, will now meet his English relatives & understand them as best he can. & perhaps i will come to understand my mother too. (11)

The voyage to England frames the narrative as a *quest for understanding*, and analysis can proceed from this point.

Formal narratological criteria, such as those suggested by Claude Brémond in *Logique du récit* (1973), can verify fabula structure. Brémond suggests that a narrative fabula be considered a series of events that constitutes a process in three phases: possibility or virtuality;

event(s) or realization; and result or conclusion. In Brémond's terms, the fabula of *How Hug a Stone* can be described as follows:

MODEL I

1. Condition of virtuality: the possibility that the narrator, in making this journey, will better understand her mother
2. Process of realization:
   June 14, flying to England
   June 15, landing at Gatwick
   June 16, staying at the stepmother's house; taking the train to Exeter
   June 17, visiting Poltimore village, the grandmother and uncle
   June 21, the grandmother giving photos, telling stories
   June 22, travelling to Ilfracombe, Combe Martin, where the narrator had stayed with her mother, sisters and grandparents as a child
   June 24, staying at Ellesmere
   June 26, on the train
   June 28, Pilgrim Cottage with Jean and Nick
   June 30, "circling the power thresholds of Stonehenge— embracing the squat stone mothers of Avebury" (64)
3. Conclusion: unspecified date, Trafalgar Square. "we want to be where live things are" (79)

In this model, the majority of fabula events constitutes the realization of the process, and the beginning and the ending function as markers in a chain of related events.

Narratology also distinguishes between non-functional and functional events that involve a change of condition caused or experienced by an actor. Barthes argues that to be considered functional, an event must pose a choice between two possibilities (*IASR* 15-16). Once made, such a choice determines the course of the narrative within a logically causal ordering of narrative functions. When causality is unclear, narratology questions the *logic of events*, for which Bal suggests a tautology: fabula events are logical when they are "experienced by the reader as natural and in accordance with the world" (*N* 12).

The pattern *choice—event—choice* is implicit in the travel narrative of *How Hug a Stone*. From Combe Martin, the narrator could have returned to London or Canada, but she chose to go on to the Cotswolds and Avebury, and so on. The events of the fabula as outlined in Model I are functional, according to the criteria of choice and change of condition.

A third criterion for selecting events was developed by William Hendricks (1973), who argued that fabula structure is determined by the confrontation of two groups of actors. Functional events thus always involve two actors and one action, two arguments and one predicate, or two objects and one process. Bal points out that linguistically, this unity can be formulated as two nominal components and one verbal component, with a basic structure as follows:

subject—predicate—direct object

The subject and the object are considered actors. Only events that can be represented in this manner are considered to be functional (*N* 17). Hendricks's criteria are oriented towards structures in which a subject is directed towards an object.

According to these criteria, the fabula of *How Hug a Stone* is as follows: the narrator flies to England to understand her mother. Variations that preserve this essential structure include: the narrator travels to Poltimore/ to Combe Martin/ to Ellesmere/ to Avebury, in order to understand her mother. She listens to stories/ relives her memories/ reads and writes/ becomes more conscious of her own mothering, and so on, in order to understand her mother. There are events in the narrative that do not fall into this pattern: Edrys herself confronting *her* mother, Kit telling his dream, British Rail returning mother and son to their itinerary. Such events might be considered subordinate clauses within the narrative sentence. Using Hendricks's formula, the activities undertaken by the narrator in her effort to understand her mother are the only functional events in this fabula.

According to each of these methods, the narrator's transformation from a condition of non-understanding to a condition of understanding is the central event of *How Hug a Stone*. The fabula established by intuition and tested against the criteria of Barthes, Brémond and Hendricks can be considered to have a quest structure. The narrator, who is the actor/subject, experiences a lack of understanding, and sets out to find what she is missing. After a series of adventures in which she receives help from donors and overcomes obstacles or opponents, she succeeds in her quest and the story is complete. As a quest, *How Hug a Stone* can be schematized as follows:

MODEL II

the narrator	—	seeks	—	understanding of her mother
actant	—	function	—	actant (object)

This elementary series of events identifies the narrator as the subject and actor of the fabula.

The narrator can also be said to fulfill the function of the subject actant. Actant is a narratological term related to the inherent teleology or goal orientation of the model. Several actors may be considered to be the same actant. "An actant is a class of actors that shares a certain characteristic quality . . . related to the teleology of the fabula as a whole. An actant is therefore a class of actors whose members have an identical relation to the aspect of *telos* which constitutes the principle of the fabula. That relation we call the *function* (F)" (*N* 26). As I have noted, the six actantial classes fall into binary pairs: subject/object, power/receiver and helper/opponent. Quest grammar identifies each character with one of these six actantial roles.

In *How Hug a Stone*, the narrator can be defined as the subject actant of the head series, understanding her mother as the object actant and seeking as the function. The power actant and the receiver actant can be defined, respectively, as that force in the narrative which enables the subject to achieve the object, and that entity which benefits from the subject's success. Power, Bal argues, is "power over the whole enterprise, is often abstract, usually remains in the background, [is] usually only one" (*N* 31). In this narrative, the power can only be language, the medium of the subject's voyage of discovery and the means through which stories of her mother come to her. Language plays an actantial function. The narrator herself is the receiver, as she alone benefits from her quest. The roles of the power and receiver in *How Hug a Stone* can be schematized as follows:

power —   function   — receiver
language — enables understanding — for the narrator

Of the four actantial functions of subject, object, power and receiver, the narrator fulfills two and the other two are intimately connected with her: her language and her understanding (which comes through language). Thus the thematic interiority of the narrator and her emphasis on language are reflected in the structure of the narrative.

Many of the other characters can be classifed as helpers. Helpers, like power, make it possible for the subject to achieve its aim, but helpers are usually multiple, often come to the fore, are mostly concrete and give incidental aid (*N* 31). The helper is paired with the opponent class, and together the helpers and opponents add interest to a story.

Here again language is related to actantial function: the stories that Kit tells, for example, are helpers because they contribute to the narrator's understanding. Other helpers include the narrator's grandmother, with her stories and photographs, the other family members, Edrys's friend, Jean, all of these characters' stories, and, finally, the landscape itself, with its residents, sites, names, flora and fauna. Stories and names are important helpers in this quest, where "everything calls, shines, points to itself" (*HHS* 43).

Since the narrative subject struggles with opponents and, overcoming them or not, achieves or fails to achieve its object, opponent actants are important to narrative structure. In "grounded in the family," the step-brother seems to be an opponent, playing his game of death with moths and "hailing" or "interpellating" Kit in Althusser's sense of the word (174-75). Marlatt's text in fact displays this ideological process or mechanism which works to form Kit as the subject of a pre-existing, patriarchal ideological formation, at the same time that the narrator, who "thought" she was "free," is hailed as mother and moth in the role of feminine prey. Female bodies, "soft and angry," are captive in a setting both domestic and feral, signifying simultaneously the marital bedroom and the hunt: "under the moon a grown man now lures *moththe, math-*, worm. with a white sheet spread on the lawn, with a bedroom lamp he lures their bodies, heavy, beating against the walls. he wants to fix them in their families" (17). The male position into which Kit is interpellated is linked to a suggestion of sexual violation, as the moths are, "wings-pulled-open, pinned on a piece of cotton, mortified. as then, i protest this play as death—despite his barrage of scientific names, his calling to my son, you game? as if he held the script everyone wants to be in, except the moths" (17). Both as a personal threat and as a representative of patriarchal ideology, the stepbrother resembles an opponent; yet, his play enriches the narrator's understanding as she realizes that Kit's turning from her parallels her own pushing past her "mother's quick restraint" (18), at the age of nine. In this way, her stepbrother furthers the narrator's quest for understanding. Since, in addition, the narrator does not struggle with or overcome her stepbrother, he should probably also be classified as a helper.

The real opponent in *How Hug a Stone* is fear: fear that vanquished Edrys and that threatens her daughter. In "back to Reading," the narrator articulates her struggle with fear:

> i think of the shape of her life, her brooding silence. how i felt i was
> struggling often with her sense of fatality, either about herself or
> about us, her children. the struggle with her fear which i suspected
> of being so strong it could actually shape what happened to me.
> coming to meet it, i see what i've been struggling with here. (76)

The rough notes for the book, now part of the Daphne Marlatt collection
in the Literary Manuscripts Division of the National Library of Canada,
support the assignment of an actantial role to fear. There, Marlatt writes
of fear as an obstacle to spiritual growth: "fear is the great debilitator—
poisoning 'the well of being' so that we lose sight of our own potential
(the wellspring, the source)." As an actantial opponent, fear must be
overcome if the narrator is to succeed in her quest.

Kit's actantial function proves impossible to define within the given
terms of narrative grammar, and it is in relation to Kit that the quest structure can most clearly be shown to have serious limitations as an explanatory
model for the fabula of *How Hug a Stone*. Kit is more than a helper; the
stories he tells and the comments he makes repeatedly emphasize that Kit
is a subject (actor) with a program (function) of his own to fulfill. He is the
subject of language and of a number of sub-fabulas embedded within the
head series constituted by the subject's quest. He is not a double of the
subject/actant, since he doesn't have the same functional relationship to
the object: Kit is not questing to understand his mother, or his grandmother.
He might be defined as an "anti-subject," that is, an actor who pursues
her/his own object and, at a certain moment, stands at cross-purposes to
the subject (*N* 32). However, Kit is not independent of his mother; in his
illness, his play and even his dreaming, he is caught up in her reality.

The complex play of identity and difference that characterizes the rapport of Kit and his mother is typical of parent-child relationships, yet it
cannot be accounted for within the model implied by narrative quest
grammar. We are led to the startling conclusion that narratology is ill-
equipped to describe the central human relationship of parent to child.
This conclusion is a dismal but coherent one, in that it is consistent with
the Freudian alignment of parent and child inside an Oedipal narrative
paradigm that forms the boy as the subject-hero and his mother as the
object-matrix, but which fails in its description of the little girl. The
subject/matrix opposition, as a prototype or variation of the hero/obsta-
cle opposition basic to quest narrative grammar, cannot account for
democratic or dialogic parent-child relationships.

Neither can the quest paradigm fully account for the second well-
developed parent-child relationship in the book, that of Edrys and her

daughter. Edrys, like Kit, fits awkwardly not one but several possible actantial roles. None accounts well for her. She is not the object, although she is related to it; she is not the subject, although she shares actantial functions with her daughter. According to the Oedipal logic that characterizes quest grammar, Edrys should be the opponent or obstacle, but she is surely not: she shares her daughter's struggle against the real obstacle, fear—but is less successful in warding it off. Insofar as Edrys's fear is what her daughter must struggle against, Edrys is a kind of obstacle; insofar as she too struggles against that fear, she is a subject. Quest structure cannot accurately represent this mother-daughter relationship.

It becomes apparent that although the fabula of *How Hug a Stone* can be described as a quest, the narrative grammar of the quest cannot fully describe the events of the poem. The inaccuracy of the quest model with respect to parent-child relationships points to the patriarchal limitations of the model and perhaps of Western narrative itself. Marlatt's awareness of these questions is articulated in her thematization of narrative teleology, in her deconstruction of the narrative transformation in which a generically male subject transgresses a generically female topological boundary or obstacle. The poem's prescient definition of a feminine matrix which "we come through to & . . . come out of, ground & source" (73) suggests a rapport between the mother's body and the earth-body of the arché-mother, earth-womb-tomb. The notebooks also treat the question. Through her inclusion of her son in the subject pronoun "we"—a "we" strongly focalized as female—Marlatt constructs a gender-inclusive subject that transgresses the generically female boundary without being constructed as male. Without ambiguity, she interprets the matrix prior to "all possible relation"—including relations of gender—as that which embraces all of us, women, men and children. The representation of the relation mother:daughter:son in *How Hug a Stone* breaks apart the narrative paradigm that normally reproduces a generically male subject and generically female object or obstacle.

Congruent conclusions are reached when the fabula structure of *How Hug a Stone* is considered from the point of view of the motivating desire that moves the narrative forward. The quest paradigm describes events in terms of the desire of one subject: at its most abstract, the desire of a singular subject to successfully transgress an obstacle or boundary. This structure subordinates all other fabula elements to the desire or *telos* of the subject. In *How Hug a Stone*, the *telos* is the narrator's desire to understand; according to the logic of the quest, all other characters in the poem are functionally related to her desire, and only to her desire. Structural subordination on this level runs counter to the spirit of *How Hug a Stone*, which emphasizes a plurality of voices and celebrates a listening and ultimately collective subject. However, *How Hug a Stone* has other deep structures that contest this structural teleology. The first of these becomes apparent when we bring forward the full complexity of the quest narrative itself.

The narrator's desire to understand her mother is the head series of events in this narrative; however, a head series is the dominant, but not necessarily the only, fabula constituting a narrative text. Secondary fabulas, embedded into the head series, increase the complexity of the fabula. When the embedded narrations are written into the formula, two different fabula models suggest themselves. Models III and IV represent the events of Edrys's life as constituting a second fabula embedded in the head series, creating a complex fabula structure with not one hero but two: the narrator and her mother. Read in this way, the fabula metamorphoses and the structural dominance of quest teleology declines.

In Model III, while the narrator's story moves forward in time and space, Edrys's story appears to unfold in the reverse direction. Considered as one narrative with a second embedded within it, the fabula appears as follows:

MODEL III

June 14 subject travels to Reading
    (narrator's memories of 1948: Edrys on vacation)
to Poltimore
    (grandmother's memories of the late 1930s and 1940s:)
    (Edrys becomes a woman)
to Pilgrim Cottage
    (Jean's memories: Edrys in school)
to Avebury
    (cultural, ancestral memory)
to London
    (vestige of dinosaurs)
to 1951
to the present, "where live things are."

Represented in this way, the fabula appears to escape the strict control of chronological time. As the narrator encounters the embedded fragments of her mother's fabula, she does so in reverse chronological order, beginning with the most recent, and receding steadily in time so that Edyrs disappears, eventually, not into death but into the timelessness of the not-yet-born, the older worlds of the ancestors and the dinosaurs beyond them. While the deviation from strict chronology is an effect rather than a fact, it nonetheless suggests a double movement that generates an effect of synchrony.

Model III can be differently represented to correspond to Brémond's analysis of narrative cycles, either in sequence or embedded within one another, which are constituted by "processes of improvement" and "processes of deterioration" (*N* 22). Model IV describes the fabula structure in terms of such cycles, as follows:

MODEL IV

Improvement
fulfillment of the task (crossing over)
intervention of allies (stories)
elimination of the opponent (fear)
negotiation ("Pilgrim night" to "long after The Brown Day of
     Bride")
satisfaction (feeding the pigeons)

Deterioration
misstep (Edrys's marriage)
creation of an obligation (to be a wife and mother)
the sacrifice (going to North America)
the endured attack (madness, fear)
the endured punishment (silence)

Model IV, like Model III, represents the fabula of *How Hug a Stone* in terms that undermine quest teleology. Model IV represents aims other than those of the narrator as equally important. Both Models III and IV are characterized by balance and synchronicity, which correspond to the timeless mood of the text as a whole.

In this context, it is interesting to consider the correspondence between narrative events and verbal forms in this text. *How Hug a Stone* characteristically presents events in a paratactic series of nominal or adjectival phrases. In "Combe Martin," for example:

> let off the bus with our bags & pack & where shall we go? here at
> the heart of what i remember of Combe Martin, curve of Seaside
> Hill running down to the cove where tide daily climbs the shingle
> beach to a seawall clutter of small hotels, new plate glass fish &

> chip place, shops off High Street stretching back up the combe.
> let's eat, he says. (45)

The elision of finite verbs is a stylistic aspect of this narration that moves from scene to scene with a sense of timelessness. Grammatical form indicates accurately the equivocal status of discrete events in the best possible readings of the narrative fabula, readings that bring to light a mythological narrative structure somewhat like that of Lotman's mythological plot type. In *How Hug a Stone*, events are absorbed into cycles of death and renewal which are nonetheless transformations rather than a repetition of the same.

A fifth fabula model accounts more carefully than the first four for the narrator's trip to Avebury and her exploration of Neolithic culture. Since the narrator's visit to the Neolithic site enables her to realize her goal, the event of this visit should be satisfactorily accounted for in terms of the narrative structure and represented by an accurate model of the fabula. During the visit to the Avebury complex, two specific narrative events occur, a ritual at the West Kennet Long Barrow and the construction of Silbury Hill; these become the first events in the chronological and open-ended fabula Model V.

The final section of the poem, "Black Hole at Centre," begins with the narrator in crisis, her guiding *telos* disoriented, her quest in danger of failure. "Lost" and "nameless" (65), in a nautilus of language, she fears to be lost as Edrys was and is, gone beyond words. Later, when Kit becomes ill, the narrator is like Dante in the dark forest: "the terror of being, alone on your own in the dark. the terror of dragging your child along in the panic woods in the night crying" (71). Gilbert and Gubar argue that when in crisis, male poets turn to a *patrius sermo*, finding Virgil to be their guide, but female poets turn to the Cthonian Mothertongue (1989). Marlatt's narrator turns implicitly to the Neolithic goddess when she asks, "who mothers me?" (71), and it is a ritual rebirth from the "tomb-body" (72) of that Mother which reorients her passage back into the daylight and eventually enables her to achieve her desire. This shift into archaeological time is marked by the movement from "Pilgrim night" to "long after The Brown Day of Bride" (72-73). The poem which follows, named by the etymological opening of *Avebury*, re-establishes a balance between the narrative functions of the narrator and those of her son, alternating Kit's childish story with that of his mother, who is now able to weave together a sense of narrative continuity:

narrative is a strategy for survival. so it goes—transformative sinuous sentence emerging even circular, cyclic Avebury, April-May leaps *winged* from *buried*. sheds lives, laps, folds, these identities, sine: fold of a garment / chord of an arc (active misreading). writing in monumental stones, open, not even capstone or sill, to sky (-change). (75)

The figure of Edrys, linked early and late in the poem to images of birds, folds into images of the Bird Goddess, Bride or Brigit, the British incarnation of the Old European goddess. The narrator's quest to understand her mother leads her beyond Edrys and beyond *her* mother, to the "squat stone mothers of Avebury" (64) and to the interior narratives of language. The focus widens to the integrating rhythm of myth.

In Model V, ceremonies at West Kennet in approximately 3500 B.C.E. are the first fabula event. They are followed by the construction of Silbury Hill in late July 2660 B.C.E. Subsequent transformations are arranged along a timeline that dissociates them from the narrator and her quest. The fabula duration of five to six thousand years is dominated by the enormous ellipsis separating the Neolithic period from our own. The ellipsis itself functions as the sign of our collective loss of rapport with the earth and the matrix of creation, as symbolized by the arché-mother, or goddess. The subject/actant is the speaking community manifested by all the characters. Language is the power that makes transition from generation to generation possible. This version of the fabula merges with Model I, as follows:

MODEL V

3500 B.C.E. West Kennet Long Barrow: "running to meet them"
2660 B.C.E. Silbury Hill: "April-May leaps *winged* from *buried*"
1890 Grandmother born
1941 Edrys brought out
1942 narrator born
1948 holiday in England
1951 emigration
June 14, 1981 the narrator and her son fly to England
June 15 landing at Gatwick
June 16 staying at the stepmother's house; taking the train to Exeter
June 17 visiting Poltimore Village and the grandmother and uncle
June 21 the grandmother giving photos, telling stories
June 22 travelling to Ilfracombe, Combe Martin, where the narrator had stayed with her mother, sisters and grandparents as a child

June 24 staying at Ellesmere
June 26 on the train
June 28 Pilgrim Cottage with Jean and Nick
June 30 "circling the power thresholds of Stonehenge—embracing
the squat stone mothers of Avebury" (64)
Conclusion: unspecified date, Trafalgar Square. "we want to be
where live things are" (74)

In this representation of the fabula, a collective subject-actant crosses
the boundary of the generations, thereby reconciling chronological time
with the narrator's desire to avoid teleological closure. The model
describes the process through which the narrator is freed from the claus-
trophic identification with her mother, indicated by the Models III and
IV, and notable at the registers of story and text. With the exception of
Edrys and Kit, all subjects of language are unnamed but familiar and
familial, characterized by the "reciprocal ties" thematized in the poem
through the extended etymological play on the Indo-European root
ghosti-, "stranger, guest, host; one with whom one has reciprocal ties of
obligation." The fabula reflects the thematic evolution of consciousness
which is able to go beyond telos, "our obsession with the end of things,"
to finally hear, "the old slow pulse beyond word become, under flesh,
mutter of stone, stane, stei-ing power" (75).

Paradoxically, this model of the fabula, which explicitly reaches
towards the Neolithic origins of culture, reveals the illusory nature of any
quest for origins. If the family or the speech community is the subject
actant of the fabula, origin and teleology disappear in the mists of time:
someone always gave birth to the one before. This "mise en abyme" is
suggested in the evolutionary image of the final passage: "ruffled neck
feathers ripple snakelike movement of the neck last vestige of dinosaurs"
(79). As long as humans survive, the story will continue, but human survival, the text points out, is in doubt. "This earth hospitable. . . . takes
back what is given, ghost-i, hostly and hostile at once" (48-49). By
neglecting reciprocal duties to the earth, modern society puts all life in
jeopardy, "(getting rid of us)" (48).

The fabula of How Hug a Stone can be modelled in various ways,
ranging from the list of events in Model I, to the quest in Model II, to the
more complex Models III and IV, and finally to the linear yet open-ended
Model V, resembling the mythological plot-type hypothesized by Lotman.
Although each model has something to recommend it, they are not
equally able to account for all aspects of the poem. The quest models are

the least adequate, in that they are unable to describe the central relationships of the poem. Model V is the best, because it is the only model that can account for the importance of Avebury. In constructing this model, narratological analysis is able to describe the mythological fabula structure of *How Hug a Stone*. A collective actant does not live and die but is absorbed into a wavelike movement through time. The many characters of the story, including the narrator, Kit, Edrys, the grandmother, the builders of Silbury Hill and the ritual celebrants in the West Kennet Long Barrow, are rendered by a single mythological actant, thus enacting the significant numerical inequality between characters and actants which characterizes mythological narrative (*N* 32). Isomorphic structure identifies the many and the one, so that the mythological paradigm will always signify in larger terms than those of any single hero; the narrative has no particular end or *telos*; no one human desire can affect its form. Not least, the subject actant is both female and male, thus imagining and representing in narrative embodiment a non-binary gender-inclusive human subject.

CHAPTER 5

Story: Where the Body Is Written

> A great aid to my meditations is the beauty of our
> location.   — Gita Mehta, *A River Sutra*

STORY IS THE REGISTER OF geography and emotion, where abstract actants are coloured in to show characters caught up in events. At the register of story, the body *is* written because there the fabula is embodied through the medium of narration and the technique of focalization. Focalization represents fabula events through the perceptions of particular characters. The term is meant to distinguish between the witness of fabula events and their narrator, the linguistic subject. In addition to seeing, the focalizer may also hear, taste and feel the events of the narrative. The story level of *How Hug a Stone* is characterized by powerful focalization through the character narrator known as "i," whose sensory body articulates the story and governs the complex temporal relations of the poem. In this way, the gigantic, unwieldy mythological fabula is rendered coherent as the story of one woman's quest to understand her mother.

For a character narrator (CN)—in Genette's terms, an intradiegetic narrator—to be also the focalizer (CF) is not an unusual narrative situation. What is striking in *How Hug a Stone*, however, is the intensity of the focalization. The narrator's presence motivates every word. Whether or not she is linguistically represented, the reader is never in doubt that the i-narrator is telling her own story.

The poem does record the words of many other linguistic subjects. One example, the line, "let's eat, he says," can be encoded as follows:

CN (i), CF (i), CN2 (Kit) speaks, "let's eat."

The fragment of dialogue, "let's eat," is a short dramatic text embedded in the primary narration. The i-narrator is linguistically signalled by the expression, "he says," since these are her words. In other examples,

66

however, the reader is aware of the i-narrator even when she is not linguistically represented. In the following example, focalization never falters although the lines float alone on the page:

> CF (i), CNx (unknown) speaks, *"if it wasn't for the clouds England*
> *wouldn't be so green, you see, it would be all dry grass now wouldn't*
> *it?"* (62).

The speaker is unidentified, yet the reader knows that these words were
spoken by someone on the train, and that they were listened to and noted
down by the i-narrator, intrigued, we might imagine, by their lilt. As
character narrator, focalizer and implied author, she is the listening and
notebook-carrying interlocutor of all the voices in the poem.

Narrative embedding of this kind implies narrative levels: a primary
narrator reports the words of a secondary narrator who reports the words
of a third and so on. Such structures are hierarchical, and although Bal
argues that the hierarchy is only technical, she points out herself that the
power of narrative hierarchies is such that one word from the primary
narrator can invalidate or render ironic the embedded text of another
character (*N* 149). The primary narrator always has power over the other
narrative levels: power to interpret, to present or misrepresent, or to censor entirely. In the first example above, the narrator both reports Kit's
words and comments implicitly on his unruffled response to an environment that is so stimulating to her. In the second example, she transforms
someone's words into an artifact or a found poem. In transferring the verbal expressions of others to the signifying context of her own quest, she
constructs her story as intertext and resists narrative closure through her
intense attention to the daily manifestations of the real. As she comments, "i'm intrigued, writing it down" (23).

How Hug a Stone is full of narrative embeddings, yet the words "he
said" or "she said," which signal a shift in narrative levels, are often
elided, replaced by italics, quotation marks, a change in rhythm or a different sounding voice. The favouring of such methods over the hypotactic
grammatical subordination of normal reporting is crucial to the text's
non-authoritarian political stance, which unites many voices through the
sensory and sensual focalization of the i-narrator.

I have argued that quest structure cannot account for the generations
of parenting relationships central to the poem. Fabula Model V replaces
the quest with a chronological, open-ended structure reaching back to
the Neolithic Age. At the story level, however, the quest reappears as
plot: the narrator journeys to England in order to understand her mother.

The emotional intelligence of the poem is wound up with the narrator's need to come to terms with her mother's death and her life, equally unresolved in a labyrinthine centre: "enraged mother at the heart of it: lost" (15). Threatened, like many daughters, by identification with her "furious" (24, 67), "lost" (71, 78), "wild" (19, 78) and "panicked" (55, 71, 77) mother, the narrator must decode "this plot we're in" (15), through signs traced in memory and across the maps of a long-ago childhood vacation.

The narrator's reconstruction of her mother's life corresponds to fabula Model III in which Edrys's story is told in "subjective anachronies" (*N* 57), in counter-chronological order and in fragments of ever-increasing span. She is first vividly recalled when Kit catches a cinder in his eye on the train to Reading; next, when the narrator is reminded of driving in the car during the family's trip to England in 1948. Edrys's mother, the narrator's grandmother, picks up the thread, telling how Edrys was taken out at the age of eighteen and how she started her own family during the Second World War. Finally, Edrys's closest school friend, Jean, recalls her as a girl, and her "image comes clear" (67). The first anachrony spans a moment; the second, a short scene; the third covers a period of several years; the fourth, iterative and vague as to temporal details, refers to the approximately seven years that Edrys spent in boarding school.

From June 30 to the end of the journey, elision of dates and factual details corresponds to the protagonist's increasing preoccupation with the past and with her pilgrimage to Avebury. The memory work continues through that passage, culminating in the final poem, "feeding the pigeons," where it strikes like a "thrum way back in the tunnel rocketing forward, fear, rocketing through my whole being/ lost" (77). In Bombay again with her panicking mother, she relives Edrys's fear of losing her children: "unbearable loss don't take them from me" (78). The narrator's overwhelming fears for her own child force her into a painful identification with her mother, but it is mercifully followed by recognition and release: "her i lost, not him" (78). Kit is safe, "blue joggers planted firmly on cement" (78). Mourning her mother's love, "first love that teaches a possible world" (78), the narrator can return home with the text of *How Hug a Stone*, a gift of understanding and reconciliation:

> & i can do nothing but stand in my sandals & jeans unveiled, beat
> out the words, dance out names at the heart of where we are lost,
> hers first of all, wild mother dancing upon the waves, wide-wander-

ing dove beat against, & the dance beats with you, claims of the
dead in our world (the fear that binds). (78-79)

The emotional and intellectual quest which the narrator's journey frames
is an aspect of the fabula's focalization through her. When the quest is
fulfilled, *telos* is achieved and the poem ends.

Skillfully conducted by Marlatt's musical ear, the play of time in *How
Hug a Stone* is a study in temporal complexity. Fortunately, narratology
has developed a large vocabulary to describe narrative time. The remain-
der of this chapter will look at the various aspects of temporality in *How
Hug a Stone*, noting that they, too, are rendered coherent by the strong
focalization through the i-narrator, and that the thematic development of
the poem is closely correlated with the temporal rhythms.

Narrative time has always at least two components, fabula time (TF)
and story time (TS). Fabula time is defined by the duration of the fabula
events, and is necessarily chronological and diachronic. Story time is
inherently more complex, because it is the correlation of fabula time to
the speed of story presentation. Fabula time can be developmental, corresponding to events with long and regular duration, or critical, corresponding to events that come to a head dramatically, in a short period of
time (N 70). Story time is not necessarily chronological or even logical.
Bal encodes the varieties of story time as follows:

ellipses	$TF = n$ $TS = 0$	thus	$TF > \infty TS$
summary			$TF > TS$
scene			$TF = TS$
slow-down			$TF < TS$
pause	$TF = 0$ $TS = n$	thus	$TF < \infty TS$ (71)

Dramatic presentation of dialogue always implies a *scenic* rhythm in
which story time is more or less equal to fabula time. In an ellipsis, the
fabula proceeds while the story does not, which is to say that events are
unreported. A pause is when the story is elaborated while the fabula
stands still. In *How Hug a Stone*, alternating critical and developmental
events combine with story rhythms ranging from pause to ellipsis. The
poem exploits every possible complexity of narrative time, maintaining
narrative unity through focalization.

The most striking feature of narrative time in *How Hug a Stone* is the
fact that the fabula endures for five thousand years, yet is emptied out by
an ellipsis almost as long. Focalization is said to have an architectural
aspect, and the study of temporal relations in *How Hug a Stone* can clar-
ify what this expression might mean, since focalization in effect *engineers*

a bridge to span this impossible temporal gap. Of course, the narrator does not literally visit the Neolithic period, but she is there emotionally—her archaeological and linguistic research, woven into a chiasmatic structure of transformation, is what allows her to come to terms, finally, with her mother. She does literally visit the archaeological site at Avebury, which comprises the largest stone-chambered collective tomb of its kind in England and Wales, the largest human-made hill in Europe and the Avebury Stone Circles or Stone Henges, which cover an area of about 28½ acres (see Fig. 1). As Vatcher and Vatcher put it in the official handbook to the site, the ruins testify to the "probable sancity and, no doubt, vast prestige" of Neolithic Avebury (*The Avebury Monuments* 30).

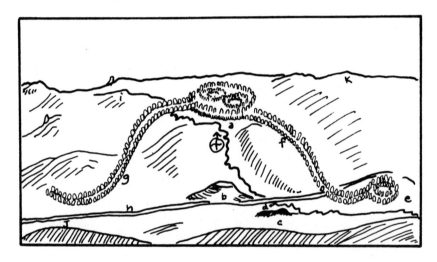

Fig. 1. The Neolithic complex at Avebury Parish, Wiltshire, England (after Stukeley).

Key

a. Avebury Henge
b. Silbury Hill
c. South Long Barrow
d. Kennett Spring
e. West Kennett
f. Kennett Avenue

g. Beckhampton Avenue
h. Bath Road
i. Windmill Hill
j. Saint Ann's Hill
k. Temple Downs

The visit to Avebury is recorded in the book's fifth section, "Black Hole at Centre," which traces the three-phase structure that Arnold van Gennep identified in 1908 as typical of a rite of passage: separation, transition and incorporation into society (see also Leach). "Pilgrim Cottage" and "Pilgrim night" inscribe the initiatory motifs of isolation, water and death in the "insulation," "unwept tears" (66) and danger represented by Kit's fever. An initiatory structure for the narrative as a whole has already been signified by the initial watery crossing, the intermediate status of the *ghosti-*, and the sacrifice and death of the narrator's mother, not to mention the sacrifice of the moth and the behaviour of the mob in Kit's dream. The narrator's entrance into the stone circles may be doubly or triply arduous in that she is framed on either side by the "ghostly child" (49) of familial generation. Exit out of the barrow, through the stone circle and "back to Reading" signifies reintegration into society—"the dark weight is gone" (76). Passing by "the white stone lady" (76), they move on to Trafalger Square, "the downspout of Empire" (78), to freedom "where live things are" (79). At the close of their rite of passage, the narrator and Kit move back into the world of the living and the light.

The rite begins with a visit to "the ex-governor [of Penang] and his lady, simply Jean & Nick growing old together in a cottage in the Cotswolds" (64). Jean went to boarding school in England with Edrys, whom she remembers sympathetically as a "resister" (66) of "subversive . . . imagination" (67): "a noncompliance Jean admired, being the dutiful daughter" (66). As her mother's image comes into focus, the narrator loses her own way, "torn between" rebellion and being "the perfect little mother" (66), even while she worries obsessively about her son:

> i feel lost. layer on layer of place, person. dramatis personae. the nameless creature i am at the heart of this many-chambered shell is getting overlaid, buried under. coming down with a cold? kit coughs his way through the night restless as if the room were packed with dream people. dream words. (65)

The narrator's quest for her mother has become a personal crisis in which she needs to be mothered (66), and is mothered, by Jean, who guides her to Avebury rather than Stonehenge. But insofar as Jean is a surrogate mother—"tall, sane, with a body mine resembles much more than my mother's" (66)—she is caught in the old mother-daughter scripts, and the narrator becomes irritated with Jean, although she needs her support (68).

"Pilgrim night" is a dark night of the soul. The "terror of being" (71) strikes with full force, and "there is no limit. something in me is in shock, like a bird beating wildly against a branch—lost, panicked" (71). The bird signifies both the mortal and the transcendent mother, but there is little comfort in her presence here. Impossibly and simultaneously both child and mother, the narrator's courage fails her:

> the terror of being, alone on your own in the dark. the terror of dragging your child along in the panic woods in the night crying, having a child when you *are a child*—terror a kind of trembling in the heart, helpless, listening to him cough. he coughed so much he couldn't catch his breath. heart pounding, & very hot. (71)

The sacred is imaged in the child-parent dyad through which the generations cascade. The narrator questions: "i say the mother-things to him but what do i say to the child in me? who mothers me?" (71). She is answered in the following poem with its visit into the home of the earth mother at the West Kennet Long Barrow. Here, too, a key psychological structure is doubly inscribed, since the journey of the child-mother through the earth to the Long Barrow has already been traced in "Combe Martin, house martin, Martinmas, Saint Martin, martial swords & plowshares":

> i see my ghostly child in him, not gone & not quite him, as she in me, mother, grandmother, grand, full grown we stand in, not for. that earth takes back what is given, *ghos-ti*, hostly & hostile at once. *guests will be provided with a hot water bottle*, immaculately shining bath, long boat, long barrow at the end of the day's rambles. (49)

The barrow, and especially the West Kennet Long Barrow, is provided by the hospitable earth as a resting place at the day's end. In the chiasmatic rite of descent and return, the barrow is the turning point where danger becomes safety and death itself sends forth shoots of new life.

West Kennet Long Barrow, the narrator notes, was not only a burial place but was also "a place to visit" (72), the site of community rituals honouring the dead and celebrating new life.

> quick, running to meet them, with pots, meat bones, flint implements, with stone, bone & shell beads. rubbish, *from which new life annually rises*,

The celebrants gather in the world of the dead, making ritual connection between the generations and embodying the cyclic life passage from winter to spring. The list of items such as pots and meat bones is an archaeological inventory of the debris left behind from years of community and ceremonial use. The homeliness of it all is reflected in the Neolithic imagery surviving in children's games of cup and ring, and Farmer's in the Dell, images behind which the goddess playfully peeks:

> cup-&-ring, stone ring within a ring, the Farmer's in the Dell (is that
> you, Bride of the Brown Day, of the White Hills?) (72)

The visit to the barrow is a return to the body of the mother in its aspect
as a "safe" (72) place: home. While death as homecoming is also a
Christian doctrine, the barrow-as-home images the stones and the earth
of the barrow as literally *"her tomb-body"* (72). Mothered again, the narrator finds the safety she has been seeking. She emerges from the barrow
into the light and the *temenos* of the great stone circles.

This ritual of initiation and healing requires the descent not only into
the earth mother's body but also into that of the mother tongue; like the
fabula, the story of *How Hug a Stone* is very much about language. As
Marlatt notes in "Narrative in Language Circuits," this is a text of
"word/thought unravellings . . . touch words in the secret narrative of the
compositional process" (61). Through difficult passages, the implied
author—"Daphne Marlatt," poet and scholar—traces a way "along the
neural net language makes of experience, where light flares" (61).
Rebirth is affirmed in "Avebury *awi-spek*, winged from buried
(egg."—the poem and its title unravelling out of *Avebury* a divine and a
divining narrative of who we are. An etymological search begins with
ave-, from the Latin *avis*, or bird; an Indo-European root, *awi-*, with a
compound, *awi-spek*, or "observer of birds." The observation of birds or
bird augury reminds us that the stone circles themselves are oriented
towards the stars for divination and study. Bird augury, one of the oldest
and most persistent forms of divination, has already been introduced by
"Magpie Augury" and linked to women's untold stories. Among the many
cognates, we find "egg," thus "hatching, winged from buried," like
bones in a barrow, the broken eggshell miming the open-ended parenthe-
sis of the story yet to be told. The bird images signify also Edrys who
"loved birds" (40), who perched like a gull (45), whose wings were
clipped (67). The pigeons' upward spiral in the end signifies both (her)
flight and the metanarrative of evolution: "ruffled neck feathers ripple
snakelike movement of the neck last vestige of dinosaurs: then lift, this
quick wing flap, heart at breast strike up a wild beating, blood for the
climb, glide, rest" (79).

A parallel narrative opens out of the second part of the name, "Avebury." "Bury" comes from the root *bhergh-*, which means to hide or to
protect, and which gives us the words "burial," "borrow," "bargain,"
"burrow." The root also means high, as in a hill, hill-fort (which protects)
or burrow, in which people were buried to rise again. Cognates include

borough; thus Avebury means Bird-Town. Not least, *bhergh-* is also the root of the Celtic name for the ancient goddess: Briget or Bride. In her body, the people are safe—hidden *in* and *under*, like the keel of the ship in the water or a woman's sex, "this *kiel*, to *ku-*, to, a hollow space or place, enclosing object, round object, a lump. mound in the surrounding sea of grass. *ku, kunte*" (72). In this syntax, the burrow is the gateway to "wave-breaking womb," life-giving, hidden from the light. The story winds through the descent into the darkness of "Pilgrim night" through "long after The Brown Day of Bride" and "continued" to ascend finally in an initiatory spiral into the light of the summer harvest, winged out of buried. The initiatory structure of descent and return ends with the image of Silbury Hill and a summer ritual which took place there in late July 2660 B.C.E., some 4,641 years before the narrator's visit to the site.

These initiatory transitions constitute the central theme of the narrator's quest for reconciliation and understanding. Technically, they are also co-extensive with the most outstanding feature of the temporal structure, the ellipsis/gap which is bridged by the narrator's rite of passage. Story rhythm, in this and other ways, frames the poem's meaning and guides interpretation.

The pause, verbally represented by the present participle form, characterizes the narrator's interior world of thoughtful emotional quest, and is the poem's most characteristic rhythm. Events are transformed into pictures by participle or nominal phrases that reinforce the rhythm's dreamy stasis: "the feel of this cottage full of dogs, cats, flowers, currents of emotion. the drama of English manners" (24). Events are implied: " 'sorry, darling.' scones with Devonshire cream & strawberry jam for tea." Or again, "such tides of feeling—grey despair even, listening to Kit coughing through the door in fits, attacks" (51).

The present tense of the dramatic scene is often used when the narrator thinks of her mother, a technique that Marlatt develops in *Ana Historic*. A good example from *How Hug a Stone* occurs when Kit catches a cinder in his eye, triggering a memory that slows the story to a scene: "*didn't i tell you?*" (16). After this interruption, the rhythm slows even more as associations gather around the fragment of dialogue. This rhythmic emphasis, combined with the ambiguity surrounding who actually spoke these words—Edrys, her daughter, or both of them?—highlights the narrator's identification with her mother. Edrys's voice syncopates the regular rocking rhythm of the first stanza, written in the dreamlike flow of participle and pause:

> it is the rackety clacking of the wheels that is familiar, or this side-
> ways motion, this compartment speeding down the line, of brick
> houses, rows of washing, embankment flowers. it's my son discover-
> ing the window open, staring head out into wind, ecstatic, until the
> cinder bit in eye:
>
> didn't i tell you?
>
> that was it, my vision smeared with soot like some kind of powdered
> ink, my mother's handkerchief a scalding rubdown, tearful eyes to
> the horizon line of the cut, those fences other kids were climbing
> free as they went in their unwritten world. (16)

The reader can initially hear the train in the metrical stress and in the
tonal rise and fall (typical, in fact, of Malay). Syncopation begins with
the dramatic question, *"didn't i tell you?"* and continues with the metri-
cally irregular and tone-rising "that was it," followed by the repetition
and imperfect rhymes of "my vision smeared with soot" and "like some
kind of powdered ink." The ink that smears the vision signifies writing,
while the context associates freedom with that stone-age goddess who
preceded writing and who, in this poem at least, is at odds with Edrys.

The narrator must distinguish her identity from that of her mother, but
the narration tends to obscure distinctions between them. The following
passage merges all three generations of mothers and daughters into their
shared actantial function:

> & so coal lights, *geulo-*, ember from India born "somewhere in the
> north" in the 1890s, schooled in the hills, has a daughter born in
> Bombay, schooled in the Nilgiri Hills ("like the English downs,"
> she said) & England, carried all the way to Malaya, thence to Aus-
> tralia when war breaks out, where i appear. (29-30)

It is impossible to identify who said that the Nilgiri Hills are like the
English downs. Within continuity, there are births: the grandmother born
in the north of India in the 1890s, Edrys born in Bombay and the narrator in Australia. The subject actant here is *geulo-*, promethean fire of life
or simply, as Marlatt wrote in her notebook, "the same old coal."

Identification and conflict between Edrys and her daughter is developed through their mutual resistance to the roles offered by the patriarchal script. Edrys ended by "lending her body" (29) to the inherited
dream, but her daughter

> refused, on a new continent suffocated in changing rooms thick with
> resentment: you don't understand, *everybody* wears jeans here & i

want a job. refusing the dream its continuity in what i thought was
no man's land (not Rupert's, not the King's), just the trees'. (29)

The identification between the narrator and her mother with respect to
their fears for their children also relates to their shared actantial function
as mothers in the spiral of generation. Throughout, focalization maintains story coherence while permitting the reader to glimpse the actantial
functions underlying the dramatic personnae of the individual characters. Thus, although the blurring between characters might be thought of
as a temporary weakening of the focalization, it is the opposite; strong
focalization makes it possible for the focalizer to trace the collective subjectivity that unfolds through and beyond her body, incorporating the difference she made in refusing the patriarchal dream.

An ample, scenic rhythm gives a feeling of presence to one critical
conversation between Edrys and her mother, which took place in the late
1930s:

> "We went to Penang and she said, 'Mother, I'm so *tired* of this life,
> of just wasting my time going out dancing every night, getting
> engaged to play tennis, somebody ringing up and wanting to take me
> out to golf. It seems so futile. I want to learn dress designing and
> dressmaking. I've seen advertisements and I've written off to Eng-
> land. I won't be coming back with you when we go on leave.' This
> was when we were in the hotel in Penang sitting on the grounds fac-
> ing the sea just where her wedding photograph was taken a few
> months later. Isn't it extraordinary?" (29)

These embedded words record Edrys's unsuccessful decision to write her
own script. The dialogue occurs in the scene of the narrator's visit to her
maternal grandmother, and within the embedded narration of Edrys's life.
Narrative mirroring (discussed in the next chapter) and a shift to a dramatic, scenic rhythm both mark the importance of this speech, and direct
attention to this moment in Edrys's story, memorializing her unsuccessful
but courageous independence speech to her domineering mother.

Scenic presentation consistently characterizes the narrator's interactions with Kit. Their mother-and-son dialogues mirror in a distinct register the structural preoccupations of the poem. Notably, Kit has his own
quest, which he pursues in "boy with tape recorder stalking horses in a
field of cows." Kit always acts in the present tense and in dramatic
scenes; the one exception occurs when he brings forward his own memories of Edrys and thus, to a limited extent, participates in his mother's
quest (76). That passage has a summarizing rhythm which is gentle and

reflective, unlike the panicky summary of "close to the edge," which condenses the adventure of Edrys and her daughters at Wild Pear Beach and the later scattering of Edrys's ashes.

Anachrony also undermines linearity and supports the timeless, synchronic mood of the pause. Anachrony is the non-coincidence of fabula and story time. Two types of anachrony, retroversion (flashback) and anticipation, contribute to the temporal complexity of *How Hug a Stone*. Internal retroversion fills in missing information elided in its sequential place (paralipsis), or it presents an event twice, for example when events recorded in the journal entry, "*June 17, Poltimore village. evening— warm, silent, fragrant with hay & silage, timothy grass (June the worst month for pollen count)*" (22), are repeated and expanded in "June near the river Clyst, Clust, clear. Clystmois this holding wet & clear." Internal anticipation also occurs when this journal entry comments on "Poltimore, Pwyll Ti Mawr, Pool by the Great House" and identifies the grandmother's actantial function of helper or donor: "*June 21, my grandmother is giving back my early self to me in photographs she foresees drained of meaning in strangers' hands*" (22). Another entry, "under her mothering wing" (64), brings together in one image the symbolic, emotional and proairetic codes of the narrative, creating a densely synchronic moment.

Much of "Black Hole at Centre" has a timeless, eerie mood, twice characterized as "surreal" (66, 76). "Pilgrim Cottage" summarizes Edrys's life in a sketch of her years as mother and wife. Verbal structures of recurring gerunds and participles convey an effect of timelessness consistent with the rest of the section:

> wondering even as a mother was she "doing the right thing"? hiding her doubts to wrestle with the angel authority of father, teacher, doctor, dentist, priest. furious, raging at the false front of society, tearing out the placid assumptions of family . . . & then lapsing, controlled, into silence. (67)

In fact, the narrator has come to a place of portraits, where she herself is temporarily captured by a pause. Although Pilgrim Cottage is beautiful, it is so static that it is literally "like walking into the very picture of . . . / slate roof, roses twining up the stone wall to the eavestrough, *delphiniums blue*. larkspur & lupins in the honeyed light. Nick on his knees among the cabbage" (65). The lack of linear progress is compounded by a sense of misdirection; the narrator is "circling the power thresholds of [Bronze Age] Stonehenge" (64), caught up in the field of the wrong power. Redirected by Jean, "the gate-keeper," she will go to Neolithic Avebury, through the ellipsis and into mythological time.

The register of story unifies *How Hug a Stone* by focalizing six thousand years of duration through a narrator whose scholarly and emotional reach spans the world from Vancouver to southern England to Bombay. Her overriding desire to understand what happened to her mother ensures that the quest remains in view as a motif signalling the paradox of teleological narrativity deconstructed by the poem.

CHAPTER 6

Textual Subjectivity, Marlatt's i/eye

Each moment is magnificent
—George Elliott Clarke, *Whylah Falls*

IN ANY NARRATION, SOMEONE who knows tells something that is known, so that narrative is itself an epistemological structure. At the textual level of analysis, the focus is on the one who knows: the narrator(s). In *How Hug a Stone*, the narrator is "nameless" (65), identified only as "i," but because she is such a powerful focalizer, the text tells us a lot about her way of knowing. She resembles Daphne Marlatt, but it would be a mistake to claim that she *is* Daphne Marlatt. In a series of texts and over a number of years, Marlatt has developed her knowing and narrating "i." This chapter examines Marlatt's i-narrator in relation to linguistic and feminist theories of subjectivity in language, with particular attention to the extensive work of Monique Wittig in this domain.

Indications of the knower in language are defined linguistically as deixis: the function that locates persons, objects and events in relation to the space-time context implied by a particular utterance. Deictic signs denote only in relation to specific speech acts; they are always relative indicators of place, person and time. The range of deictic signs includes "here" and "there," and the personal pronouns "I," "you" and "we." Proper names are deictic, as are relative temporal terms such as "now," "the day after tomorrow" and "yesterday." Deixis is the register of subjectivity in language, so we might tend to think of it as abstract, but it is not. In fact, deixis refers us to what is most physical about language, the some*body* who is speaking or writing. The roots of the word highlight this aspect of the concept, from the Greek *deiktikos*, meaning "able to show," from an Indo-European root, *deik*, meaning "to show" or "to pronounce solemnly." Etymology emphasizes the way that deixis relies on the physicality of language: the body pointing, the mouth articulating, the vocal chords vibrating and the hand working. Deixis points to the person who is speaking in the here and now of language as it is produced.

In *Problèmes de linguistique générale*, Emile Benveniste outlined the relationship between subjectivity and language:

> C'est dans et par le langage que l'homme se constitue comme *sujet*; parce que le langage seul fonde en réalité, dans *sa* réalité qui est celle de l'être, le concept d'"ego."
>
> La "subjectivité" dont nous traitons ici est la capacité du locuteur à se poser comme "sujet." Elle se définit, non par le sentiment que chacun éprouve d'être lui-même (ce sentiment, dans la mesure où l'on peut en faire état, n'est qu'un reflet), mais comme l'unité psychique qui transcende la totalité des expériences vécues qu'elle assemble, et qui assure la permanence de la conscience. Or nous tenons que cette "subjectivité," qu'on la pose en phénoménologie ou en psychologie, comme on voudra, n'est que l'émergence dans l'être d'une propriété fondamentale du langage. Est "ego" qui *dit* "ego." Nous trouvons là le fondement de la "subjectivité," qui se détermine par le statut linguistique de la "personne."[1] (259-60)

Benveniste locates our common-sense impression of subjectivity in the activities of deictic language reflecting back towards the person who is speaking or writing. His argument implies that subjectivity is experienced at the moment of speech by the person who mobilizes the deictic network of words. Subjectivity is experienced most profoundly when we access the most deictic of signs, the personal pronoun "I."

In *La révolution du langage poétique*, Julia Kristeva analyzes this self-creation as it continually occurs in the form of a "rupture and/or boundary"[2] in which the subject separates from the object (43-45). This

---

1 It is in and through language that man constitutes himself as a *subject*, because language alone establishes the concept of "ego" in reality, in *its* reality which is that of the being.

  The "subjectivity" we are discussing here is the capacity of the speaker to posit himself as "subject." It is defined not by the feeling which everyone experiences of being himself (this feeling, to the degree that it can be taken note of, is only a reflection) but as the psychic unity that transcends the totality of the actual experiences it assembles and that makes the permanence of the consciousness. Now we hold that that "subjectivity," whether it is placed in phenomenology or in psychology, as one may wish, is only the emergence in the being of a fundamental property of language. "Ego" is he who *says* "ego." That is where we see the foundation of "subjectivity," which is determined by the linguistic status of "person" (224).

2 "rupture et/ou frontière" (41).

phase, which Kristeva calls the thetic, constitutes the threshold of language. Behind every language act, there is a subject in formation. With respect to narrative language specifically, Mieke Bal argues in a similar vein that the narrator who is the knower in the narrative utterance, whether speaking in the first or the third person, is always in reality an "I"; the narrating "I" is an *effect* of the narrative utterance. She discusses this phenomenon in a section entitled " 'I' and 'He' are Both 'I,' " and her argument, for which she is perhaps indebted to Benveniste, is as follows:

> In principle, it does not make a difference *to the status of the narration* whether a narrator refers to itself or not. As soon as there is language, there is a speaker who utters it; as soon as those linguistic utterances constitute a narrative text, there is a narrator, a narrating subject. From a grammatical point of view, this is *always* a "first person." In fact, the term "third-person narrator" is absurd. . . . [A]t best the narrator can narrate *about* someone else, a "he" or a "she." . . . [T]he distinction between "first person" and "third person" narratives . . . rests in the object of the utterance. (*N* 121-22)

The subject-in-formation in narrative language is a narrator and a first person. What can be said about the gender of this narrating subject?

Emile Benveniste frequently employs the masculine generic in outlining his theory of human subjectivity; for example, he writes, "C'est un homme parlant que nous trouvons dans le monde, un homme parlant à un autre homme, et le langage enseigne la définition même de l'homme"[3] (259). He does not question whether women might have a different rapport with language or subjectivity. However, feminist theory has addressed the specific rapport between women's subjectivity and language, often drawing on Benveniste's work. An important feminist reading of Benveniste is given by Monique Wittig in "The Mark of Gender" (1985).

In this essay, Wittig defines gender as a "primitive ontological concept [which] enforces in language a division of beings into sexes" (3). Lexical manifestation of the law of gender has "a plastic action on the real" (4), working through language to continually reconstitute the world according to the binary opposition of male and female. It places women in the ontologically impossible position of being a partial or "relative"

---

3 It is a speaking man whom we find in the world, a man speaking to another man, and language provides the very definition of man (224).

subject. "The result of the imposition of gender, acting as a denial at the very moment when one speaks, is to deprive women of the authority of speech . . . to deny them any claim to the abstract, philosophical, political discourses which give shape to the social body" (6).

Wittig's argument complements Virginia Woolf's portrayal, in *A Room of One's Own*, of the divided condition of women's subjectivity:

> [I]f one is a woman one is often surprised by a sudden splitting off of consciousness, say in walking down Whitehall, when from being the natural inheritor of that civilization, she becomes, on the contrary, outside of it, alien and critical. Clearly the mind is always altering its focus, and bringing the world into different perspectives. But some of these states of mind seem, even if adopted spontaneously, to be less comfortable than others. (93)

According to Woolf, a woman experiences a contested status as subject; both inheritor of and alien to her own culture, she has involuntary knowledge of states of consciousness which are "less comfortable" than others and which, she argues, are considerably less creative. Woolf's theory of women's divided consciousness and Wittig's argument that the law of gender intervenes at the moment of speech to make women relative subjects both describe a consciousness divided against itself. Both describe an uncomfortable, habitual and involuntary shift out of the subject position.

In *Alice Doesn't*, Teresa de Lauretis suggests that such a perilous or split relationship to subjectivity is in fact a product of the "symbolic function" inherent in narrative grammar:

> The hero's . . . descent through the landscape of her body symbolizes the (now) unimpeded descent of the fetus along the birth canal. In short, the effectiveness of symbols,—the work of the symbolic function in the unconscious—effects a splitting of the female subject's identification into the two mythical positions of hero (mythical subject) and boundary (spatially fixed object, personified obstacle). (119)

De Lauretis correlates this argument to the double or split identification of the woman who, faced with the cinematic image of Woman, sees herself being seen:

> [W]e can again recognize a parallel with the double or split identification which, film theory has argued, cinema offers the female spectator: identification with the look of the camera, apprehended as temporal, active or in movement, and identification with the image on the screen, perceived as spatially static, fixed, in frame. (199)

Wittig, Woolf and de Lauretis all argue that the action of gender on women's subjectivity can be described in terms of a counter-productive object identification that potentially intervenes at the most intimate stage of subjectivity formation. How can a woman overcome this condition of split identification? On this subject there is less unanimity.

Monique Wittig takes from Benveniste the critical notion of an abstract but whole subjectivity made accessible through the exercise of language. In "The Mark of Gender," she integrates his theoretical work into her own analysis of gender, subjectivity and language:

> For when one becomes a locutor, when one says I and, in so doing, reappropriates language as a whole, proceeding from oneself alone, with the tremendous power to use all language, it is then and there, according to linguists and philosophers, that there occurs the supreme act of subjectivity, the advent of subjectivity into consciousness. It is when starting to speak that one becomes *I*. This act—the becoming of *the* subject through the exercise of language and through locution—in order to be real, implies that the locutor be an absolute subject. For a relative subject is inconceivable, a relative subject could not speak at all. I mean that, in spite of the harsh law of gender and its enforcement upon women, no woman can say *I* without being for herself a total subject—that is, ungendered, universal, whole. Or, failing this, she is condemned to what I call parrot speech (slaves echoing their masters' talk). Language as a whole gives everybody the same power of becoming an absolute subject through its exercise. But gender, an element of language, works upon this ontological fact to annul it as far as women are concerned and corresponds to a constant attempt to strip them of the most precious thing for a human being—subjectivity. . . . [E]ach time I say *I*, I reorganize the world from my point of view and through abstraction I lay claim to universality. This fact holds true for every locutor. (6)

Wittig identifies a critical dynamic between women and language, in which language reproduces patriarchal structures that split women's consciousness. In spite of this, however, at the moment of her access to language, a woman experiences herself as a "total subject . . . ungendered, universal, whole."

In emphasizing the role of the first-person subject pronoun above that of other deictic signs, Wittig follows Benveniste who argues as follows that the first-person pronoun is the key term in the linguistic construction of subjectivity:

C'est en s'identifiant comme personne unique prononçant *je* que chacun des locuteurs se pose tour à tour comme "sujet." ... Si chaque locuteur, pour exprimer le sentiment qu'il a de sa subjectivité irréductible, disposait d'un "indicatif" distinct ... il y aurait pratiquement autant de langues que d'individus et la communication deviendrait strictement impossible. A ce danger le langage pare en instituant un signe unique, mais mobile, *je*, qui peut être assumé par chaque locuteur, à condition qu'il ne renvoie chaque fois qu'a l'instance de son propre discours. Ce signe est donc lié à l'*exercice* du langage et déclare le locuteur comme tel. ... Quand l'individu se l'approprie, le langage se tourne en instances de discours, caractérisées par ce système de références internes dont la clef est *je*, et définissant l'individu par la construction linguistique particulière dont il se sert quand il s'énonce comme locuteur. Ainsi les indicateurs *je* et *tu* ne peuvent exister comme signes virtuels, ils n'existent qu'en tant qu'ils sont actualisés dans l'instance de discours, où ils marquent par chacune de leurs propres instances le procès d'appropriation par le locuteur.[4] (254-55)

Benveniste here identifies the first-person pronoun as the most powerfully deictic of linguistic signs; it represents the subject at its most abstract and, in that sense, the subject who is beyond gender. Since Benveniste does not address gender, Wittig moves outside his theoretical framework to correlate subjectivity in language with the question of women's divided subjectivity. She argues that in saying "I," a woman becomes an undivided subject in spite of the law of gender; the use of language works directly against the exclusive appropriation of subjectivity by men.

In her fiction, Monique Wittig has experimented with ways to empower female subjectivity in language by universalizing female sub-

---

4 It is by identifying himself as a unique person pronouncing *I* that each speaker sets himself up in turn as the "subject." ... If each speaker, in order to express the feeling he has of his irreducible subjectivity, made use of a distinct identifying signal ... there would be as many languages as individuals and communication would become impossible. Language wards off this danger by instituting a unique but mobile sign, *I*, which can be assumed by each speaker on the condition that he refers each time only to the instance of his own discourse. This sign is thus linked to the *exercise* of language and announces the speaker as a speaker. ... When the individual appropriates it, language is turned into instances of discourse, characterized by this system of internal references of which *I* is the key, and defining the individual by the particular linguistic construction he makes use of when he announces himself as the speaker. Thus the indications *I* and *you* cannot exist as potentialities; they exist only insofar as they are actualized in the instance of discourse, in which, by each of their own instances, they mark the process of appropriation by the speaker (220).

jectivity without lending allure to the patriarchal construction of "woman." She has used the grammatical feminine generic, but prefers to disrupt the masculine generic by theorizing a future beyond gender. In "The Mark of Gender," she argues that the feminine generic is a temporary phase that serves a particular purpose but then must end. "Gender must be . . . destroyed" (6). This vision of a post-gender future can be compared to Woolf's argument in *A Room of One's Own* that only the "androgynous mind," "man-womanly" or "woman-manly," is truly creative (98-99). For women—as for men—such a quality of mind must lie in the future, for, as Christine Delphy has also recently argued, the subjectivity of the non-gendered human being is something we can only envision (204). Gender creates not one but two problematic categories of human being: "Gendered societies, such as Western societies, create their own subjectivities" (203), according to which "the notion of 'human being' does not exist . . . or rather, there are two ideas of 'human being.' There is a 'male human being' and a 'female human being'" (203). And if it is true that contemporary female human subjectivity is often divided against itself by the action of gender, this is not to imply that male subjectivity is without problems.

Again, contemporary theorists are in step with Virginia Woolf who, in *A Room of One's Own*, recounts how she discovered, in some men's writing, an "I" that neglects the androgyny characteristic of the creative mind. Woolf describes the "other" side of women's consciousness as "alien" and "critical," and one of the things it is critical of is the imperial, male "I." In Woolf's view, women's imaginations are limited by gender oppression, and men's imaginations suffer from other and related distortions:

> [I]t was delightful to read a man's writing again. It was so direct, so straightforward after the writing of women. It indicated such freedom of mind, such liberty of person, such confidence in himself. One had a sense of physical well-being in the presence of this well-nourished, well-educated, free mind, which had never been thwarted or opposed, but had had full liberty from birth to stretch itself in whatever way it liked. All this was admirable. But after reading a chapter or two a shadow seemed to lie across the page. It was a straight dark bar, a shadow shaped something like the letter "I." One began dodging this way and that to catch a glimpse of the landscape behind it. Whether that was indeed a tree or a woman walking I was not quite sure. Back one was always hailed to the letter "I." One began to be tired of "I." Not but what this "I" was a most respectable "I"; honest and logical;

> as hard as a nut, and polished for centuries by good teaching and good
> feeding. I respect and admire that "I" from the bottom of my heart.
> But—here I turned a page or two, looking for something or other—the
> worst of it is that in the shadow of the letter "I" all is shapeless as
> mist. Is that a tree? No, it is a woman. But . . . she has not a bone in
> her body, I thought. (95-96)

This male "I," unlike the "I" of a woman, is healthy, well fed and not at
all stunted. Yet, it is flawed: it impedes perception, making it impossible
to distinguish a woman from a tree. Woolf condemns this "I" for its
"dominance . . . and the aridity, which, like the giant beech tree, it casts
within its shade. Nothing will grow there." She argues that the author of
the male "I" is writing strictly from the male side of his brain. There is
no androgyny to such a mind, and it is "a mistake for a woman to read
[such writing] for she will inevitably look for something that she will not
find" (96).

Woolf's point might seem to be contradicted by the fact that diaries,
diary novels and autobiography are all forms of writing at which women
have excelled and which are written in the first person. However, feminist
scholarship has recognized a female writing tradition in which women's
autobiographical strategies are characterized by recourse to an other—
God, father, husband or greater cause—which serves as a justification for
the autobiographical act (Jelinek, 3). Typically, a woman's autobiographical "I" is, in the words of autobiographer Mary Meigs, only "seemingly
audacious" (7). Insofar as women writers have been truly at ease in the
literary idiom, they have been subject to vitriolic misogynist attacks by
their male contemporaries, as Sandra Gilbert and Susan Gubar demonstrate in "Sexual Linguistics." I would not foreclose the possibility of a
female literary tradition such as that traced by Gilbert and Gubar, but
would rather point out that the existence of such a tradition does not
upset Woolf's contention that within the male literary tradition, which is
uncontrovertibly the dominant one, women have occupied a curiously
unfruitful and divided subject position.

Monique Wittig strongly endorses the power of the pronoun "I," but
for many years, she avoided it almost entirely in her fiction. Catherine
Legrand, the protagonist of *L'opoponax* (1964), refers to herself as "je"
only once, in the crucial last sentence of the book: "On dit, tant je
l'aimais qu'en elle encore je vis"[5] (281). Until this point, the character

---

5 You'd say, I loved her so much that I live still in her. (My translation, as this sentence
  is left in French in Helen Weaver's translation.)

speaks only of "on," building in this way a non-specific, non-gendered sense of subjectivity. In "The Mark of Gender," Wittig comments on her experimentation with pronouns, explaining that the single use of "je" at the end of *L'opoponax* indicates a hope that "the transformation into the sovereign subject (which it implies) was accomplished for the character Catherine Legrand and all the others of her group" (8). The characters of *Les guérillères* (1969) are referred to as "elles," the feminine plural being gradually invested with a universal and undivided point of view as the female collectivity engages in the civilization-building activities of making laws, developing religions and writing history as they see it. A grammatical feminine generic is employed near the end of the book when the women are joined by several young men, but are still referred to as "elles." The subject of *Le corps lesbien* (1973) is a double lesbian subject, "j/e" and "tu," who, in Wittig's words, is "an *I* become so powerful that it can attack the order of hetero-sexuality in texts and . . . lesbianize the gods and goddesses, lesbianize men and women" (*MG* 11). We should not assume a facile understanding of Wittig's verb, "to lesbian-ize." In my view, it signifies a kind of cyborg-"I" which has been destroyed only to be recreated in a more powerful, completely translat-able form; this "I" has shed its contested human status and adopted a powerful, post-gender reversibility. Significantly, Wittig does not fully appropriate the personal pronoun "I" until *Virgile, non* (1985), a text that also transposes Dante's central metanarrative of knowledge and transcendance to a contemporary lesbian point of view.

Like Wittig and Woolf, Daphne Marlatt has explored in her poetry and theoretical writing the complex interrelations of the pronoun "I," subjec-tivity and gender; Marlatt, however, does not attribute the problems of the "I" solely to gender, and takes account of other unequal relationships of power and privilege. She almost always uses the first-person pronoun in her writing. *How Hug a Stone*'s narrating, focalizing protagonist is known only as "i," underlining her status as subject of language. Neither Wittig's rather aggressive lesbianizing "I," nor the "I" that Woolf criti-cized for its blighting effects on growth and perception, have much in common with the "i" that Daphne Marlatt constructs in this text. Mar-latt's "i" is an "i"/eye; a channel for perception, a conduit that gives voice to a woman's senses: her eyes, ears and skin. Marlatt developed this "i" in explicit opposition to the blindly ethnocentric and colonizing postures of white Europeans. The power relations that she criticizes include, but are not limited to, those of gender.

"In the Month of Hungry Ghosts" (1979) records Marlatt's replacement of "I" with "i," and her text makes it clear that the transition is not simply stylistic but is rather a critique of colonial power relations. The narrator of "In the Month of Hungry Ghosts," returning to her childhood home in Malaysia after her mother's death, feels herself and her sister to be "uncomfortable parodies of the leisured class. Is this the only way to be a white woman here?" she asks, "Or is this the condition of being a member of an exploitative & foreign moneyed class?" (63).

> there's no authentic ground here for "Europeans." I want to rip out
> of myself all the colonialisms, the taint of colonial sets of mind.
> That's why as kids we hated everything "English"—not because it
> was English but because we equated what was English with a colo-
> nialist attitude, that defensive set against what immediately sur-
> rounds as real on its own terms—because to take it on as real would
> mean to "go native" & that was unthinkable to them. (62)

The colonial tried to maintain as "real" what was elsewhere, denying the daily evidence of the senses, eating tinned food while ignoring the fresh tropical produce of the land. Marlatt opens her senses to the present, to construct a subjectivity that is radically immediate. "I stands for domi-nant ego in the world when you is not capitalized" (70), she writes, and doesn't use the capital letter for herself again.

The character of the grandmother in *How Hug a Stone*, on the other hand, uses the capital "I" repeatedly: " 'brought up in luxury with ser-vants & comforts of every sort. When I see what people are going through now I think how lucky I was to be born when I was.' sitting straight in the room where the tv is, my grandmother imperious" (27). The critique of colonialism is developed through this grandmother who defends her identity as a privileged, white and female subject in the colonial order. The privileges that she accepts as her due extend also to her role within the family: " 'I always came first with Grandpa & your mother. I always want to come first with people'—mauve & blue, she tells the story from her point of view, how else?" (34). In this family history, the grand-mother's attitude earns her the bitter anger of her daughter Edrys, and of her son, Edrys's brother, now the uncle to whom the narrator speaks: " 'queening it around the lodge,' he says. star of a shattered system of domestics, memorial orbits of love" (34).

The egotistical "I" represented by this grandmother is a product of British imperialism, class stratification and patriarchy. "Monolithic" (29), "imperious" (27), "queening it around the lodge" (34), she represents the powerful Victorian colonial order. Showing a lack of empathetic intelligence that recalls the emotional blindness of Woolf's male "I," she is what Brossard would call, in *L'amèr*, a *patriarchal mother*. She is completely unlike her notebook-carrying granddaughter, which is, of course, the point: in naming herself "i," the narrator defines an identity in opposition to everything this grandmother represents, a move that leads to the further necessity to reconstruct a female, familial genealogy that can explain her own presence in the world: the thetic theme of *How Hug a Stone*.

As I argue in the previous chapter, the narrator of *How Hug a Stone* is a focalizing "i"; aware, listening and feeling, she channels her perceptions of the world into her text. "In the Month of Hungry Ghosts" also interprets the adoption of the lower-case "i" as an affirmation of the sensory and immediate present, as a way to be more alive. *Ana Historic* preserves the upper-case "I" for historical language, maintaining the lower case for all those who evolve in the dialogic present of that book: Annie, Ina, Zoe and even Birdie Stewart, who brazenly intrudes into Annie's present tense in order to suggest an ahistorical but immediately desirable lesbian *telos* for Annie and her novel (134). In Marlatt's work, the lower-case "i" is used consistently for reality as it is manifest to the present-tense sense perception of the focalizing narrator/implied author.

Marlatt theorizes her view of the relation between sensory input and writing in a 1985 essay, "Writing Our Way through the Labyrinth." She argues for a writing which is more like reading and, in this essay, she links the egotistical "I" to gender:

> writing can scarcely be for women the act of the phallic signifier, its claim to singularity, the mark of the capital I (was here). language is no "tool" for us, no extension of ourselves, but something we are "lost" inside of. finding our way in a labyrinthine moving with the drift, slipping through claims to one-track meaning so that we can recover multiple related meanings, reading between the lines. finding in write, rite, growing out of *ar-*, that fitting together at the root of read (we circle back), moving into related words for arm, shoulder (joint), harmony—the music of connection. making our way through all parts of the figure, using our labyrinthine sense, we (w)rite our way *ar*-way, "reading" it, in intercommunicating passages. (49)

This essay encodes the values Marlatt invests in the subjectivity of the writing woman she created in *How Hug a Stone*: harmony, music, fitting together, circling back. Marlatt moves away from a critique of women's

subjectivity as constituted by the law of gender and damaged by hierarchical systems of class, power and privilege. She articulates instead an
eco-feminist vision of what might be possible, using a non-hierarchical
grammar at the level of the sentence and at the level of narrative. The
subjectivity signified by the lower-case "i" is constructed as the sensing
body listens for meaning(s), multiple and dialogic.

The narrator upholds the value of being in harmony with her world,
but of course she is often not in harmony, as the text makes clear. She is
repeatedly confronted by other voices and values with which she cannot
identify, and she subjects each of them to a rigorous reading for whatever
might further her struggle to find her own ground. I have already noted
that the i-narrator is not the only linguistic subject in *How Hug a
Stone*—the text is full of other voices, woven in without grammatical subordination by the focalizing "i." I pointed out that stories or fragments
narrated by others are technically defined as *embedded texts*. Mieke Bal
explains that embedded texts often serve as *signs* to the reader, informing
her/him how to interpret the primary fabula; similarly, embedded narratives can serve as signs to other characters in the story, enabling them to
resolve a problem or solve a mystery. When the embedded and the primary fabula resemble each other, that is, when they can be paraphrased
in such a way that the summaries "have one or more striking elements in
common" (*N* 146), then narratology defines the embedded text as a
mirror-text and a *sign* of the primary fabula (142-48). According to this
definition, *How Hug a Stone* is not only a symphony of voices but is also
a hall of mirrors in which the i-narrator narcissistically explores her own
image and confronts that which she both rejects and fears. The embedded mirror texts record the challenges faced by the i-narrator in her
effort to put her values into practice.

In psychoanalysis, narcissism is the developmental stage that precedes the thetic emancipation of the subject from the undifferentiated,
semiotic realm of the mother. In relation to *How Hug a Stone*, such an
interpretation is consistent with the preponderance of narcissistic or mirror texts that explore the narrator's problematic identification with Edrys.
This primary relationship is explored, for example, by the mirror text in
which the narrator's grandmother recounts Edrys's coming out at an
upper-class British wedding in Malacca. Edrys's story resembles the narrator's in one striking respect: a young woman confronts her prescribed
identity. The story of her mother serves as a sign to the narrator, who rec-
ognizes that she escaped where Edrys did not:

> "Do you know what she wore? I can see her *now*—a lovely pale
> coffee-coloured organdy dress . . . and she looked a *dream*."
> *her* dream, the one my mother inherited, *her* dress, my mother lend-
> ing her body to it. as i refused. (29)

The narrator's refusal of the dream is a moment when the actantial
identity of the two characters is confronted and rejected by the narrator.
Her refusal is not without consequences; in fact, it puts stress on the
mother-daughter relationship. The existence and eventual resolution of
this stress is one of the motivating forces of the text, in relation to which
it is useful to examine the framing narration that circles the story as a
whole.

The narrative told by "i" is itself framed by another narration, told in
another voice. The book opens with the words of a Vancouver medium
who, in 1975, immediately following Edrys's death, foretold the voyage
which is the subject of the book. Although the i-narrator is already present in her role as focalizer and implied author, this medium is, in fact,
the first narrator, and hers is the primary, framing narration.

> "you'll cross to England & you *will* walk in
> 'England's green & pleasant land' & she'll
> go home with you, though she has been already."
> Vancouver, 1975

Such a summary of events at the beginning of a narrative is a common
form of narrative anticipation, implying that what is about to be told was
fated to be (*N* 63). In *How Hug a Stone*, the epigraph frames the story as
a prophecy and as foreknowledge of the voyage to England, of Edrys's
presence there and of the successful outcome of the quest. The fabulas of
the prophecy and of the main narrative can therefore be said to mirror
one another.

The prophecy must be interpreted in relation to "six years earlier in
Vancouver the English medium began," a poem also narrated by the
medium with further embedded texts by Edrys and her father. The
medium recounts Edrys's recollections of her own death:

> "she said it was wonderful. she's telling me . . . & as she turned
> around, & she said she fell, she bowled over, but as she looked up
> she said it was her father, her father picked her up. & she said it
> didn't matter, it didn't matter at all, i only knew he was there. she
> says don't cry, no regrets, it couldn't have happened better. some-
> thing that i dreaded for so long caught me unawares. because,
> sweetheart—did she call you sweetheart? suddenly she said that i

was walking down an English lane with my father. you couldn't be
unhappy with that, could you now?" (40)

In her death, the terrifying fall "over the edge" loses its sting, and
Edrys's fear is calmed. She is reconciled with her daughter, whom she
addresses as "sweetheart," and with her father: "your grandfather stood
tall but your mother stood small in him. he's protecting her" (40).
Indeed, Edrys's father is here represented as loving, charming and
funny:

> there are an awful lot of her people over there 'cause she walked
> into the church to meet them, your father took her into the church &
> they were all there. he said—that was your grandfather—that's one
> way of getting them all together & you don't have to buy them
> drinks. (40)

Conflict is resolved to such an extent that the narrator's attention to the
stress in her relationship with her mother seems unnecessary or even
misguided. Appearances, of course, can be deceiving. The peaceful walk
of father and daughter down the English lane will be repeated in "back
to Reading," when the narrator and Kit mark the anniversary of Edrys's
death, "walking up the road in the sweet-smelling night recalling her"
(76). The two passages' mirroring of each other implies that the story
changes but the fabula remains the same. When the medium, however,
specifies that "the very old English church" is full of "her people," she
alludes to a matrilineal concept instantly overwritten when Edrys
"walked into the church" is corrected to read that her father *took her
in*" (my emphasis). A more gyno-centric world is fleetingly signified
again when the medium confirms the association between Edrys and
birds, in a wonderfully rhetorical unfolding of her death: "her passing
was swift, so swift. your mother loved birds. as i was talking i saw the
swift, you know the swift of England? a 'blue' bird" (40). The medium's
story doesn't address the real lack of harmony that disrupted Edrys's life,
and carried over into the life of her daughter. As a mirror text, it does,
however, signal to the narrator and to the reader the eventual success of
the narrator's quest, a success framed in broader, societal terms by the
epigraphic prophecy which frames the book as a whole.

The prophecy is partially composed by a transposed line from the final
stanza of the lyric in the "Preface" to William Blake's *Milton*, which was
incorporated into a hymn sung by Edrys while in boarding school:[6]

---

6 Thanks to Valerie Raoul for bringing the hymn to my attention.

> I will not cease from Mental Fight,
> Nor shall my Sword sleep in my hand,
> Till we have built Jerusalem
> In England's green & pleasant Land. (62)

Blake's words connect the narrator's quest with the utopian desire to naturalize Jerusalem, to build an earthly paradise in England. Such a context rereads the narrator's quest as wider than her personal story, so that *How Hug a Stone* itself becomes a mirror text and a sign that Jerusalem will be built. The effect of the epigraphic frame is to highlight the political issues that weave their way in and out of the narrative: feminist and environmental issues and the danger represented by the arms race. In this context, the book's title *How Hug a Stone* can be translated to mean how can we be closer to the earth, our mother? How can we build a more dialogic world?

The value that the narrator places on listening to the language of others ensures that the narration is dialogic, and this applies most significantly to Kit. Clearly, one of the ways that the narrator tries to do things differently is in relation to how she parents her son, to whom she frequently listens. Kit is often included in his mother's discourse. Benveniste argues that the first-person plural subject pronoun is in reality a first-person singular "I" speaking on behalf of him/herself and others (*Problèmes* 233). The narrator and Kit embody the first and second persons of such a discursive context, so that when the narrator refers to "we," she generally means herself and Kit. For his part, Kit tries out every kind of pronoun on his mother, speaking of her and her partner as "they," but modifies this to "you, or whoever" when queried (59).

Kit's dream on the train is also a mirror of the primary fabula; in both narratives, Kit and his mother seek to feel at home, and to avoid sacrifice. Stylistically, Kit's action-packed and heroic language contrasts sharply with his mother's nominalized and detailed observation, suggesting and perhaps parodying traditional gender opposition. Whereas the narrator is focused on her identity, Kit is equally focused on his own: "sitting face to face across a moving table, recognizing our difference" (61). The often hierarchical relationship of mother to child is represented as a face-to-face dialogue, although focalization rests with the narrator. The creation of a first-person plural pronoun that includes the narrator and Kit is essential to the political stance of the text, for it is the basis on which Marlatt is able to envision a generic human subject which includes both women and men.

How Hug a Stone's emphasis on relation as opposed to subordination reflects the thematic play of *host, hostile, ghostly* and *hospitable*, developed through cognates of the Indo-European root *ghost-i*, and recalls Marlatt's interest in a writing that is more like reading, a writing of connection. The narrative upholds the values of discourse, resists a "historical" accounting that might pass itself off as Truth, and takes a stance against the invisible (white, male, heterosexual, able-bodied, bourgeois) generic subject of historical language. *How Hug a Stone* constructs a subject who listens, who refuses to silence others, who takes a feminist stance. Like Heidegger's artwork, which "opens up a *world*" to ground our "dwelling" (44, 46), *How Hug a Stone* opens up an ideal textual space where there is enough room for the narrator and her son to live.

CHAPTER 7

Intertextual Narrative

Intelligible: logos there in the gathering hand,
the reading eye.
— Daphne Marlatt, "Musing with Mother
Tongue"

THE WORLD OF *How Hug a Stone* is full of voices, many and various,
hailing from a wide range of sources. Some belong to characters in the
story, family members and friends with whom Kit and his mother interact
while travelling in England. Others are more ephemeral: Marlatt over-
heard the phrase "narrative is a strategy for survival" (75) on a car radio
(personal interview with Daphne Marlatt, July 12, 1988). Still other
voices are transferred into the poem from books and pamphlets, many of
which are listed in the bibliography that Marlatt appended to the text
(see Appendix). The bibliography should have been published, for it
would have permitted readers to move more quickly into the most
thoughtful level of the poem. Together with the manuscript notes, also
housed in the Literary Manuscripts Collection of the National Library of
Canada, the bibliography confirms that, on one level, *How Hug a Stone*
encodes critical readings of Michael Dames's *The Avebury Cycle* and
Robert Graves's *The White Goddess*.

Both Dames and Graves characterize Neolithic religion in Great
Britain as goddess-worshipping and agricultural. Dames focuses on the
complex of Neolithic sites at Avebury, arguing that the society which
built this complex left behind a fragmented but richly suggestive record
of its beliefs. Robert Graves documents the innumerable names of the
Great Goddess, which can be found, helter skelter, in the literary records
of Western civilization. The two belong, along with Frederick Engels and
Lewis H. Morgan, to a long scholarly tradition of fascination with the
Neolithic, not so much for its achievements in agriculture, animal hus-
bandry, pottery and stone toolmaking, but for its social structure, which

was effectively transitional between that of the Paleolithic, or Old Stone Age—characterized by goddess worship and primitive communism—and that of the Bronze Age, which saw the development of writing, private wealth, weaponry and patriarchal chiefdoms. As Marlatt observes in her notebook, the archaeological record shows that the builders of Avebury were succeeded in the Iron Age by a warrior-oriented, patriarchal and class-stratified society, and preceded by many thousands of years of Paleolithic culture. Marlatt's notes reveal the extent to which Graves's and Dames's theories about Neolithic culture are transferred into her poem, where they are rejected or, at least, revised. Importantly, many of the transpositions signify together, forming a discrete, largely concealed, secret narrative of harvest sacrifice and transformation.

Each of the transferences into *How Hug a Stone* exemplifies the signifying process that Julia Kristeva defines as *intertextuality*. In *La révolution du langage poétique*, Kristeva argues that the signifying processes of displacement and condensation must be supplemented by a third process involving transference from one sign system to another:

> Nous connaissons les deux "procédés" fondamentaux que Freud désigne dans le travail de l'inconscient: le *déplacement* et la *condensation*. Kruszewski and Jakobson les ont, d'une autre façon, introduits dans les débuts de la linguistique structurale par les concepts de *métonymie* et de *métaphore* qu'on a pu depuis interpréter à la lumière de la psychanalyse.
>
> Il nous faut ajouter un troisième "procédé": le *passage d'un système de signes à un autre*.[1] (59)

The intertextual process is composed of displacement and condensation but, in addition, also involves an altering of the thetic *position*—"la déstruction de l'ancienne et la formation d'une autre"[2] (59).

The inherent association between intertextual transference and the reformation of the thetic has a particular significance for feminist texts. As the enunciative boundary of the subject, the thetic represents a critical stage in the formulation of a female subjectivity seeking to overcome

---

1 As we know, Freud specifies two fundamental "processes" in the work of the unconscious: *displacement* and *condensation*. Kruszewski and Jakobson introduced them, in a different way, during the early stages of structural linguistics, through the concepts of *metonymy* and *metaphor*, which have since been interpreted in light of psychoanalysis. (See Lacan, *Ecrits: A Selection*, 156-57, passim.)

   To these we must add a third "process"—the *passage from one sign system to another* (59).

2 the destruction of the old position and the formation of a new one (59).

the split condition of object-identification discussed in the last chapter. This means that if the canonical texts of Western culture can be rearticulated from a [+female] thetic horizon, the difference may empower women who find themselves defined by a civilization that both is and is not their own. Intertextual writing in this sense will be a significant form within Western feminist writing, and, for similar reasons, within the literatures of all marginalized cultural formations. Transposition or intertextuality is a particularly appropriate vehicle for *How Hug a Stone* because it is a poem that recounts the i-narrator's passage from the margins to the centre of her own history and family story.

The poem "at Cogswells (*'whose* wells?')" illustrates the transposition from spoken language to text while it evokes the collectivities of family and village in their necessary proximity to both language and water. The title is dialogic or double-voiced: someone, probably Kit, interrupts what might have been a magisterial and authoritative naming of this ancestral place. The question reminds us that wells, like village commons—also celebrated in *How Hug a Stone*—long resisted the institution of private property. In the landscape architecture of the Neolithic, wells were sacred.

> the feel of this cottage full of dogs, cats, flowers, currents of emotion. the drama of English manners. "sorry, darling." scones with Devonshire cream & strawberry jam for tea. "o bloody hell, there goes the phone." a constant stream of speech, my aunt in alliance with her teenage girls, the jokes, the stories—"that old bag," "what rubbish," "a perfectly horrid little house." the comings and goings of my uncle, pater familias, Mephistophelian brows (my grandfather) with the full feminine mouth i see in my sister, the moods of my mother, charming & furious at once.
>
> my son imitates an English accent, intrigued (to be in the swim) & yet stuffed up, finding it hard to breathe. allergic to the nearest thing we have to a hereditary home. (24)

At Cogswells, the narrator listens, focalizes and writes down the voices of family members who belong there, transposing between the signifying systems of her family's language and her own. She is caught in a network of deictic relations: "this cottage," "my aunt," "my uncle," "my sister," "my mother" and "my son." The "constant stream of speech" washes over her and she transposes its music for her own soundings: "*currents* of emotion," "*stream* of speech," "in the *swim*." The flow of nominal phrases builds the mood of shape-shifting fluidity.

The poem's only complete sentence reports Kit's response to the watery surroundings: "my son imitates an English accent, intrigued (to be in the swim)." Kit "find[s] it hard to breathe," and his condition suggests an ominous aspect to the watery character of their ancestral home. The idea that Kit might be in danger signals the presence of the hidden, intertextual narrative.

In "June near the river Clyst, Clust, clear. Clystmois this holding wet & clear," the equally intense transposition is no longer between spoken language and writing but is from text to text. The first part of the poem is largely composed of phrases transposed from Gail Duff's *Country Wisdom* (1979), an encyclopedia of "traditional good sense," which in turn acknowledges a long list of contributors for their "words of country wisdom." The heard voices are thus even more ancestral. This poem is a meditation on haysel, or hay-making, the hay harvest which, taking place in June, the month of Oak, coincides with the summer solstice and the journey of the narrator and her son. A powerfully ritual time in the ancient world, the haymaking season is here overdetermined by the secret narrative of sacrifice, signifying excessively both in relation to the archaeological/mythological researches of the narrator and to the dangers the allergens in the air pose to Kit's health:

> it's haysel, haymaking time, "Sweet an' dry an' green as't should be,
> An full o' seed an' Jeune flowers." tedding & cocking going on,
> shaking, turning, spreading, haytrucks go lorries lumbering by these
> twisty lanes line high with hedgerow, no seeing over, cow parsley,
> stinging nettles, campion, "day's eyes" & snails all colours coiled
> in their leaf byways. jeune the young, green June delayed by rain.
> June why do you punish me? "Take heede to the weather, the wind,
> and the skie." indeed, make hay while the sun shines you write,
> while the moon is on the wane. (25)

The opening of the poem partially integrates the following lines from Duff: "Tedding is shaking, turning, spreading the grass out to help drying. Cocking is making the grass into piles" (22). Most quotations are indicated by quotation marks. "Sweet an' dry an' green as't should be,/ An' full o' seed an' Jeune flowers," is cited in Duff along with a series of other proverbs to do with haymaking: "Take heed to the weather, the wind and the skie,/ If danger approacheth, then cock apace crie," and "Mow grass and make hay while the moon is on the wane" (22-23). "Make hay while the sun shines" is not in Duff's list, although it is cited in the *Oxford English Dictionary* under "hay"; it appears in the poem courtesy of a letter from Roy Kiyooka (personal interview with Daphne Marlatt, July 12, 1988).

"June near the river Clyst, Clust, clear. Clystmois this holding wet & clear" traces an etymological map of the Old English word *hieg*, or "hay," which evolved from *kau-*, meaning to hew or strike. Marlatt takes the Indo-European root to be a clue linking haymaking to the harvest sacrifice of a son/king—a practice theorized by both Graves and Dames. Like the cyclic moon, the narrator's son wanes; the time is ripe, then, for (hay) mowing:

> he wanes, my son redeyed & watery, phlegmatic in the face of *phleum pratense* grass of the meadow, timothy spikes erect a masculine given name, god honouring. not her who is cut, full of young vigour, from the living book, from the play of light & shadow, nothing less than herb-of-grace, rue i find, there with the queen's pinks in the clock that is a garden. (25)

Timothy spikes refer to the grass *phleum pratense*, "having narrow, cylindrical flower spikes and widely cultivated for hay." "Timothy" is "a masculine given name" meaning "God-honouring" and stemming from *kwei*, to pay, atone, compensate. It is cognate to "punish," which perhaps accounts for "June, why do you punish me?"

The poem is signifying what it does not make explicit: a mythological identification between harvest wheat and a young, male surrogate who— it is theorized—is sacrificed in a harvest ritual. Such an identification is attested to by Duff, who records a local tradition that blades of harvest wheat are young men (23), and by the many surviving folk songs which commemorate the life and death of John Barleycorn. Dames argues explicitly that a male harvest surrogate was sacrificed at midsummer rites observed by early Neolithic, agricultural cultures (70, 104-105). The poem's snail image also suggests Dames who comments on the ubiquity of the snail, with its natural spiral form, in burial sites from Neolithic Avebury (71). Graves maintains that the sacrifice of a surrogate son/king took place for the common good of the people and the recurrence of agricultural, life-supporting cycles. On June 24, he argues, an "Oak King" was burned alive, then after a seven-day wake the second half of the year began: the Celtic New Year (*WG* 177). The month of Oak is from June 10 to July 7, which roughly corresponds to the dates of the narrator's journey. It is the month of looking both ways, Duff's country wisdom reports, which is why oak is good for making hinges (135).

"June near the river Clyst" signifies as it conceals—and ultimately misreads and refuses—this theory that Neolithic religion involved the sacrifice of a harvest surrogate. The narrator notes the masculine emphasis in the materials she is studying, a focus which directs her own panicking attention to her son, rather than to "her who is cut, full of young vigour, from the living book" (25). "Her i lost, not him" (78). Edrys is the one whose life was sacrificed to "the common good," which tyrannized who she was (70). Mythologically, Edrys is Persephone. Now the narrator, rueing her loss, finds rue: herb of grace in the kitchen garden (personal interview with Daphne Marlatt, August 3, 1988). In the *Oxford English Dictionary* under "rue" one finds Shakespeare's *Richard II*: "Ile set a Bank of Rew, sowre Herbe of Grace; Rue, e'en for ruth, heere shortly shall be seen, In the remembrance of a Weeping Queene" (III, iv, 105-108). The final image of Marlatt's poem, "there with the queen's pinks in the clock that is a garden," resonates with the image of Demeter, weeping Queen and keeper of cyclical, time-keeping nature. The narrator mourns her mother who in this moment is Persephone, too. The mythological narrative does not function as a hidden "truth" but rather as a deeper layering of the questions and issues that are the constant preoccupations of *How Hug a Stone*. The inaccuracy and the androcentric bias in the scholarly materials to which she has referred lead the narrator through the theorized harvest sacrifice, terrifying in its implications, to a richer and deeper sense of the cyclic year both as immediately present, in the "clock that is a garden," and as told in the Greek myth of Persephone and Demeter.

According to Dames, "the monuments [in Avebury Parish, Wiltshire] were created as a coherent ensemble to stage a religious drama which took one year to perform" (9). The earth and stone constructions represent the body of the earth mother, an image that Marlatt strikingly represents as she and her son visit the sites: "nose stuffed eyes holes in the chalk ridge of sinal bones rushed down back roads' upland grass wind weaving snakelike through" (74). Dames argues that Neolithic ritual was organized as an earth-centred narrative focused on images such as the earth-as-pregnant-mother and the serpent. The images of the deity "were regarded as living characters, brought, each in its turn, to a state of maximum vitality by the annual sequence of human rites" (9). Annual ritual dramatized the monuments at Avebury in order to bring them and the images they embodied to such a vital state, "so as to describe and contain the divine narrative in a sequence of architectural stages (symbols) shaped to correspond with the changing condition of the deity's form" (13). This changing condition corresponds to the seasonal, agricultural cycle. "The Avebury cycle," writes Dames, "provides a glimpse of the Mother we have lost" (218). Marlatt develops her narrative in intertextual rapport with Dames's divine narrative, relating it to her narrator's search for her lost mother. The intertext is essential in the Avebury poems, "long after The Brown Day of Bride," "continued" and "Avebury *awi-spek*, winged from buried (egg."

I have suggested that in "long after The Brown Day of Bride," the narrator successfully negotiates a necessary rite of passage which permits her to come to terms with her mother and her mother's death. The intertext makes clear the extent to which this rite of passage is developed in relation to Dames's theories of Neolithic goddess religion. Dames understands that the goddess, like Persephone, spends the winters underground. As winter approaches, she descends to her underworld retreat, inviting her community to visit her at the West Kennet Long Barrow, the oldest monument in Avebury. In her poem, Marlatt cites portions of the following passage from Dames:

> The nature of the Winter goddess at West Kennet is revealed as much by her furnishings (now housed in Devizes Museum) as by her overall form. Her tomb-body was built to contain that primary chaos of natural and man-made things—the undifferentiated rubbish from which new life annually arises. Within the tomb there was a blurring of distinction between corpse and corpse. (43)

Mentioning also those objects housed in the Devizes museum—pots, meat bones, flint instruments, bone and shell beads[3]— Marlatt writes:

> *her tomb-body . . . built to contain that primary chaos*, long barrow
> of bones, dismembered or not, of potsherds, all mingled together.
> winter, this time of the year, submerged. as i am, heavy with cold. on
> the other side "down under" watching almond blossom in the chill
> streets of their world. a place to visit, blurring distinction between
> corpus & corpse.
> quick, running to meet them, with pots, meat bones, flint imple-
> ments, with stone, bone & shell beads. rubbish, *from which new life
> annually rises*. (72)

Like the harvest goddess, the narrator's mother has retreated to her underworld home, here confounded with what is literally "down under,"

---

3 I visited the Devizes Museum in November 1986.

the narrator's childhood haunts in Austronesia, long gone but not out of reach, for in this system, death is "a place to visit."

Marlatt deliberately misreads Dames, mingling "corpus and corpse," in order to observe how we must study the past to learn what we need to know. Her word play may be particularly poignant for the feminist, postmodern or postcolonial subjects whose (dis)inheritance poses them the task of sorting out the detritus, artifacts and treasures of Western culture. As Adrienne Rich observes, "no one ever told us that we had to study our lives, make of our lives a study" (73). The civilizing practices of housekeeping—sorting, recycling, composting, nurturing and throwing away— are themselves recycled into a spiritual and ethical *bricolage* thrown up in response to the present crisis. "[T]he nest we live in full of holes these days" (70), as the narrator puts it.

Dames is also the source for the suggestion that the traditional children's game of "The Farmer's in the Dell" might have its origins in Neolithic ritual. He writes:

> On balance . . . the life-giving force enjoys no absolute triumph, but always survives. This is shown in the traditional game, "The Farmer's in his Den," where the child selected to be Bone is destined to be chewed by Dog, and to receive a shower of blows from the others who shout: "We all pat the bone." The bone disintegrates, but the end of one game is the start of another, because that very bone is changed into a new being. Bone becomes Farmer in the next round. (45)

Marlatt incorporates this suggestive notion into a densely transitional passage which requires a bit of detective work from the reader:

> cup-&-ring, stone ring within a ring, the Farmer's in the Dell (is that you, Bride of the Brown Day, of the White Hills?)
> & *we all pat the bone*, thinking to make it ring us round, earth word (home again), seed word (safe again). (72)

Each motif in this shifting cascade ignites another intertextual system. Arranged paratactically as they are, these motifs form a narrative that traces the goddess's path from the Paleolithic through the Neolithic and early historical Gaelic cultures to her progress in the Christian era.

The cup, ring and bone are Stone Age symbols that may be seen incised on the rock surfaces of Avebury and at many other European archaeological sites and museums. Such symbols form an important part of the evidence for Marija Gimbutas's argument that Old European culture evolved continuously from the Paleolithic. In *The Language of the*

Goddess, Gimbutas maintains that the female-positive aspects of Old European culture reflect the crucial role of females in "the slow advance from upright hominoids to the fully developed humans of the Neanderthal period (100,000 B.C.)," postulated by Gerda Lerner (39). Basing her hypothesis on the evidence of prehistoric art, Gimbutas argues:

> the major aspects of the Goddess of the Neolithic—the birth-giver; portrayed in a naturalistic birth-giving pose; the fertility-giver influencing growth and multiplication, portrayed as a pregnant nude; the life or nourishment-giver and protectress, portrayed as a bird-woman with breasts and protruding buttocks; and the death-wielder as a stiff nude ("bone")—can all be traced back to the period when the first sculptures of bone, ivory, or stone appeared, around 25,000 B.C., and their symbols—vulvas, triangles, breasts, chevrons, zigzags, meanders, cupmarks—to an even earlier time. (xix)

Early human cultures, Gimbutas argues, interpreted their experience through very different symbolic systems from those with which we are historically familiar. These symbolic systems were organized around the mystery of birth and death in human life, on the earth and in the heavens. Cyclical and mythical, the renewal of life is symbolized by spirals, snakes, circles, crescents, horns, sprouting seeds and shoots.

> The snake was a symbol of life energy and regeneration, [and] even the colors had a different meaning than in the Indo-European symbolic system. Black did not mean death or the underworld; it was the color of fertility, the color of damp caves and rich soil, of the womb of the Goddess where life begins. White, on the other hand, was the color of death, of bones—the opposite of the Indo-European system in which both white and yellow are the colors of the shining sky and the sun. In no way could the philosophy that produced these images be mistaken for the pastoral Indo-European world with its horse-riding warrior gods of thundering and shining sky or of the swampy underworld, the ideology in which female goddesses are not creatrixes but beauties—"Venuses," brides of the sky-gods. (xix-xx)

In *How Hug a Stone*, the overall emphasis on birds, serpents, spirals, caves, crevices and, finally, on Avebury itself suggests a mobilization of such a prehistoric symbolic system. At the same time, the white stone lady whom the narrator meets at the end of the garden reminds us not to expect continuity between the Neolithic goddess, the goddesses of patriarchal times, and anything at all in our world today. That enigmatic lady may be silent because she is a patriarchal goddess, having changed into the colour of Robert Graves's White Goddess and muse (*HHS* 76; *WG* 24).

In her notebook, Marlatt records some of the White Goddess's names:
Belili, the Sumerian White Goddess who preceded Ishtar; Brigit, known
as Bride. Marlatt borrows from Graves the title that Graves gives Mary in
her aspect as Brigit: "Bride of the White Hills" (*HHS* 72; *WG* 394). The
white hills are probably the same chalk hills of Wiltshire where the narrator travels with her son, and where archaeologists and farmers continuously unearth evidence of Paleolithic, Neolithic and Bronze Age cultures.
The related Gaelic title, "Bride of the Brown Day," reminds one of the
curious etymology of "brown," from the Proto-Indo-European root
bher-3, meaning bright, which Marlatt will trace again in *Touch to My
Tongue*, igniting a chain of associations leading from brown to bright to
bride, Belili and Brigit. *The White Goddess* is also the source for the
Night Mare (*HHS* 33), "one of the cruellest aspects of the Goddess" (*WG*
26), whose association with the horse suggests that she too is a patriarchal goddess. Graves affirms as well the traditional identification of the
serpent as the Goddess's consort or son (387).

Graves observes the well-known phenomenon whereby many of the
names of the Goddess gradually became associated with the Christian
Mary. He records, for example, a tradition that the medieval Brigit shared
the muse-ship with "Mary Gypsy" or "Mary of Egypt," as Marlatt puts it
(*WG* 394). This is the transition that closes the poem with an open-ended
ellipsis:

> Bride who comes unsung in the muse-ship shared with Mary Gypsy,
> Mary of Eygpt, Miriam, Marianne suppressed, become/Mary of the
> Blue Veil, Sea Lamb sifting sand & dust, dust & bone, whose
> son. . . . (72)

The theory that the sacrifice of a son or consort was central to the
Neolithic goddess religion is ultimately lent credence in this series of
transformations which culminate in the Christian sacrifice of Mary's son.
When Marlatt reaches this point in her reconstructive work, however, she
stops, refusing the son's sacrifice. Her transformation of Dames's text
traces the signs of the goddess from the Neolithic cups and rings, through
the children's game with its ancient refrain, to Christian iconography
which preserved elements of the goddess, and transformed the sacrificed
serpent/son into the passion of Jesus Christ. But, her poem stops there.

The following poem insists that reified, deified sacrifice is not the point
of the story the narrator seeks to reconstruct. Or perhaps, reconstruction is
not the point: "active[ly] misreading" (75), she wants to "make us new
again: to speak what isn't spoken, even with the old words":

> . . . that is the limit of the old story, its ruined circle, that is not how
> it ended or we have forgotten parts, we have lost sense of the whole.
> left with a script that continues to write our parts in the passion we
> find ourselves enacting, old wrongs, old sacrifices. (73)

"Avebury awi-spek, winged from buried (egg" moves the focus of the text from death to ritual marriage followed by the summer harvest. Winter subsides, and the goddess moves from the West Kennet Long Barrow through the stone henges to Silbury Hill, following the ceremonial procession through the Avebury architecture which embodies the life-giving seasonal change. A version of the whole was reconstructed in the nineteenth century by William Stukeley (Fig. 1). From what he called the sanctuary, he proposed that a procession led up West Kennet Avenue to meet with a second parallel procession which began at the now-obliterated second stone circle and continued up Beckhampton Avenue. The two lines met in the henge for a ritual sexual/symbolic reaffirmation of life, and then continued to Silbury Hill, the goddess's pregnant belly. Dames argues that this ritual procession has been associated since time immemorial with a "serpentine" dance known as "dancing the hay" (168), described in the *Oxford English Dictionary* as "a country dance having the winding or serpentine movement, or being of the nature of a reel." The narrator and her son follow this ancient dance-like route, "rushed down backroads' upland grass wind waving snakelike through" (74).

In any agriculturally based religion, harvest festivals are thought to play a central role, and they are believed to have been significant in Neolithic religion. Dames argues that the Tan Hill Fair, a harvest festival held until 1932 in Wiltshire, near Avebury, evolved from a Neolithic festival anciently observed there (210-18). He theorizes that the hill is the goddess's pregnant womb from which she gives birth to the harvest (131). Alternatively, she gives birth to spring. Marlatt cites a Gaelic poem that is thought to remember the ritual of the birth of spring: "The Day of Bride, the birth of Spring/ the serpent emerges from his knoll . . . / The serpent will come from his hole/ on the Brown Day of Bride" (Mackenzie, 188). She writes, "the line hypothesized druid lore (in Christian times), today a collective need to endure winter to spring, when *from his knoll . . . / the Serpent will come from his hole/ on the Brown Day of Bride* singing, wave on wave emerging: & at centre, earth, only earth" (75). Marlatt reads the serpent dancing forth to his bride as the life principle, "wave on wave emerging," like the "*sine*" of continuity and renewal: *"man's life like the life of cereals. woman's too"* (74). Silbury Hill is both a discrete *topos* and sacred body; activated in ritual it is an image of a singular event and of the endlessly repeated and therefore timeless movement of the seasons. The sacred narrative thus embodies an equivocal or mythological relation to teleology that recalls the resistance to teleology in the fabula and theme of *How Hug a Stone*.

Three different archaeological excavations of Silbury Hill suggest that that its construction was related to a ritual midsummer celebration. Marlatt's phrase "at centre, earth, only earth" (75) refers to the archaeologists' expectation that Silbury Hill would contain burials, which it does not. Unlike the Egyptian pyramids and unlike the West Kennet Long Barrow nearby, the Hill contains no bones, only (sacred) earth, a matrix of chalk blocks and a moat, resembling the one around the Avebury henge, which was filled in with more earth at the time of construction. *The Avebury Monuments* relates that Silbury Hill is "made up of a matrix of chalk block walls arranged in the pattern of a spider's web with a number of concentric circumferential and interrupted radial walls in plan" (Vatcher and Vatcher, 26). The handbook continues:

> the highly preserved state of the organic material was quite exceptional. As well as the grass which was still pliable, though brown in colour, there was all the insect and floral life that goes with it; beetles, many other insect components, and flying ants with their wings. Although the date of construction of the hill is still only known within a bracket of a few hundred years, the ants with their wings tell us that the building started at the end of July or early in August, at a time of year when the wings of this ant develop. (28)

This is the information that Marlatt transposes to her poem:

> *matrix of chalk block walls arranged in the pattern of a spider's web* around & over a mound of turves, *grass still pliable though brown in colour . . . beetles . . . flying ants with their wings* showed them buried late July of 2660 B.C. why? (74-75)

If death is not at the centre of this mandala, neither is it empty, and the discovery of the earth at the centre harmonizes with the primary positive association with the earth in a symbolic system of the kind that Gimbutas suggests characterized Paleolithic and Old European culture. Dames interprets the structure as a ceremonial representation and a symbolic summary of what he calls the "divine narrative" (13), which served these early communities as a social paradigm, or, as Marlatt puts it, "a strategy for survival" (75).

It may be that Graves, Dames and others are correct in their argument that a young man was ritually sacrificed at summer harvest; it is conceivable that such a thing played a role in the survival strategies of communities struggling in difficult material circumstances. It has not, however, been proven. The theme of the harvest sacrifice for the Mother is woven into the narrative of *How Hug a Stone* at the same time that the poem reaches steadily towards an epiphanic refusal of its supposed necessity; in the end, the sacrificial teleology is clearly rewritten and rejected. "Sacrifice of son refused," Marlatt wrote in her manuscript notes:

> the fear that if i was to (identify with) embrace Her, then he would have to die, be sacrificed. but she was never a person as (even,) He, Jehovah, became, dictating to Abraham. She was the source of all life, a cunt, wellspring, daemon of the earth out of which everything flows (Olson's Gaia?) Rhea (flowing) & her son in the old Mediterranean religions was both son & lover individuated, mortal, therefore of seasonal duration only. (n.p.)

The motif of sacrificing the son motivates the narrator's fear that she has put her son at risk in bringing him on her quest for the/her mother: "i only want to fly home with him, to keep him safe. where does this feeling come from that i have put him at risk? that the longer we stay here the more i tempt fate?" (54). The sacrifice motif lies behind Kit's dream in "on the train," as the notebooks make clear: "Kit's dream—the King/ the sacrifice. 'idol idol idol' etc"(n.p.). Kit's fever, in "Pilgrim night," where he is "very hot" and "scared," as well as his dream of idolatry and sacrifice, are proairetic developments of this subnarrative. The appearance of animals sacred to the goddess, specifically the serpent, in "as commonly told," and the horse in "boy with tape recorder stalking horses in a field of cows," combined with the emphasis throughout the poem on the importance of birds, can all be read in relation to the narrative of the harvest sacrifice of a surrogate son for the mother. Marlatt's text reconstructs as it refuses, as she comments in her notes: "subtext—illuminates / collision of subtexts" (n.p.).

The notes also relate the growing historical significance of the sacrifice of the son to the depersonalization of the goddess as matrix and matter:

> as we get caught up in the passion & pathos of His sacrifice, she fades into undifferentiated background, because she is not a person in that way. we can't relate the tragedies of our lives, our Mortalities, to Her because she is pure source. (n.p.)

Refusal of the sacrifice is thus correlated with refusal of the hero/obstacle opposition and the plot position defining woman as object or matter rather than as striving human subject.

Marlatt's narrative rereads the "writing in monumental stones," reaching back to the "transformative, sinuous sentence emerging even circular, cyclic Avebury" (75). She follows Dames in reading the procession to Silbury Hill as the serpent/ine narrative of the year's progress, but her narrative line leads to a radically reformed symbolic system based on the evidence:

> *she lives* stands for nothing but this longstanding matter in the grass, settled hunks of mother crust, early Tertiary, bearing the rootholes of palms, they bring us up, in among stone-folds, to date: the enfolded presented waits for us to have done with hiding-&-seeking terrors, territories, our obsession with the end of things. how hug a stone (mother) except nose in to lithic fold, the old slow pulse beyond word become, under flesh, mutter of stone, *stane*, *stei*-ing power. (75)

Marlatt indicates that the cultural changes that are bringing us up to date are structural ones, winding down the narrative syntax based on terrors, territories and *telos*, all outmoded by the actual demands on our life resources. Neither is it a question of substituting female icons for male in the same old structure, as the critique of the grandmother's imperial "I" earlier made clear. And, of course, Kit will not be sacrificed. How could he be when he signifies the future?

Kit's play is essential in the poem because it is the free play of a child of either gender raised outside of the "weariness of Weirfield school morality" (66). The democratic family dyad of mother/son signifies an *ethos* freed from fear, opening into renewal and light:

> red windbreaker fleck a sea of green & climb some moat in
> his imagination scaled he calls me to: come & get me
>   the, all-powerful tickle, gulp, wriggle
> gulping in the whole world hugged in ecstatic limit,
> breath's. nothing still, no duration now (a line) creeps
> through fields of (waves of) renewed green, cloud, light. (74)

For a moment, as in the divine narrative of the intertext, the human body is in harmony with the sacred body of the earth, and the syntax of the poem works to describe an event outside the epistemological framework of known narrative syntax.

A final, illuminating motif from Graves is that of the riddle or poem that conceals the name and attributes of the goddess. The question framed by the book's title, "how [do you] hug a stone?" is nothing less than a riddle, and as a riddle it recalls the many Old English riddles that are proper to the places the poem memorializes. In relation to the mythological intertext, the riddle of *How Hug a Stone* is the specific type known as the "Câd Goddeu," or "The Battle of the Trees," in which the poem itself, which is nothing less than the correct response to the riddle, both preserves and conceals the mysteries of the ancient and forbidden goddess (*WG* 27-48). In like manner, *How Hug a Stone* presents and disguises the goddess's attributes: bird, horse, snake, cave, cow, white lady and so on. The riddle's answer may finally be a homely one: it is difficult to hug a stone, and much more rewarding to hug a child.

PART THREE

A Narratological Reading of *Picture Theory*

CHAPTER 8

Fabula: Hologram

> Nous partons, Danièle Judith, Claire Dérive et
> moi vers la mer, retrouver Florence Dérive et Ori-
> ana dans la grande maison, sur une île, au sud de
> Cape Cod.   — Nicole Brossard, *Picture Theory*

IN AN INTERVIEW RECORDED in Montréal in the summer of 1988, Nicole
Brossard comments on the appearance of metaphors based on aspects of
nature "which are not visible, like waves, *des ondes, des vibrations*," but
which have become accessible to the human imagination because of
advances in science and technology.

> We live in general in our society with metaphors which belong to the
> industrial and agricultural periods. We don't live with the metaphors
> of our new technology, and I think that the new technology provides
> us with information which somehow we will fantasize. When we do,
> then we'll come up with new metaphors which will tell more about
> space and time, will tell about them in a different way. There are
> things we can do because of gravity, and now we are discovering
> things we can do without gravity and we will be able to do them. It's
> very challenging. Just the fact that we know so little about the
> brain—we can imagine a certain potential. It doesn't mean that we
> would be happier, it only means that we can dream. (Personal inter-
> view, June 8, 1988)

The hologram of *Picture Theory* is clearly such a metaphor: "Ainsi voit-
on surgir d'inédites métaphores ayant partie liée avec le cerveau: l'hologramme, l'ordinateur"[1] ("Synchronie" 82). Drawn from the dreaming of
lensless photography, fibre optics and virtual reality, the hologram is a
high-tech fantasy of women's being in a post-patriarchal age—a new picture theory of nature, reality and life.

---

1 Thus we are witnessing the appearance of entirely new metaphors, some associated
  with the brain: the hologram, the computer (99).

In terms of the development of Brossard's oeuvre over a thirty-year period, the hologram stands in a pivotal position. It is a metaphor that enriches much of her earlier work, giving deeper sense to *Le centre blanc* and *Aube à la saison*, satisfying the complex desire that is the final expression of *L'amèr* (1977):

> je travaille à ce que se perde la convulsive habitude d'initier les
> filles au mâle comme une pratique courante de lobotomie. Je veux
> *en effet*
> voir s'organiser la forme des femmes dans la
> trajectoire de l'espèce.² (109)

The three-dimensional woman in *Picture Theory* celebrates her gender's trajectory in the evolution of the species. At the same time, looking in the direction of *Le désert mauve* and *Baroque d'aube*, the hologram illuminates the figure of translation that dominates Brossard's writing in the period following *Picture Theory*. Both figures—the hologram and translation—are types of "making sense," and both display the structure of a Brossardian narrative event, based on light-wave interference patterns which produce three-dimensional meanings or holographic pictures in the brain. For the hologram in *Picture Theory* is more than a metaphor. It is also a narrative structure, the basis for a non-linear narrative grammar inspired by lensless photography and the workings of the human mind. Narratological analysis of *Picture Theory* allows us to appreciate the depth of Brossard's challenge to traditional narrative, in reimagining completely the fundamentals of narrative form.

Narratological analysis of *How Hug a Stone* began with the fabula, the deepest level of narrative, and with identification of the events out of which fabula is constructed. Chapter 4 outlined procedures to establish fabula events, arguing that, in most cases, an intuitive, one-sentence summary of the action produces a model of the fabula, which can be corrected or verified using formal criteria. Such a summary of events in *Picture Theory* inevitably directs attention to "livre deux," "L'émotion," the most narrative of the book's eight sections, in which the five protagonists travel from their homes in Québec and New York to enjoy their summer vacations together on an island off Cape Cod. In *Picture Theory*, as in *How Hug a Stone*, a collective subject undertakes a journey to fulfill an

---

2 I am working so that the convulsive habit of initiating girls to the male as in a contemporary practice of lobotomy will be lost. I want to see *in fact* the form of women organizing in the trajectory of the species (101).

object; a head series of functional events articulates an actantial change of condition detailed by the sequential structure of a vacation. In both narratives, the quest-journey can serve as a preliminary fabula model.

MODEL I: THE VACATION AS QUEST

five women   —   travel to an island   —   to vacation together
    subject   —   function   —   object

However, quest structure, as I have argued, cannot be mobilized in a literary text as if it were ideologically neutral. In spite of its archetypal figurative power, and its character as a naturalized generic narrative sentence, the quest is a semiotic mechanism for the construction of patriarchal gender. Ruled by the desire of the generic hero, for the present it must remain a problematic vehicle for feminist narrative. In *How Hug a Stone*, Daphne Marlatt disarms the intransigent teleology of the quest while recuperating its charm at the story level, where it functions as a plot-motif and an aspect of focalization. In *Picture Theory*, the quest is displaced as the deep or determinant structure by the hologram. The repositioned vacation-quest is thereby freed to supplement the Brossardian repertoire of initiatory figures such as the sunrise, the island, love, translation, writing, reading and the horizon. The primary event, which is the building block of the holographic narrative structure, is an abstraction of this repertoire of figures.

Brossard's text deconstructs the inherent teleology and inherited gender bias of the quest. From the beginning, she puts a *ludique* spin onto her characters' quest-voyage, since the five women, once settled in their vacation home, do little more than read books, prepare meals and eat them and visit the beach in the afternoons. One memorable night, they venture to a nightclub, emerging in time to witness the dawn. The substitution of these daily activities for the *agon* of the Aristotelian hero signals Brossard's interest in Joyce's epic modernism; as Lorraine Weir has argued, several of Joyce's texts, including *Ulysses*, *Finnegans Wake* and "The Dead," provide critical points of departure for *Picture Theory*'s far-reaching transformations. Brossard goes beyond Joyce in reconfiguring narrative grammar according to the model of the hologram.

The intertextuality of *Picture Theory* is such that virtually every aspect of the island vacation is overdetermined, and must be decoded in relation to a series of texts, particularly Brossard's key 1982 essay, "De radical à intégrales." As I note in chapter 1, this essay traces the passage from a cultural condition in which only a few individual women are able to achieve an awareness of themselves as fully human, to an evolved community of women who can claim full humanity for themselves. This is the development of culture in the feminine, for which Brossard specifies the following process:

>   1. L'éclat du sens unique
>   * briser l'homme comme universel
>   ** rompre le cercle de la féminité
>   2. Produire un vacance, soit un espace mental qui peu à peu sera investi de nos subjectivités, constitutant ainsi un territoire imaginaire à partir duquel nos énergies pourront prendre forme.[3] (96)

Feminist rejection of the masculine universal corresponds in *Picture Theory* to the women's departure "vers la mer," while the vacation itself suggests the play on *vacance*, pointing to the polysemic potential of *void* and *vacation*, which gets lost in the English. The edge of the enclosing circle of patriarchal meaning is represented, in *Picture Theory*, as the sunrise. The departure "vers la mer" also recalls the triple play of "la mer," "la mère" and "l'amer," which Brossard uses to signify the deconstruction of patriarchal motherhood in *L'amèr*; in broad terms, the earlier text corresponds to the rupture with patriarchal meaning, while *Picture Theory* itself corresponds to the vacation in which women's energies can be elaborated. This permits the evolution of woman as subject, and Brossard writes of the vacationing women that "Les subjectivités s'interpellent ainsi les unes les autres **toute une nuit chaude de juillet, lentement**"[4] (*PT* 107). Following Althusser, we understand the verb "s'interpeller" to mean that the women call each other into being as functional subjects. The *vacance* is the energized space around which the spiral will begin to take form (Fig. 2).

The passage to the island is also written into a Sapphic intertext associating the island environment with Sappho's legendary poetic academy for women. It is a remarkable fact that Sappho was a celebrated female lyric poet who wrote lovingly of women, and who lived in the thriving

---

3   1. Exploding one-way sense
        * shattering the concept of man as universal
        ** interrupting the circle of femininity
    2. Producing a void, a mental space which, little by little, will become invested with our subjectivities, thus constituting an imaginary territory, where our energies will begin to be able to take form (111).

4 Subjectivities were interpellating each other in this way throughout *toute une nuit chaude de juillet* slowly" (79).

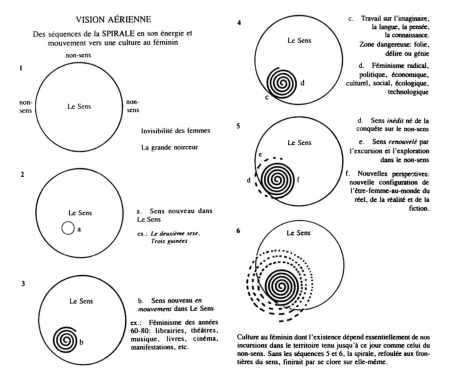

Fig. 2. Nicole Brossard's *"Vision aérienne,"* from *La lettre aérienne.* Used with permission.

Aerial Vision

The sequences of the SPIRAL in its energy and movement towards culture in the feminine

1. Non-sense/sense: the invisibility of women, *La grande noirceur* in Québec.

2. a. New sense within sense: *The Second Sex, Three Guineas*

3. b. New sense in movement within sense: feminism from the 1960s to the 1980s: bookstores, theatres, music, books, films, demonstrations, etc.

4. c. Work on the imaginary, language, thought and knowledge. Danger zone: madness, delirium or genius.

   d. Radical feminism, politics, economics, culture, society, ecology, technology

5. d. *Never-before-seen* sense born from the conquest of non-sense.

   e. Sense *renewed* by exploratory excursions into non-sense.

   f. New perspectives: new configurations of women's-being-in-the-world, of reality and of fiction.

6. The existence of culture in the feminine essentially depends upon our incursions into the territory which has until now been held as non-sense. Without sequences 5 and 6, the spiral, suppressed within the confines of sense, would end up closing in on itself. (My translation.)

port city of Mytilene, on the Greek island of Lesbos, in the seventh century B.C.E. The fragments of her work that survived destruction by the early Christian church, and the stories which have never ceased to circulate about her, have given rise to a rich literary tradition to which many writers, both male and female, have contributed (see Robinson and Carman). In developing the motif of five women reading, writing and otherwise spending intimate time in the privileged milieu of the island, Brossard unmistakably evokes Sappho's island academy and participates in what Susan Gubar refers to as "Sapphistries"—the "fantastic collaboration" (95) between Sappho and women writers such as H.D., Renée Vivien, Marguerite Yourcenar, Natalie Barney and Amy Lowell. Since the 1991 publication of "Booking Passage," Daphne Marlatt's place among Sapphic collaborators is equally well assured. Gubar suggests that even as they supplement the loss of Sappho's texts, the feminist modernists who look back to Sappho create "an empowering literary history" (95). Their project resembles that of the narrator of *Picture Theory*, who struggles with disempowering male-centred history: "faire entrer de l'histoire dans ma vie est la chose qui m'est la plus difficile. Pourtant, j'y travaille réellement. Je lie l'histoire à ce qui m'entoure; elle est toujours ailleurs"[5] (158). In this respect, the island vacation off Cape Cod signifies a privileged milieu for the cultural reintegration of history and experience. It provides an environment fulfilling the material conditions needed, as Virginia Woolf speculates, for the emergence of a woman poet of Sappho's stature: predecessors, membership in a group where art is freely discussed and practised, and freedom of action and experience. "Perhaps in Lesbos, but never since, have these conditions been the lot of women," wrote Woolf ("The Intellectural Status of Women" 46).

Monique Wittig's Sapphic collaborations also figure in this intertext of feminist writing and reading. Namascar Shaktini has elaborated how Wittig's *Le corps lesbien* signifies the voyage to Sappho's island in order to reconstruct human subjectivity around the image of the lesbian body, thus writing over culturally dominant, generic and unmarked phallogocentric subjectivity (152). Sigmund Freud, in an infamous moment, commented, "We know less about the sexual life of little girls than of boys. But we need not feel ashamed of this distinction; after all, the sexual life

---

5 to let some story enter my life is the most difficult thing for me. Still I work on it really. I link history to what surrounds me: it is always somewhere else" (125).

of adult women is a 'dark continent' (English in original) for psychology."[6]
Wittig's *amantes*, or "companion lovers"—to borrow the term chosen by
Wittig and Sande Zeig to translate "amantes" in *Lesbian Peoples: Materials for a Dictionary*—break with Freud's claim that women's sexuality is a
"dark continent," and appropriate Watteau's *Embarquement pour Cythère*,
in a compact, intertextual gesture:

> adieu continent noir de misère et de peine adieu villes anciennes nous
> nous embarqons pour les îles brillantes et radieuses pour les vertes
> Cythères pour les Lesbos noires et dorées."[7] (20).

The lovers leave behind the dark continent and the binary symbolic structures it signifies, embarking for radiant islands coloured in green, gold and
black. Wittig's imagery suggests the Paleolithic colour symbolism
described by Gimbutas, associated with the chthonic goddesses of the
ancient world, and mobilized by Daphne Marlatt in "long after the Brown
Day of Bride."

Brossard's own transformations of Freud's "dark continent" begin seriously in her 1980 text, *Amantes*, when she feminizes the grammatically
masculine "le continent" in order to dwell there with like-minded women
writers, co-signers in connivance with Sappho and each other:

> ma continent multiple de celles qui ont signé: Djuna
> Barnes, Jane Bowles, Gertrude Stein, Natalie Barney,
> Michèle Causse, Marie-Claire Blais, Jovette Marchessault,
> Adrienne Rich, Mary Daly, Colette et
> Virginia, les autres noyées, Cristina Perri Rossi,
> Louky Bersianik, Pol Pelletier, Maryvonne si
> attentive, Monique Wittig, Sande Zeig, Anna d'Argentine,
> Kate Millett, Jeanne d'Arc Jutras, Marie Lafleur, Jane Rule,
> Renée Vivien, Romaine Brooks, écrire: le réel / la peau
> clairvoyante prunelle essentielle dans le déploiement
> de ma consciouce et *expression*: mon double
> une singulière mobilité et le continent
> certes une joie[8] (108)

---

6 Sigmund Freud, in *The Standard Edition* (1959), Vol. 20, 212; also Sigmund Freud,
   "On Femininity," in *The Standard Edition* (1964), Vol. 22, 112-35. Cf. Donald
   Stephens on the moderns' interest in "the ambiguity of Sappho's character; though
   [her] age, the 'dark age of Greece,' was condemned, for the perversions of its women"
   (74).

7 farewell black continent of misery and suffering farewell ancient cities we are embarking
   for the shining radiant isles for the green Cytheras for the dark and gilded Lesbos.

8 my continent multiplied by those who have signed: Djuna Barnes, Jane Bowles,

In Brossard's thought here and elsewhere, the transformation of consciousness is a thought-full and incarnate desire associated with light.
The companionship expressed by the long list of names shows that
women writers have achieved the critical mass necessary to refashion
Freud's continent in the feminine, and to neutralize the binary oppositions to which he refers. The poem's transformation of the continent—as
opposed to a migration to the islands—may reflect a lesbian-positive but
non-separatist political strategy. Certainly, Brossard embraces that old
continent and watches it fill with daylight, putting an end to marginality,
secrecy and fear:

> ma continent, je veux parler l'effet
> radical de la lumière au grand jour
> aujourd'hui, je t'ai serrée de près,
> aimée de toute civilisation, de toute
> texture, de toute géométrie et de braise,
> délirantes, comme on écrit: et
> mon corps est ravi.[9] (109)

Picture Theory fulfills the promise of *Amantes*, articulating the consequences of its progressions: *"du continent des femmes à la pensée
conséquente"* (168). In *Picture Theory*, *"la pensée conséquente"* is in
effect an island that the women can access only after separation from the
continent, or dominant culture, and traversal of the water with all of its
symbolic associations. The journey is a rite of passage, complete with
separation, water, suspension and reintegration. The lesbian women, who

---

Gertrude Stein, Natalie Barney, Michèle Causse, Marie-Claire Blais, Jovette
Marchessault, Adrienne Rich, Mary Daly, Colette and Virginia, the other drowned
ones, Cristina Perri Rossi, Louky Bersianik, Pol Pelletier, Maryvonne so attentive,
Monique Wittig, Sande Zeig, Anna d'Argentine, Kate Millett, Jeanne d'Arc Jutras,
Marie Lafleur, Jane Rule, Renée Vivien, Romaine Brooks
to write: the real/the skin clairvoyant
pupil essential in the unfolding
of my consciousness and expression: my double
a singular mobility and the continent
indeed a joy" (108).
9 my continent, i mean to talk about the radical
effect of light in broad daylight
today, i've held you close,
loved by every civilization, every
texture, every geometry and ember,
delirious, as it is written: and
my body is enraptured (109).

live in symbolic obscurity on the continent, appear in the brightness of a July day on the other side of the water's initiatory divide.

In "L'émotion," the night is illuminated by flashes of lightning as the women traverse the forests of Québec and Maine (95). The historical and cultural significance of their collective movement is signified intertextually through the deployment of classical figures and motifs such as these dark, continental forests, which recall the wood where Dante is lost in the opening lines of *The Divine Comedy*. The activation of an intertextual reading linking *Picture Theory* to *The Divine Comedy* aligns the female characters with the [+male] subjectivity of the central traditions of European culture, preparing the reader for the female achievement, later in the novel, of a vision of paradise in the form of a rose. When the travellers reach the coast in the middle of the night, they are awaited by an eery ferry that suggests Charon's ferrying of the dead across the River Styx. This may mean that the break with the past is irrevocable. The travellers disembark, however, with the rising sun, and are interpellated into a collective *vita nuova* as the subtle elaborations of the vacation begin.

The *women* entering the *daylight* as they cross over to the *island* are symbolic of *three* binary pairs—masculine/feminine, day/night and centre/margin—deactivated by this crucial event.

> Nous partons, Danièle Judith, Claire Dérive et moi vers la mer, retrouver Florence Dérive et Oriana dans la grande maison, sur une île, au sud de Cape Cod. Il y avait des autoroutes, de la forêt, des odeurs, des champs; nous avancions sur le continent vers la mer et nous regardions devant nous. Les autoroutes prennent la couleur des bois et des villes que nous traversons. Les autoroutes faisaient des boucles dans l'horizon et parfois nous avons l'impression de ne pas avancer. Chacune de nous prenait le relais vers la mer. L'autoroute était *d'ombre et de lumière* vers la fin du voyage, au crépuscule lorsque nous l'avons quittée pour des routes plus lentes et qui serpentent vers la mer. En arrivant à Woods Hole nous avons vu le bateau qui devait nous mener dans l'île et qui flottait devant nous comme un éclairage suspendu.[10] (95)

---

10 We are leaving, Danièle Judith, Claire Dérive and I for the sea, to find Florence Dérive and Oriana in the big house, on an island, south of Cape Cod. There were superhighways, forest, scents, fields; we advanced over the continent toward the sea and we looked straight ahead of us. The highways took on the colour of the woods and cities we passed through. The highways made loops on the horizon and sometimes we had the impression we were not moving forward. Each of us took turns relaying the other on the way to the sea. The highway was *shadow and light* towards the end of the

The passage to the island is a key occurrence of what I identify as the primary event of *Picture Theory*. Traversal of the liminal—island marge or *hall d'entrée*—synchronized with the historical passage into daylight, encodes the spatial/neurological organization of the primary event, which is key to the fabula's modelling on the holographic picture of an integral woman.

In order to produce a hologram, one must split a beam of light into a reference beam and another that reflects the object to be holographed. The two light beams interact on a filter or screen, creating a light-wave interference pattern which, under appropriate conditions, can reproduce a three-dimensional image of the holographed object. Since the 1960s, holograms have been made with laser light characterized by coherent wave patterns. The holographic screen is reexposed to a laser beam to produce the hologram. The primary event of *Picture Theory* reproduces the mechanisms of hologram production: a beam of light (the collective feminist subject) which has been exposed to the object to be holographed (a more meaningful idea of what *woman* means) separates into two beams and then comes together again and interacts, producing energy in the form of light.

The plot of "L'émotion" provides a readerly model for the primary event in a longer, narrative context. Beginning with the night departure of the travellers, who have divided into two groups, "L'émotion" ends with the collectivity emerging from the nightclub into the dawn. This overall change of condition inscribes the elements constituting the primary event: separation into two groups, traversal of space, reassembly and interaction, energy in the form of light. The basic series reoccurs nine times in "L'émotion," so that the narrative structure of the section as a whole could be described as a spiral with nine loops, or as a sequence of nine big waves.

In the first wave, the five women, in two groups, set out on a journey. When they have crossed the water, they reassemble, interact and watch the sun rise. In the second wave, they again reassemble; they interact, and the house fills with light. As the third wave begins, the women separate into two groups, and each sets out on a journey. One group enters light (the sunny beach), while the other enters shadow at the speed of light (98). The group in the shadows waits, while the others at the beach

---

voyage, at twilight when we had left it for the slower roads which wound their way to the sea. Arriving at Woods Hole we had seen the boat we had to take to the island floating in front of us like a hanging light" (67).

interact; memories flow, the tide comes up and the two groups reassemble. The narrator's comment at the close of the fifth series suggests what all of this repetition might mean: "une lumière blanche les rendait réelles"[11] (105); the seventh series, too, contains an indication that the women are spiralling into new and collective sense: "Les subjectivités s'interpellent"[12] (107). The ninth and last series ends with the rising of the sun and the imperfect rhyme of "corps céleste" to "le cortex," the brain which is seeking to comprehend "la nature des phrases"[13] (116).

I refer to this visualization of the fabula structure as Model II. Model II is characterized by an open-ended repetition of the abstract narrative unit or primary event. The structure becomes visible when events are isolated in chronological order, as in the working model below. Events involving a choice which determines the subsequent evolution of the action are identified as functional (F); those which seem to participate in an order of the real beyond the ordinary are in parentheses; series of functional events are numbered.

Model II: Events in "L'émotion"

1Fa.	Danièle, M.V. and Claire leave for the ocean
1Fb.	They cross the water in a boat
1Fc.	They meet Florence Dérive and Oriana on the island
1d.	All five watch the sun rise
2Fa.	The five assemble around the breakfast table
2(F)b.	Discussion
2c.	("Toute la maison, fenêtres ouvertes, s'ensoleillait") (98)
3Fa.	Danièle, Oriana and M.V. drive the car to the village
3Fb.	Florence and Claire go to the beach
3Fc.	Danièle, Oriana and M.V. enter "dans l'ombre à la vitesse de la lumière" (98)
3Fd.	They wait at a garage for their car to be fixed
3Fe.	Florence talks about their mother and their brother John
3Ff.	Claire is overwhelmed
3Fg.	Claire gives the impression she hasn't heard
3Fh.	(Her lips full of salt)
3Fi.	Memories flow
3Fj.	(The tide comes up)
3Fk.	Claire shuts her eyes and cries

11 a white light made them real (77).
12 Subjectivities were interpellating (79).
13 the nature of sentences (88).

3Fl.   Florence falls silent
3m.   Florence looks at the ocean
3n.   (The island reappears)
3Fo.   They go back to the house
3Fp.   Danièle, Oriana and M.V. arrive back from the village with groceries (the five assemble)

4a.   Oriana and Danièle go to the beach
4Fb.   Claire and M.V. interact (talk)
4Fc.   Claire spills beer
4d.   Claire opens another beer
4Fe.   Claire and M.V. interact (make love)
4Ff.   Claire and M.V. sleep
4Fg.   M.V. opens her eyes
4h.   She hears, *"la table est mise"* (101)
4Fi.   The five assemble around the supper table
4j.   They talk

5   ("Le lendemain, les jours s'écoulent au bord de la mer") (102)
5Fa.   Oriana proposes that they visit the cliffs
5Fb.   Danièle Judith drives to the cliffs
5Fc.   They arrive, park and look around
5Fd.   They advance towards the cliffs
5e.   (The cliffs tell a story of rainy days; there is writing/a woman in the rock)
5Ff.   They cross the island in returning to the house
5g.   ("Aujourd'hui une lumière blanche les rendait réelles") (105)

6Fa.   They arrive back at the house, named "Tournant des chats" (105)
6b.   They have naps
6c.   They talk
6d.   They read books all the next day
6Fe.   M.V. writes about Curaçao
6Ff.   Claire visits her in her room
6Fg.   Claire and M.V. interact

7.   They assemble at the supper table
7Fb.   Oriana talks
7Fc.   Claire/Florence and Danièle/M.V. hear her differently
7Fd.   They talk
7e.   ("Les subjectivités s'interpellent ainsi les une les autres toute *une nuit chaude de juillet*, lentement") (107)

8Fa.   The next day they go to the beach
8Fb.   Except for Florence who listens to Carlos Gardel on the balcony
8Fc.   Florence joins the others on the beach

8Fd.	Florence sits down to write on the beach
8e.	M.V. desires Florence
9Fa.	Florence comes back from the city with food
9Fb.	They assemble at the supper table
9Fc.	They talk
9Fd.	Enthusiasm mounts
9Fe.	(Two sentences encounter each other)
9Ff.	They open more wine
9Fg.	They talk
9Fh.	At the far end of the night, M.V. opens more wine
9Fi.	("[L]es cités convergeaient dans nos verres") (112)
9Fj.	They talk/transform ("des femmes émergeaient de partout, l'architecture") (112)
9Fk.	They go to a nightclub
9Fl.	They see a man dressed as a woman
9Fm.	Oriana investigates his theatrical effects
9n.	She reports that his breasts are plastic and his voice sounds like a recording
9Fo.	A man cries out an invocation to night from *Finnegans Wake* in French translation (115)
9p.	("La nuit s'ouvre sur l'horizon") (115)
9q.	The sun comes up/ they watch the sun rise
9r.	They change the course of fiction
9s.	("le cortex cherche à comprendre la nature des phrases") (116)

Modelled in this way, the fabula structure is repetitive and isomorphic. Each series—spiral or wave—corresponds to the collective subject reassembling, interacting and generating energy, only to split apart again. That each part, or turn of the spiral, recapitulates the overall structure of the whole points to the hologram, which shares this characteristic, and to that other, significant spiralling structure: DNA.

As a narrative form, this model is thought-provoking in other ways, too. For example, it is largely non-linear and non-causal: the second series does not cause the third, nor the third the fourth and so on. The first series is causally linked to the others, but series two to nine occur at the same causal level and are non-functional relative to each other. In this sense, the structure resembles a tree; the first series is the trunk and the others are branches. Two Brossardian metaphors, "la racine aérienne" and "le cortex," draw on such a form. The first series, or tree trunk, is the "racine aérienne" on which further development of the aerial network depends (*RI* 97). The tree structure also resembles that of the synapses of the brain (Fig. 3); in fact, the cortical synapses are conventionally described by terms relating to trees, "dendrites," for example, and "arborization" (Pribram, 27). The fabula structure of "L'émotion" resembles both the brain and the tree in that a series of isomorphic events depends upon the trunk, the departure "vers la mer" to take a vacation, with all of its intertextual overdetermination. Just as the spiral inscribes revolutions around a fixed point, while drawing further and further away from it, this structure circulates around the initial break with patriarchal meaning, so that the model signifies a culture still related to the patriarchy it is leaving behind.

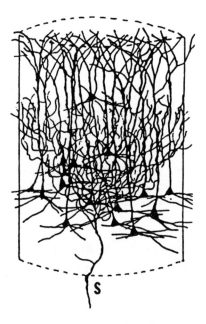

Fig. 3. A diagram of the microstructure of the synaptic domains in the cortex, after Pribram (redrawn after Schneibel and Schneibel in Chow and Leiman), showing the junctions between "branches" of input axons and cortical "dendrites." The terms and the form both suggest a tree-like structure similar to that of the fabula of "L'émotion."

The darkness of the first wave is broken first by flashes of lightning as the boat approaches the island: then again and more definitively by the rising of the sun. The second wave is complete when the house floods with sunlight; the fifth ends with the "lumière blanche [qui] les rendait réelles" (105). When one part of the group takes the car to the mechanic's, traditionally a male preserve, Michèle comments, "nous entrions dans l'ombre à la vitesse de la lumière"[14] (98). The third and fourth waves end with the characters gathering around the supper table, signifying a scene of communal interaction; the sixth ends as Michèle Vallée and Claire Dérive build their relationship by communicating with each other, and the seventh with the intense supper party at which "les subjectivités s'interpellent"[15] (107). These four waves build the association between language, communication and light. The eighth wave is complete when M.V. feels sexually attracted to Florence Dérive. Sexual attraction between women is a type of interaction on which Brossard places a special emphasis, following Gertrude Stein whose comments on this subject frame the book. It is also associated with light.

The ninth wave brings together again many elements from the previous ones, closing with the exit from the night(club) and the link to the brain: "le cortex cherche à comprendre la nature des phrases"[16] (116). Here it is a question of a collective ritual descent and passage. Such a chiasmatic structure supports Brossard's feminist transference of the classical and modernist epic, particularly Dante's spiralling tour through the Inferno to Purgatory and Paradise, Odysseus' underworld passage on his way home to Ithaca, and Bloom's meanderings through the city of Dublin.

Sunrise occurs twice: at the close of the first series, "nous sommes cinq au lever du soleil à la voir éperdument la mer"[17] (96), and during the ninth: "Au lever du soleil nous sommes cinq femmes à voir éperdument l'origine des corps"[18] (116). The repetition of "éperdument" underlines the danger in this zone of "la folie, délire ou génie"[19] (RI 103), when the sun overtakes the horizon of patriarchal sense. The liminal horizon—like the island, skin, screen, forest's edge and hall d'entrée—is the very edge of "l'inédit" (RI 103).

The spiral structure of the fabula can perhaps be seen more clearly

---

14 we entered into shadow at the speed of light (70).
15 Subjectivities were interpellating each other (79).
16 The cortex seeks to understand the nature of sentences (88).
17 we are five at sun rise madly to see the sea (68-69).
18 At sunrise, we were five women madly seeing the origin of bodies (88).
19 madness, delirium, or genius (117).

when characterization, details of time and place and textual effects are suppressed, abstracting fabula events.

MODEL III: ABSTRACTION OF EVENTS IN "L'ÉMOTION"

1. A collective actor travels, in two groups
1. They assemble
1. They interact
1. They interact with their environment (sunrise)
2. They assemble
2. They interact
3. The group separates into two
3. They set out on journeys
3. One group enters light (the sunny beach)
3. One group enters shadow at the speed of light.
3. The group in shadow waits.
3. The ones at the beach interact
3. Memories flow
3. The group reassembles
4. They separate into two again
4. One group enters the light
4. The other group interacts
4. They sleep
5. The whole group reassembles
5. They interact
5. They set out on a journey
5. They interact
5. They interact with their environment
6. They return from their journey (reassemble)
6. They read books
6. They sleep
7. One actor writes
7. She is joined by another and they interact
7. The group assembles
7. They interact
8. The group separates into two
8. One part goes to the beach
8. One actor writes
8. She joins the others and they interact
9. The group assembles
9. They interact

9. They interact with their environment (the night)

9. (The sun comes up)

This model represents an abstract, repetitive, isomorphic fabula structure. Each series repeats the PRIMARY EVENT: a collective actor splits in two parts, reassembles, interacts, generates energy and splits again.

Insofar as events are the building blocks of narrative, the reformulation of the elementary event is a radical but crucial step in the reinvention of fundamental narrative structures. This primary event which Brossard explores in *Picture Theory* is a striking variation of the elementary narrative event as defined by Jurij Lotman: entry into a closed space and emergence from it, or traversal of a spatial field. The actors of *Picture Theory* also enter and exit closed spaces and traverse fields, not just once but over and over again. The crucial difference between the Brossardian primary event and Lotman's elementary narrative event is that in Brossard's text the collective subject splits and comes together again in an assembly and interaction, which generates light or energy and builds in a wave or spiral formation.

The energy-producing interaction of the two groups often takes place when the women are seated around the dining table. Series two and nine frame typical interactions as conversations or embedded texts which develop Brossard's feminist themes. These embedded conversations are integrated into the fabula structure in that they produce the energy of the primary event and contribute to the evolving "spirale ignée, picture theory"[20] (116). They are metonymic of the feminist thought that progressively illuminates reality according to the principle of discursive accrual, whereby each conversation or wave is affected by the fact of being in a series. Wave theory defines the difference between an event in isolation and an event in a series as a mathematical function called "neighbourhood interaction." Neighbourhood interaction is critical to the development of a hologram (Pribram, 140-49). In Brossard's fiction theory, women use neighbourhood interaction to build momentum for their feminist project.

Typically, energy produced by the actors' interactions appears in the form of light. The first time that all five women are seated around the table, light energy is generated by the voice of Claire Dérive. The abundance of light in this passage, "la mer . . . au comble de la lumière," "la maison [qui] s'ensoleillait," suggests a wave of light that swells in

---

20 igneous spiral, **picture theory** (88).

response to Claire's passionate voice rising in the "grande salle de bois"[21] (98). Like the light which renders the women real at the close of the fifth wave, the light building as Claire speaks presages the appearance of the hologram formed by a "volume *torrere* lumière cohérente"[22] (221). Coherent or laser light, related in Brossard to the synaptic white light of the brain making sense, signifies the symbol of the hologram.

The primary event of *Picture Theory* can also be described in the language of neuropsychology as a wave-front interaction synonymous with consciousness or, as Brossard puts it, with *making sense*. To produce or to change consciousness—a key feminist project—"the conduction of nerve impulses [must] pass the *barrier* of the synapse" (Pribram, 8). In the language of narrative grammar, the subject must traverse a boundary to achieve its object; in the terms of *Picture Theory*, the women must cross "la mer" to get to the island. The production of the hologram is synonymous with increasing consciousness because the brain's representations to itself are produced by a two-process mechanism of brain function, in which the interference patterns of two or more wave-front formations create an effect that Pribram describes as "akin" (105) to a hologram, in a decoding process that produces a representation operating as a filter or screen (152). Consciousness, awareness and brain modification through experience (i.e., memory) are accounted for as functions of parallel processes organized spatially within the brain.

The cortical processes responsible for changes in consciousness are paradigmatic of Brossard's primary event:

> nerve impulses arriving at junctions generate a . . . microstructure [which] interacts with that already present by virtue of the spontaneous activity of the nervous system and its previous "experience." The . . . whole procedure produces effects akin to the interference patterns resulting from the interaction of simultaneously occurring wave fronts [i.e., holograms]. The slow potential microstructures act thus as analogue cross-correlation devices to produce new figures [which correspond to] . . . changes in awareness. (Pribram, 105)

In *Picture Theory*, the new figure which corresponds to a change in awareness is the "picture theory" of the integral woman. The energy field or slow potential microstructure generated by electrical energy in the

---

21 The voice of Claire Dérive rose with passion in the great panelled room. . . . The whole house burst into sunshine. . . . The sea . . . is at the acme of light (70).

22 volume *torrere* coherent light (182).

neurons is crossed by the incoming information which is provided by the characters' interactions and which takes certain highly significant forms such as the ability to trust the words of another woman (98), or the sexual ecstacy of the *scène blanche*. This incoming information can be described either as wave activity or by using a quantum mechanical approach. In either case, the interaction of wave fronts produces awareness, intention, emotion, motivation and desire—all Brossardian motifs. An isomorphism becomes apparent among the primary event of *Picture Theory*, the production of the hologram and the changing of consciousness in the brain; each event typically depends upon the interference pattern generated by two interacting wave fronts.

The human brain contains between fifty and one hundred billion brain cells, or neurons, grouped together in regions and sheathed by the cerebral cortex, the extensive outer layer of the cerebral hemispheres that is largely responsible for higher nervous functions. In an active brain, electrical impulses flow through the neural networks to trigger chemical reactions across the synapses, or gaps, separating the neurons. The resulting synaptic contact mobilizes millions of brain cells in specific regions of the brain, which can be linked to specialized roles such as language function and the regulation and co-ordination of voluntary and involuntary muscular movement. In these neural relays, individual cells can communicate with thousands of other cells in a complicated electrochemical interplay that produces consciousness and thought. Information is not stored in particular places; the cortex is capable of three-dimensional image production and reproduction. As Brossard puts it, "la mémoire est en vue comme un site: toutes les régions du cerveau"[23] (*PT* 147).

Neuropsychological research suggests that consciousness is a constant match, or mismatch, between prior experience and incoming data:

> Experimental evidence shows that, at any moment, current sensory excitation is screened by some representative record of prior experience; this comparison, the match or mismatch between current excitation and representative record—guides attention and action. (Pribram, 49)

This model clarifies the crucial role of positive experience in the development of further positive experience. Applying this paradigm to women's break with patriarchy, Brossard traces the cultivation of utopian

---

23 memory is in view like a site: all the regions of the brain" (*PT* 114).

consciousness as a gradual process during which the screen or wave front encoding prior experience becomes sufficiently imbued with utopian elements to allow a match between incoming data (ecstasy) and coded prior experience which is already in place. The sequence "Screen Skin," "Screen Skin Too," "Screen Skin Utopia" and *hologramme* traces the formation of this type of cortical screen, which is also a metaphor for writing. The book's opening gesture of refusal to reconstitute memory is here apparent not only as a refusal of nostalgia but as positive orientation to the future.

Picture Theory refuses the past, transforming ordinary reality by a concentrated process to which the text repeatedly refers: "j'essaie de ne rien reconstituer. De mémoire, j'entame. Et cela ne peut être d'enfance. Seulement d'extase, de chute, de mots. Ou de corps autrement"[24] (35). The refusal to reconstruct is developed further in the first appearance of "la scène blanche":

> reconstituer serait l'aveu de ce qui n'a pu être qu'en fiction transformée par le temps. Pourtant nous voilà, l'horizon, jamais je ne saurai narrer. Ici sur le tapis, enlacées. Visibles. C'est ainsi que j'ai cherché à comprendre l'effet de la scène.[25] (40)

The cortex seeking to understand the nature of the sentence (116) is an energy field or cortical "skin" (Pribram, 194) seeking a match for the incoming wave of utopian information.

> La scène blanche est un relais qui persiste comme écriture pendant que le corps dicte ses clichés, ferme les yeux sur les bouches qui s'ouvrent à répétition touchées par le destin dans leur propre mouvement. Face à ce qui s'offre: l'extravagence des surfaces, transparence de la scène holographiée.[26] (43)

---

24 From instinct and from memory, I try to reconstruct nothing. From memory, I broach a subject. And that cannot be from childhood. Only from ecstasy, from a fall, from words. Or from the body differently (15).

25 to reconstitute would be the avowal of what could only in fiction be transformed by time. Still, there we were, the horizon, I will never be able to narrate. Here on the carpet, intertwined women. Visible. This is how I tried to understand the effect of the scene (20).

26 The white scene is a relay that persists as writing while the body dictates its clichés, closes its eyes on the mouths that open to repetition touched by fate in their own movement. Faced with what is offered: the extravagence of surfaces, transparence of the holographed scene (23).

"La scène blanche" represents the interaction of the wave front with the beam of coherent light (218) and thus heralds the appearance of the virtual image or hologram. As the "scène holographiée," "la scène blanche" is critical because it is there that the lesbian body, language and energy fuse, and "l'utopie *l'intégrale*[27] (184) becomes visible. What begins as a series of scenes is transformed by "La perspective," "L'émotion" and "La pensée" to become the screen skin that matches and makes possible the utopian transformation. The touching skin of the women is the link that permits the reconsitution of the hologram: "Skin/link: oui la langue pouvait être reconstituée en trois dimensions à partir de sa partie dite de plaisir là où fusionnent le corps lesbien, la langue et l'énergie"[28] (204).

In a lecture delivered to the Third International Feminist Book Fair in Montréal, Brossard elaborates on the rapport between memory and utopia. The title of Brossard's lecture, "Mémoire: hologramme du désir," refers to the theory of holographic memory function:

> [S]i l'on convient qu'une mémoire de femme est une mémoire inscrite dans un corps marqué, si l'on convient que cette mémoire est étroitement liée à une série d'intimidations et de contraintes répétées dans le temps patriarcal, il va sans dire que celle qui travaille à la légende des images et des scènes qui se bousculent en elle, tracera immanquablement une cartographie explicative des blessures, des cicatrices qui parsèment son corps mais aussi une cartographie des élans de joie qui enthousiasment la pensée. Aussi pouvons-nous dire que chaque mémoire de femme à laquelle nous avons accès par le biais de sa légende nous informe, nous incite à faire en sorte que ce qui fut blessure ne se répète plus, que ce qui fut émerveillement se reproduise. Ce n'est que lorsque nous pouvons dire la légende de nos vies que nous devenons capables d'engendrer des scènes nouvelles, d'inventer de nouveaux personnages, de produire de nouvelles répliques, nous frayant ainsi un chemin dans le présent.[29] (6)

---

27 Utopia *integral woman* (149).

28 **Skin/link**: yes, language could be reconstituted in three dimensions beginning with the part so-called pleasure where the lesbian body, language and energy fuse (165).

29 If we agree that the memory of a woman is a memory written in a marked body, if we agree that this memory is closely linked to a series of intimidations and constraints common to a patriarchal time, it goes without saying that she who works at writing the images and scenes which are alive in her will unfailingly trace a cartography of wounds and scars traced over her body, but also a cartography of the waves of joy which make her thought come alive. Therefore, can we not say that each woman's memory to which we have access in writing can teach us, and can inspire us to act in

Turning away from the damages done to women by mechanisms of patriarchal control, Brossard will write "des élans de joie qui enthousiasment
la pensée" on a screen which is itself fiction: "la fiction serait le fil
d'arrivée de la pensée"[30] (PT 183). Only in fiction, after all, is it possible to abstract reality in such a way that "ce qui fut blessure ne se répète
plus, que ce qui fut émerveillement se reproduise." The utopian screen
fills with bits of information encoded in a spiralling movement, guarding
at its heart a feminist desire for millennial change away from patriarchal
human relations.

The refusal to reconstitute is finally displaced by what can be reconstituted: "la langue," site of pleasure and energy. The utopian potential
of language meets an "unbounded postmodern body," "a **generic
body**," as Alice Parker reminds us: "it is a radical, urban body—the
city is where the cultural action is—a utopian lesbian body that will
'respond when a woman makes a sign'" (Installations 47; cited in NBBW
1). This encounter between language and the lesbian body brings into
being the virtual image of a woman whose subjectivity is unimpeded:
"Toute la subjectivité du monde. L'utopie luit dans mes yeux. La langue
est fiévreuse comme un recours polysémique"[31] (PT 188). She is the
integral woman or la femme intégrale, discussed in more detail in chapter 9.

Brossard here signifies the creation of a human, generically feminine
subjectivity which is nothing less than the semiotic production of the
exploratory narrative structure elaborated by Picture Theory. In this way,
her novel responds to the feminist analyses linking the generic narrative
sentence—SUBJECT overcomes obstacle to meet OBJECT—to semiotic
mechanisms for the production of generically masculine human subjectivity. Fantasizing scientific insights in wave theory, quantum mechanics,
cognitive psychology and light optics to create a non-linear and interactive narrative structure based on structures other than the hero/obstacle
dichotomy, Brossard displaces quest narrative with holographic brain
functions corresponding to changes in consciousness. Picture Theory

---

such a way that the wounds are not repeated but the wonder is. It is only when we can
give words to our lives that we become capable of inventing new scenes, new characters, new responses, thus creating for ourselves a pathway through the present. (My
translation.)

30 The fiction would be the finishing line of the thought (147-48).

31 All the subjectivity in the world. Utopia shines in my eyes. Langu age is feverish like
a polysemic resource (153).

rewrites narrative grammar as plural and interactive, composed by the spiralling repetition of the primary event:

MODEL IV: FABULA AS HOLOGRAM

a collective actor of feminist women separates into two groups, then comes together again and interacts, generating light energy and, eventually, a hologram of the integral woman who can no longer be divided against herself.

The one-way structure of Model I, which moves from subject to verb to object, is metamorphosed here into a complex sentence composed of equally meaningful words. The adjective "feminist," for example, which might seem to be structurally unnecessary, is in fact essential, because it is the feminist exposure to a more meaningful idea of women's being which carries forward the information required to create the hologram. The vacation is also a necessary element insofar as the island vacation is not a narratological object but a figure of passage, opening into a privileged context where writing—another manifestation of making sense—is made possible by the release and elaboration of five women's potential to fully be. It is the space opened up by the island vacation which allows the word *woman* to be reimagined in light of the effects of brain modification through experience, or memories of ecstacy inscribed on the cor/tex(t) of the vacationing subject.

The island and the July vacation each have a place in Brossard's repertoire of initiatory figures, alongside the dawn and the horizon, the acts of writing, reading and translating, and, most importantly, the synaptic light of a brain making sense. To these we can add the hologram of *Picture Theory*: the interaction of two wave fronts imbued with energy and meeting to make visible the integral woman, she who makes sense.

CHAPTER 9

Story: The Holographic Plate

> The only access we have to our volcanic uncon-
> scious and to the profound motives for our
> actions . . . is through the choices of our encoun-
> ters with specific people.
>
> — Louise Bourgeois, *Destruction of the*
> *Father, Reconstruction of the Father*

AT THE FABULA LEVEL, *Picture Theory* and *How Hug a Stone* share
important features: a collective subject actant and an open-ended,
exploratory narrative structure. At the story level, however, the two books
exemplify diverse strategies. The strong focalization that characterizes
How Hug a Stone, governing characterization and temporal-spatial relations, produces a coherent narrative at the story level. In *Picture Theory*,
characterization and temporal-spatial relations are exploded into a
deconstructed story-sign. Focalization and temporality reflect the multiple focus of the holographic plate in lensless photography.

The subject actant of the primary event is defined by its functional
relationship to the hologram. Although the subject actant may be embodied by an indeterminate number of characters, as, for example, in the
passage, "la salle s'excite"[1] (39)—only the five vacationers, Claire
Dérive, Florence Dérive, Michèle Vallée, Danièle Judith and Oriana
Longavi, are developed as characters. Other characters such as Sandra
Artskin and Anna Livia Plurabelle (123) are intertextual signs; the latter
signifies "Joyce's . . . resolution of all women in the *Wake*," as Lorraine
Weir argues (350). *Picture Theory* also features characters such as John
Dérive and Judith Pamela, who are actors in contrasting sub-fabulas.

---

1 The audience's excited (19). Literally, the audience excites itself.

136

The five main characters are subjects of the "discours autour de la table quotidienne"[2] (95). This discourse figures the fabula's interacting wave fronts, while also playing a role as embedded mirror text. In addition, these feminist conversations serve as the dominant medium for character development. Through them, we learn that Oriana talks too much, Danièle Judith had a difficult childhood in Gaspésie, Claire Dérive is a feminist theoretician. Michèle Vallée, unlike the others, does not relive her childhood; distinguished by her passion for ideas and her love for Claire Dérive, she exemplifies the ideal of eliding memory, focusing instead on "d'extase, de chute, de mots"[3] (35). The feminist discourse represented in *Picture Theory* is synecdochic of contemporary feminist discourse in which Brossard actually participates. The sense given to words is often foregrounded as the characters participate in "la pratique collective de l'écart sémantique"[4] (*RI* 90) essential for the development of culture in the feminine. Oriana, for example, "nuançait les mots déserteur, subversif, révolutionnaire, viril pour s'arrêter plus longuement aux genres conformiste et anarchiste"[5] (107). One discussion turns on the theoretically critical word, "matriarcat" (101-102). The focus on words opens into the fabula structure when the interaction of words themselves contributes to the generation of (light) energy: "les mots se succédant comme des phénomènes, des feux de paille"[6] (109). The discourse articulates the characters' feminist desire or quest to make sense of their lives as lesbian women, and thus defines a fundamental frame of reference.

The desire to make sense, to live meaningfully, with all that it implies, is multiply represented as the desire for the hologram, for "l'utopie l'intégrale" (184), for writing, for another woman, and by the figure of the integral woman. "La femme intégrale" is a "picture theory" of women's desire to be whole subjects of language and history: *"Figure, image, métaphore, elle fait toujours sens et corps avec le sens qu'elle donne aux mots"*[7] (*RI* 100). She is a theoretical and imaginative response to the

---

2 Talk around the daily table (67).
3 from ecstacy, from a fall, from words (15).
4 a collective practice of semantic divergence (106).
5 nuancing the words deserter, subversive, revolutionary, virile in order to linger longer over the genres conformist and anarchist (78).
6 words tumbling after each other like phenomena, flash in the pan (81).
7 *Figure, image, metaphor, with the meaning she gives to words, she always makes and in/core/porates sense* (115).

blighting effects of the masculine, universal "I" critiqued by Woolf, Marlatt and Wittig, and denounced by Brossard in "Accès à l'écriture":

> Maintenant, imaginons ce je au masculin pluriel répétant, tout au long des siècles, sa vérité répétée comme la Vérité. Imaginons que ce je masculin pluriel, plus connu sous le nom de l'Homme, occupe dans toute sa splendeur, toute sa médiocrité, avec toutes ses peurs et ses extases, le champ sémantique et imaginaire. . . . Imaginons donc l'effort d'imagination qu'il nous faudra faire pour comprendre, dire, et déployer l'image essentielle que nous, femmes, désirons de nous comme un présence au monde.[8] (132)

"La femme intégrale" intervenes in a situation that Brossard describes as a crisis of female being.

Although each of the five main characters prefigures "la femme intégrale," her manifestation is primarily focalized through Michèle Vallée, and the scene of (her) writing which opens the horizon of skin and paper to anticipate "la pensée d'une femme qui m'englobe et que je pense intégrale"[9] (184). The scene of writing is also the axis of focalization which is deictic without ever implying a unified personage. As Louise Forsyth notes, "le premier mot du texte est le pronom "Je" énoncé "ici" par la narratrice qui si situe au présent textuel, tout en attirant notre attention sur la difficulté de faire sens dans la conjoncture actuelle"[10] (*Préface* 18). "L'ordinaire" begins, "J'exerce ici ma faculté de synthèse car il me faut à nouveau procéder avec précision parmi les bruits, les corps et les institutions"[11] (33). The "je" brings together bits of a story, but it will be another hundred pages before she is identified as Michèle Vallée, if indeed she is Michèle Vallée. While the "je" of this

---

8 Now, let us imagine this "I" in the masculine plural repeating its truth throughout the centuries as though it were the Truth. Let's imagine that this masculine plural, better known as Man, takes up, in all its splendour, in all its mediocrity, with all its fears and ecstacies, the entire field of semantics and the imaginary. . . . Then let us imagine the magnitude of the imagination we will require to understand, articulate and disseminate the quintessential image that we, women, want of ourselves in terms of our presence in the world (139-40).

9 the thought of a woman who embodies me and whom I think integral (149).

10 the first word of the text is the pronoun "I" enunciated "here" by the narrator who situates herself in the textual present while drawing our attention to the difficulty of making sense in the current conjuncture." (My translation.) Louise Dupré offers another perspective on Brossard's use of the first-person pronoun (*Stratégies du vertige*, 88).

11 *I exercise my faculty of synthesis here because again I must proceed with precision among sounds, bodies and institutions* (14).

passage is unequivocally the primary or first narrator of *Picture Theory*, and while it is also clear that the project of making sense serves as a kind of framing motivation for the text as a whole, the levels of narration and focalization are more complex than these propositions imply.

Narration in *Picture Theory* alternates between strictly impersonal narration, narration signified by the use of first-person pronouns and other deictic terms, and narration by the character-narrator Michèle Vallée or M.V. Focalization is also variable, resting with the character-narrator, hovering between the narrator and another character, or looking on from another perspective altogether. This variation corresponds to the fact that Michèle Vallée is inconsistently the narrator.

In "L'ordinaire," focalization shifts as the scenes of the story rotate. Florence's trip to Montréal exemplifies character-focalization with external narration (EN/CF):

> Maintenant, Florence Dérive récapitule son texte dans un bar situé
> à l'angle de la 17e Avenue et de la 42e Rue. Elle se livre momen-
> tanément à la nécessité d'être ce que l'on nomme, parmi les encres,
> un personnage. Sa conférence est prête. Demain, Montréal.[12] (35)

Florence interprets her own behaviour; the scene is focalized through her. The deictic term "demain" also locates Florence as focalizer. On the other hand, she is spoken of in the third person as she experiences herself as a character. The narrator is anonymous.

The following passage also combines an anonymous, external narrator (EN) with a character-focalizer (CF), Florence Dérive:

> EN [CF (Florence)—young woman with briefcase]
> (I narrate: [I invent: Florence focalizes:])
> Lorsque Florence Dérive sortit ce matin-là de l'Hôtel de l'Institut,
> elle remarqua une jeune femme qui tout comme elle, tenait sous son
> bras un cartable, sans doute acheté chez Bloomingdale's, pensa-t-
> elle d'abord, puis elle se concentra sur une idée très précise dont
> elle voulait discuter avec Danièle Judith avant la conférence.[13] (55)

---

12 Now, Florence Dérive is recasting her text in a bar at the corner of Seventeenth
   Avenue and Forty-Second Street. She momentarily abandons herself to the necessity
   of being what is called, among the inks, a character. Her lecture is ready. Tomorrow,
   Montréal (16).

13 When Florence Dérive came out that morning from the Hôtel de l'Institut, she
   noticed a young woman who, just like herself, held a briefcase under her arm, doubt-
   less bought at Bloomingdales, she thought at first, then she concentrated on a very
   specific idea she wanted to discuss with Danièle Judith before the lecture (34).

An external narrator "sees" Florence leaving the hotel, and "knows" the thoughts that pass through her mind. This passage exemplifies the traditional literary style of narration in the third-person *passé simple*; the narrator is relatively omnipotent, the reader is relatively passive and focalization rests with a character.

Other passages imply an external narrator-focalizer (EN/EF) who travels freely through space and time.

> c(2) Le métro était mal éclairé. De dos, l'homme cachait la femme dont on voyait la main recroquevillée dans la sienne.[14] (50)

From whose point of view is the woman hidden? Who is the "on" referred to in the last sentence? This fragment of what I refer to as *le livre au masculin* is focalized through an anonymous narrator. In a similar passage, narration remains external while focalization is multiple:

> b(2) L'homme regardait droit devant lui son destin sur la porte de l'ascenseur qui montait. Le métal reflétait flou ses vêtements sans visage et la valise à ses pieds.[15] (48)

The character sees and focalizes his destiny reflected on the elevator door, but who is down at floor level looking at the reflection of his feet and headless body?

Certain passages that combine the narratory and focalizing functions bring the reader closer to the text through the use of the first-person present indicative:

> CN (Michèle) [CF (Michèle)—Michèle in the Paris hotel]
> L'hôtel sent la verveine. Cela peut être le fruit de mon imagination mais il sent bon comme à Curaçao, Anna sentait la fiction, sur son dos, j'anticipe.[16] (45)

In this passage, focalization and narration rest with the character-narrator who eventually, during a discussion on the island—"Stop it, Michèle, watch it" (112)—will be identified as Michèle. She can be identified

---

14 The metro was poorly lit. From behind, the man was hiding the woman whose curled up hand was seen in his (30).

15 The man looked straight ahead of him at his destiny on the door of the ascending elevator. The metal blurringly reflected his clothing without a face and the suitcase at his feet (28).

16 The hotel smells of verbena. It may be the fruit of my imagination but it smells good like Curaçao, Anna smelled of fiction, on her back, I am anticipating (25).

because Michèle is writing a book, and the scene of her writing is linked to the Paris hotel and to Curaçao, two environments that nourish her fiction.

Michèle is consistently the character-narrator-focalizer of "La perspective" and "L'émotion." From "La pensée" to the end of the text, the narratory function shifts between Michèle (CN) and an anonymous external narrator (EN). In the following passage, the narrative agent changes while focalization rests with Michèle, creating an impression that Michèle is both inside and outside the scene: she has a double perspective on reality.

> Son chandail traîne à côté du lit. M.V. lui parle doucement, raconte les insomnies du samedi soir, c'est-à-dire, celles qui précédaient toujours le néfaste dimanche, jour d'expiation dans les crinolines. Puis, Claire Dérive appuyait de tout son corps sur le mien. Ses mains sont une source de chaleur sur ma nuque. L'oreiller vient de tomber sur le tapis. Un détail. Je m'en souviens comme d'un jour de semaine. Quotidiennes et amoureuses. Sans personnage.[17] (160)

When physical contact is established between Michèle and Claire, the fiction of third-person narration dissolves into first-person narration, "sans personnage." The flexible relationship between the characters and the narratory function signifies the power of fiction to metamorphose subjectivity.

Ambiguity occurs when Michèle moves in or out of the narrator's role. While the love affair with Claire, the vacation trip to the island, the narrator's trip to Paris, the writing of a book and the desire for the hologram are all focalized through Michèle, certain scenes shift focalization suddenly, provoking increased interpretive activity from the reader.

> Les mots volaient dans toutes les directions. En vue d'un sens, sillonnant l'espace, une question restait en suspens: l'origine sur laquelle M.V. restait penchée des heures entières. Du sens était en vue, amplifiait la réalité comme une comète sonore (allant vers la source, une femme casquée). L'éclat du musée. Mille fragments retombent sur mes épaules. De la matière partout, pièces d'identité: notes, lipstick, miroir, condom, clés, argent, mille fragments s'assemblent sous vos yeux dans le musée, dans le livre, il faut les voir venir.[18] (130)

---

17 Her sweater is lying beside the bed. M.V. speaks to her softly, tells about her Saturday night insomnias, that is to say, those which always preceded black-lettered Sunday, day of expiation in crinolines. Then, Claire Dérive leaned with her whole body on mine. Her hands are a source of warmth on the nape of my neck. The pillow has just fallen on the rug. A detail. I remember it as if remembering a week day. Daily and lovhers. No character(s) (127).

18 Words were flying in all directions. With a view to one sense, furrowing space, a question remained in suspense: the origin over which M.V. brooded for hours on end.

The words "mes épaules" identify a first person in a passage that also refers to M.V. in the third person and in which the second person is also used: "milles fragments s'assemblent sous vos yeux dans le musée." Is Michèle, who does go to the museum, present simultaneously in first, second and third person? Alternatively, the addressee could be Claire, or the reader of the book. Focalization and the narrative context are both ambiguous in this passage.

Louise Forsyth theorizes that the text of *Picture Theory* is constructed on the mirroring principle of books embedded within books:

> Dans l'univers de la narratrice principale circulent, à plusieurs niveaux textuels, de nombreuses écrivaines et narratrices qui se rassemblent, se ressemblent et se répètent. C'est ainsi qu'on fait émerger une communauté et une culture. . . . Les personnages dans le texte de la narratrice sont elles aussi écrivaines assises devant leur table, seules ou avec d'autres femmes. Les personnages dans les textes de ces écrivaines sont à leur tour écrivaines, chacune passant aux actes d'écrire, de parler et de lire. Le réseau mobile d'écrivaines, de narratrices et de lectrices tissé par Brossard dans son roman l'implique elle aussi non moins que la lectrice, elle aussi "ici." Ce réseau est le noyau d'une communauté interprétative par laquelle Brossard compte transformer le paysage ontologique de l'humanité.[19] (*Préface* 18)

Forsyth clarifies *Picture Theory*'s construction of the reader as participant in the feminist interpretive community; however, the notion of books within books needs to be qualified. The character of M.V. is not large enough to contain the book she is in, and the epigraph from Wittgenstein—"What can be said can only be said by means of a sentence, and

---

Meaning was in view, amplifying reality like a comet of sound (towards the source, a helmeted woman). Shattering of the museum. Thousands of fragments fall upon my shoulders. Material everywhere, pièces d'identité: notes, **lipstick**, mirror, condom, keys, money, a thousand fragments gather under your eyes in the museum, in the book, you must see them coming (98).

19 In the principal narrator's universe circulate, at several textual levels, many women writers and narrators who gather together, resemble each other, and repeat each other's words. This is how we create a community and a culture. . . . The characters in the narrator's text are in their turn also writers, sitting at their tables, alone or with other women. The characters in the texts of these writers are also writers, each one performing the actions of writing, speaking and reading. The dynamic network of writers, narrators and readers woven by Brossard in her novel implicates her no less than the reader, both of them situated "here." This network is the embryonic interpretive community through which Brossard hopes to transform the ontological landscape of humanity. (My translation.)

so nothing that is necessary for the understanding of all sentences can be said"—further underlines Brossard's refusal of the hierarchy implied by the structure that Forsyth suggests. In addition, not all the characters are writing books, and one character who is—John—exists outside the feminist interpretive community. *Picture Theory* works on a hypertextual principle that allows the fiction of narration to change from section to section and passage to passage, as I have just shown. The characters have a variety of functional relationships to the fabula object of the hologram, reflecting the diversity of a heterogeneous world.

The characters do share attributes. Claire and Florence are sisters who grew up in New York; Oriana is their mother's good friend; Danièle Judith, who is serious, Québécoise and interested in books, is trying to deal with her traumatic memories of childhood; Claire cries over childhood memories, and is an anarchist; Michèle is serious, Québécoise and a writer. All are related by a network of shared characteristics:

1. siblings: John, Florence and Claire Dérive
2. generations: the maternal grandmother who bequeathed the house to Claire, Sarah Dérive Stein, Claire, Florence, John
3. lovers: Michèle and Claire
4. married couple: John Dérive and Judith Pamela
5. name: Judith Pamela and Danièle Judith
6. Québécoise: Danièle Judith and Michèle Vallée
7. "New Yorkaise": Florence, Claire, Oriana and Sarah
8. lesbian: Florence, Claire, Oriana, Michèle, Danièle, Sarah and Cecilia (172)
9. writers: Florence, Michèle, John, Danièle and Sandra Artskin
10. Protestant: Judith and Sandra Artskin
11. love books: Claire, Florence, Oriana, Michèle, Danièle and Judith.

Such overlapping of character traits recalls Lotman's plot typology in which a mythological actant is "unfolded" into typically doubled or twinned characters. "The most obvious result of the linear unfolding of cyclical texts is the appearance of character-doubles" (164). "[N]ot only synchronic character-doubles, but also diachronic ones like 'father-son' represent the subdivision of a single or cyclic text-image" (168). In *How Hug a Stone*, Edrys and the narrator are character-doubles, who manifest, along the diachronic line of generation, the actant who is the subject of language. In *Picture Theory*, character-doubles manifest synchronically to undermine the stationary plot position that traditionally constitutes woman: the enclosed space transgressed by the hero. As "traversières"

(105), Brossard's characters occupy the plot position that constructs them as male, in a text which insists that they are female. The paradox ignites narrative grammar: "Impérative grammaire incendiée"[20] (40).

Although they share in this network of characteristics, John Dérive and Judith Pamela do not have the same functional relationship to the fabula as do Michèle, Danièle, Claire, Florence and Oriana. Both characters have an ambivalent relationship to the primary event. John's actions are partially isomorphic with it, in that he traverses spatial fields and crosses boundaries: "John roule allègrement sur la 95 en direction du Maine"[21] (44). However, John at no point interacts with another character; he is absent from the vital realm of discourse. He is imaged not as light in dark but as shadowed and bloody: "C'est sans expression que John roule *vite* le profil sanglant découpé comme un paysage au soleil levant"[22] (44). The narrator remarks that as a (male) character, John has no idea of the novel he is in: *"omme personnage, John n'avait aucune notion du roman"*[23] (36).

> Pleine lune, Greenwich Village, John titube. La ville s'abolit dans son oeil. La vie vient avec le brouillard, la transe, la panique, la pluie, on oublie tout et puis on recommence: les enfants, le ministre, son roman. Sexual harassement. Who do you think you are? Il a suivi le garçon sur les quais de la rivière Hudson, là où entre hommes on confond les torses. Ascenseur, garçon. Black out. New York.[24] (41)

Homosexual desire leads John to a black out, in spite of the full moon. Unacknowledged and repressed, his desire incompatible with his scripted role as "un fils viril"[25] (37). He has "longtemps travaillé et beaucoup pleuré devant son roman"[26] (38): his writing is associated with

---

20 Imperative grammar incendiary (20).
21 John rolls smoothly along the 95 in the direction of Maine (24).
22 Without expression John rolls along *quickly* his bloody profile cut out like a landscape in the rising sun (24).
23 *omme personnage, ()an/'s character, John had no notion of the novel* (17).
24 Full moon, Greenwich Village, John reels. The city is abolished in his eyes. Life comes with fog, trace, panic, rain, you forget everything and begin again: children, minister, his novel. **Sexual harassment. Who do you think you are?** He followed the boy on the docks of the Hudson River, where among men torsos are (con)fused. Elevator, boy. **Black out**. New York (21).
25 a manly son (17).
26 John worked a long time and cried a lot over his already discussed novel (18).

frustration. John does not share the functional orientation to the holo-gram. He is the subject of a contrasting, embedded sub-fabula.

Judith Pamela is also outside of the primary fabula. The paradoxical statement, "Flaubert était sa femme préférée"[27] (44), links her to Emma Bovary and implies that she is dependent on male fictions of women. She reads and stares at the sea. There is magic waiting for her if she can find it:

> Quelque part en Judith Pamela, une mémoire travaille qui ne con-tient pas son enfance et qui pourtant la fait se tendre de tout son corps vers les eaux. La fiction aînée s'approche d'elle, lui applique sur la joue un papillon aussi fictif qu'un baiser décoloré par l'eau dans l'horizon incertain.[28] (49-50)

A woman who "aimait le voyage et les langues"[29] (44), Judith resembles the other women of the story. Her name and her association with the Québec border (36) are semantic bridges to Danièle Judith, who might have helped Judith Pamela across "l'horizon incertain" (50). However, she remains stationary and thus occupies the generically female, tradi-tional and stationary plot position implicated in the production of patriar-chal grammar. Because she fails to traverse the frontier, her actions are not isomorphic with the primary event. An actor in John Dérive's sub-fabula, she is symbolically at odds with the other women in the book.

Claire Dérive signifies the actantial function of the subject and its relationship to feminist consciousness. Although she is essential to the timelessness of "la scène blanche," she is the most historically moti-vated character in the book. The marriage of John Dérive and Judith Pamela is an episode in the characterization of Claire.

> le mariage de John avec Judith, la réception à Stanstead sur une pelouse verte comme dans *Blow up*, le bruit des verres brandis pen-dant qu'il posait sa bouche sur ses lèvres de mariée et que Claire, en compagnie de deux hippies qui chargeaient et rechargeaient les caméras comme des déments, n'avait cessé de prendre des photos d'une manière arrogante et insistante.[30] (99)

---

27 Flaubert was her favourite woman (24).
28 Somewhere in Judith Pamela a memory is at work that does not contain her childhood and yet makes her stretch her whole body toward the water. The elder fiction approaches, puts a butterfly on her as fictive as a kiss discoloured by the water on the uncertain horizon (29-30).
29 liked travel and languages (24).   .
30 John's marriage to Judith, the reception at Stanstead on the green lawn as in *Blow Up*, the chink of glasses raised while he placed his mouth on the bride's lips and while

This scene links John and Judith to "straight" society, and Claire to the counter-culture of the 1960s. Straight society was mocked in Michelangelo Antonioni's 1967 film, *Blow-Up*, in which a photographer, working in his lab, realizes he has witnessed a possibly imaginary assassination.[31] The analogy suggests the wedding in *Picture Theory* as the site of an imaginary assassination, perhaps that of a woman. Claire's feminist trajectory, the wedding scene implies, had its origins in her rejection of the patriarchal family.

From the first references to her in "L'ordinaire," Claire is linked to the possibility of political change.

> Florence Dérive, née de sa mère et d'un ultra modern style newyorkais passait souvent ses vacances au bord de la mer, dans la maison de sa soeur anarchiste et seule héritière de la grand-mère maternelle. Maison vue and revue en plongée par la plupart des hélicoptères de surveillance qui pendant la guerre du Vietnam faisaient la ronde au-dessus des maisons pouvant abriter des hommes pansés. Pouvoir changer l'Amérique.[32] (36)

Claire is the proprietress of the house on the island, an anarchist and heiress of the maternal line. The house, dive-bombed by surveillance helicopters, shelters Vietnam war deserters who fled across the line into Canada. The phrase "Pouvoir changer l'Amérique" recalls the exuberant expectations of those who took part in the radicalization of the 1960s.

Claire is next mentioned in relation to Judith Pamela who visits the house on the island.

> Au bord de la mer, le temps c'est du sable. Judith Pamela songe à l'immense galerie qui donne sur l'horizon, là où elle pouvait faire coïncider le silence et ses pensées, àcette époque où John et elle passaient leurs vacances dans la maison de la soeur anarchiste* qu'elle n'a pas revue depuis cinq ans.
>
> *Celle qui vit partout en même temps. Qui "passait" souvent la frontière. Un déserteur à la fois (la plupart sont devenus végétariens et ont ouvert de petits commerces sur la rue Duluth ou dans les montagnes de la Colombie-

---

Claire, in the company of two hippies who loaded the cameras again and again like lunatics, took endless photos arrogantly and insistently (71).

31 The film is based on a short story by Julio Cortazar.

32 Florence Dérive, of mother born and an ultra-modern New York style, often spent her holidays at the seaside, in the house of her anarchist sister, sole heir of her maternal grandmother. House viewed again and again in a vertical shot by most of the surveillance helicopters which made the rounds above houses that might be sheltering bandaged men during the Vietnam war. Power. To be able to change America (16).

Britannique. A Nelson, leurs femmes portent des jupes marxistes et des petits foulards tissés à la main. Elles ont toutes deux ou trois enfants très beaux qui se promènent nus pieds dans les restaurants "natural food").[33] (53)

Associated again with the counter-culture and the anti-war movement, Claire is described by epithets that prefigure the primary fabula event and associate her with the hologram: "qui passait souvent la frontière" and "celle qui vit partout en même temps."

Claire is also a human and vulnerable character who cries, quarrels and sets aside time to communicate with Michèle: "nous avions fait le pacte de nous consacrer une heure par jour à l'exercice de la réponse. C'était maintenant à moi d'aller sur son terrain trouver une résonnance à ses propos"[34] (101). Michèle and Claire are model communicators, but they argue over Claire's attitude to her mother (156-57), and, significantly, over writing:

Claire Dérive disait instinctivement: "Il ne faut citer qu'en dernier recours, s'interdire certains passages de manière à ne pas se répéter." Je disais sentant la colère monter en moi qu'aucun passage ne m'était interdit et qu'ainsi pensante je pouvais m'ouvrir à tous les sens.[35] (100)

In this curious quarrel, Michèle insists on her freedom relative to meaning. Later, she realizes she misunderstood Claire: "Aimer son projet, le répéter, le fondre en soi, le citer avait un jour dit Claire Dérive au bord de la mer. Je mourrais de honte de n'avoir entendu que le mot citation"[36]

---

33 At the seaside, time is sand. Judith Pamela dreams about the immense verandah overlooking the horizon, where she could make silence and her thoughts converge, at that time when she and John spent their holidays in the house of their anarchist sister* whom she hasn't seen for five years.

   *The one who lived everywhere at the same time. Who often "crossed" the border. A deserter with her (most of them have become vegetarians and have opened small businesses on rue Duluth or in the mountains of British Columbia. At Nelson, their wives wear marxist skirts and little hand woven scarves. They have two or three very beautiful children who run bare foot around the "**natural food**" restaurants (32).

34 we had made an agreement to devote ourselves an hour a day to the practice of replying. It was now up to me to go onto her terrain to find resonance for her words (73).

35 Claire Dérive said instinctively: "You should only quote as a last resort, forbid certain passages so that you don't repeat yourself." I said feeling my anger rising that no passage was forbidden me and thinking in this way I could open myself up to all meanings (72).

36 To like one's project, repeat it, fuse with it, cite it Claire Dérive had said one day at the seaside. I should die of shame for having heard only the word citation (151).

(186). The special sense of repetition which Claire describes here is analogous to the investment of energy into the writing of utopian desire which prepares the screen/skin/text for the hologram. It is analogous to the project of transformation which is increasingly in view: "Il n'était plus possible alors de perdre de vue l'espoir en hologramme"[37] (186).

Like the hope which she embodies, and like the picture of which the book is a theory, Claire is more and more in focus as *Picture Theory* progresses:

> Claire Dérive marcherait dans le froid absolu jusqu'à la rue Laurier. Décembre, la neige. M.V. regardait dehors les passantes toutes plus futures les unes que les autres et à l'image de Claire Dérive qui enfin, visible à l'Arrêt, relevait le col de son manteau parmi les phares des voitures. Dans le hall d'entrée, il fallait enlever la tuque, le foulard, le manteau et les gants, très amoureusement. Ce visage.[38] (175)

Claire is never the focalizer of *Picture Theory*; the reader is not invited to identify with her so much as to consider her carefully. Her appearance is linked to motifs of futurity and transformation which combine to create the love scene in which the literal and symbolic unite, becoming "le point de non-retour de toute affirmation"[39] (63).

At the end of "L'ordinaire," Claire leaves a message on Michèle's answering machine: "*Je suis Claire Dérive*. La voix était belle, presque sans accent. Dans les eaux de Curaçao la blancheur est éclatante et les yeux se ferment à demi pour jongler avec les couleurs de l'arc-en-ciel dans l'iris"[40] (57-58). Her telephone call is associated with light and desire which build throughout "L'ordinaire" to announce the next turn of the spiral: "La perspective."

Claire's name symbolizes her role in the narrative, and relates her firmly to the function of light in the fabula. Her given name derives from Latin, *clarus*, "bright," "qui a l'éclat du jour," and synonyms include

---

37 It wasn't possible then to lose sight of hope in the hologram" (151).
38 Claire Dérive would walk in the absolute cold to rue Laurier. December, snow. M.V. was outside looking at the passers-by each one more future than the next and at the image of Claire Dérive who at last, visible at Stop, raised the collar of her coat among the cars' headlights. In the entrance hall you had to take off the *tuque*, scarf, coat and gloves, very lovingly. This face (141).
39 *the vanishing point of all affirmation* (40).
40 *Je suis Claire Dérive*. The voice was beautiful, almost no accent. In the waters of Curaçao, the whiteness is dazzling and the eyes half close to dream the colours of the rainbow in the iris (36).

"éclatant," "lumineux," "brillant," "net," "apparent," "certain,"
"évident," "sûr" (*Le Petit Robert*). She stands metonymically for the light
of vision, "clairvoyance" (95-116), and the sudden illumination of an
"éclair" (96). She is light for the night voyage, "l'obscure clarté" (95),
or, as Lorraine Weir puts it, "light filtered through darkness in reJoyced
chiaroscuro" (351). She is most importantly the coherent light required
for the production of the hologram (214, 218, 221). Dérive, too, as
Michèle remarks, "était un nom qu'il fallait savoir mériter en dehors des
questions de famille"[41] (112), which must be why John Dérive is never
given his family name. "Dérive" is a polyvalent word which signifies
both the slow but immeasurably powerful drift of continents and the deviation of an air or water craft from its route. It also applies to the evolution
of words and, thus, meaning. A "dérive" is paradoxically both a drifting
off course and a device that impedes such drifting, the centre-board of a
ship or the vertical stabilizer of a plane. It is also "des rives," river
banks, littoral, another frontier borderland. In *Picture Theory*, "Claire
Dérive" signifies vision and the emerging meaning of words that guide
women through the spiral and assure that they will not circle helplessly
inside the patriarchal frontier. She inundates the scene with the bril-
liance of her gaze (76); her name appears on almost every page of "La
perspective."

The relationship between Michèle and Claire opens into the act of
reading *Picture Theory*, as the narrator and Claire Dérive, the implied
author and the reader, focus increasingly on the utopian desire steadily
coming into view: "Rivées l'une à l'autre comme mises en suspens par
une écriture, nous existons dans la laborieuse création du désir dont on
n'a pas idée. Ou de l'Idée, tout ce qui parvient à métamorphoser l'espace
mental"[42] (43). This metamorphosis is accomplished by provoking
thought, figured as light running through the body (121). Claire represents the illumination of thought united with language and emotion: the
"corps crépusculaires"[43] (116) of women in the light of a new dawn.
Claire herself brings together the mechanisms, the virtuality and the significance of the hologram: "*Claire Dérive est l'onde et l'espace la mémoire*

---

41 a name you had to know how to live up to, beyond any questions of family (84).
42 Rivetted to each other as though held in suspense by writing, we exist in the laborious creation of desire of which we can conceive no idea. Or the Idea, everything that
   manages to metamorphize mental space (23).
43 crepuscular bodies (88).

miroitante que j'entends comme un sens en liberté"[44] (88). Claire is the wave of light travelling through space, mirroring memory, liberating meaning, unfolding holographic dimensions.

The complex temporal relations of the text demand intense reading and provoke interpretation (*N* 52). The duration of the fabula is eight months to a year, and the sequence of the eight sections of the book follows fabula chronology. "L'ordinaire" is followed by "La perspective" which takes place on May 16, 1980. "L'émotion" relates the events of July 1980. "La pensée" takes place the following winter when Claire's mother dies in New York; eventually Claire returns to Michèle and Montréal. "Screen Skin," "Screen Skin Too," "Screen Skin Utopia" and *Hologramme* return to and transform these narrative events. Alternation between verb tenses positions the story variously in time relative to fabula events. The timelessness of "<u>la scène blanche</u>" adds to the complex temporality.

"L'ordinaire" is a repetitive cycle of events turning on themselves at the beginning of the spiral-in-formation, the curve of which has not yet reached the outer limits of patriarchal sense (the dérive, horizon or sunrise). Locations appear as if on a carousel—carnivalesque, but not necessarily gay:

> *L'ordinaire est un bas-relief circulaire rempli*
> *de motifs inavouables. L'ordinaire s'empare de la*
> *langue à son profit O quatre étoiles confond les*
> *noms de rues la gynécologie le devoir. D'ordinaire*
> *l'homme tient la femme dans ses bras de cascadeur la*
> *soulève l'emporte, métro ascenseur parking, lui fait*
> *lire ce qu'il veut.*[45] (201)

Short scenes, from one to eleven lines, present <u>la scène blanche</u>, the trip to Curaçao, Florence lecturing on women and torture, Oriana singing Wagner's *Die Walküre*, a trip to Ogunquit taken by Judith Pamela and John Dérive, the narrator's trip to Paris (where she visits one or several museums and registers at one or several hotels) and the telephone call from Claire Dérive. Silent scenes (which I refer to as *le livre au mas-*

---

44 *Claire Dérive is the wave and the space the memory mirroring i hear like a sense in liberty* (64).

45 *The ordinary is a circular bas-relief filled with unspeakable motifs. The ordinary lays a hold upon language for its profit Oh four stars merge the names of streets gynaecology duty. Ordinarily the man holds the woman in his stuntman's arms lifts her up carries her off, metro elevator parking lot, makes her read what he wants* (162).

culin), numbered from a(1) to d(2), involve a man and a woman who are caught up in a sinister patriarchal drama, contrasting sharply with the love scenes of la scène blanche, and in general with the evolving, woman-centred and discursive world of the book. They foreground the fact that "L'ordinaire" presents reality in need of transformation. The presentation of events in "L'ordinaire" is as follows:

Story Location in "L'ordinaire"

Page 35. Curaçao, the Hilton bar
　　　　　the scene of writing
　　　　　Montréal, Hôtel de l'Institut (Florence)
　　　　　New York (Florence)
　36. the scene of writing
　　　　　childhood (Florence)
　　　　　childhood (Florence)
　　　　　childhood (John)
　37. Oriana and Florence
　　　　　Oriana and John
　　　　　New York, Broadway (Florence)
　　　　　the scene of writing
　　　　　the scene of writing
　38. the scene of writing
　　　　　Montréal?
　　　　　Paris, le Madison
　　　　　Paris, le Madison
　39. Woods Hole (the Dérive family)
　　　　　New York–Montréal (Florence)
　　　　　Montréal, Hôtel de l'Institut (Sandra Artskin)
　40. la scène blanche
　41. *le livre au masculin, rue du Dragon, Paris*
　　　　　le livre au masculin, the elevator
　　　　　New York (John)
　　　　　Montréal (Florence)
　　　　　Michéle and Danièle ?
　42. New York, Florence
　　　　　Paris
　　　　　the scene of writing
　43. la scène blanche
　44. childhood (Florence)
　　　　　John, going to Maine

Woods Hole
John
45. *le livre au masculin*
New York
the scene of writing
airplane
Paris
Paris, hotel
46. Paris, museum of Holography
Paris, hotel
New York (Florence)
Paris, museum of Holography
47. la scène blanche
48. New York (Oriana)
le livre au masculin, the elevator
the scene of writing
49. Woods Hole, a scene from "L'émotion"
Paris
Montréal (Danièle)
Woods Hole (Judith Pamela)
50. New York
le livre au masculin, the metro
le livre au masculin, the metro
New York (Oriana, Sarah)
51. Paris, hotel
52. la scène blanche
53. Woods Hole (John and Judith)
Woods Hole (John and Judith)
Curaçao
54. Opera (Oriana)
55. Woods Hole (scene from "L'émotion")
Montréal, Hôtel de l'Institut (Sandra Artskin)
Montréal, Hôtel de l'Institut (Florence)
Paris, le Madison
56. Opera (Oriana)
Paris, hotel?
Curaçao
Opera (Oriana)
Paris, museum

57. Paris, hotel
   le livre au masculin
   le livre au masculin
   Airport, Montréal (Danièle and Michèle)
   Montréal, the apartment on rue Laurier
57. Montréal–Curaçao
   Montréal, Hôtel de l'Institut

Bal argues, "the more banal the event, the less striking the repetition" (*N* 78), but this is not the case in *Picture Theory*. Banal events, overdetermined by frequent internal retroversion, are manifestations of the boundary crossing, an element of the primary event. These include entering l'Hôtel de l'Institut, various other hotels, "le hall d'entrée" and the forest, and traversing the ocean, the border, the horizon and the book. The repetition signifies the creation of a memory screen which will interact with incoming information to produce the hologram.

All time in *Picture Theory* is contemporary, unlike the very different evocations of time found, for example, in the work of Marlatt or Wittig. In *How Hug a Stone*, the narrator experiences the past, running to meet the Earth Mother *with* the ancient celebrants in "long after the Brown Day of Bride." Marlatt's metomymic poetics frame this event as if it actually occurs, allowing the narrator the insight which permits her to go home. Alternatively, Wittig and Zeig create, in *Lesbian Peoples*, a mythical sense of time. Looking at the twentieth century from a point of view far in the future, their text declares itself to have been taken from the books and fragments saved during the last period of chaos, at the end of the patriarchal age, when the companion lovers migrated from Paris to forest-covered islands (131-32). Brossard's work is not mythological or utopian in the same sense.

Picture Theory makes the realistic proposition of a discourse, a project, a picture. Its lesbian migration and forest-covered island are symbolic yet firmly anchored in the here and now of Québec–New York, in July 1980. Classical and ancient images such as the "routes qui ... serpentent"[46] do have a place in this text, and Homer's Ulysses is introduced in a passage from "L'ordinaire" which looks forward to the island vacation:

---

46 roads which wound (67); but see chapter 7 on the significance of the serpentine.

*Des vacances au bord de la mer, sur une île où quand le soleil se
couche, on croirait voir Ulysse poindre à l'horizon de la maison (rose
wood). "La terre des Yeux-Ronds était là, toute proche: nous voyions
ses fumées; nous entendions leur voix et celles de leurs chèvres. . . . Au
coucher du soleil, quand vient le crépuscule, on s'étend pour dormir
sur la grève de mer." Les transatlantiques nous font des raies dans le
dos et sur les cuisses. Il est sept heures, Florence Dérive revient du village avec des moules.*[47] (48-49)

As the phrase "on croirait voir" indicates, Brossard focalizes the classical intertext through her characters who are aware of it. Florence returns
from the village with mussels in a scene not much changed since
Homer's time. Or Sappho's. The "filles studieuses"[48] (116) of Brossard's
fiction understand the classical associations in their lives, and they also
know that their existence thwarts an ancient and patriarchal determination of women's place. These lesbians who love books are reading themselves into an epic intertext which expresses the magnitude of women's
entrance into history, but this epic is focalized through contemporary
women who talk while they prepare the daily meals.

---

47 *Holidays at the seaside, on an island where, when the sun is setting, you would believe
you were seeing Ulysses heave into sight on the horizon of the house (***rose wood***).
"And we looked across to the land of the Cyclops who dwell nigh and to the smoke and
to the voices of the men and of the goats. . . . And when the sun had sunk and darkness
had come on, we laid us to rest upon the sea beach."* Deck chairs make stripes on our
backs and thighs. It is seven o'clock. Florence Dérive comes back from the village with
mussels.* (29)
*Homer, *The Odyssey.*
48 studious girls (88).

CHAPTER 10

Text: *In Which* the Reader Sees a Hologram in Her Mind's Eye

> La langue est ce qui nous permet d'acheminer
> l'image mentale vers la pensée.
> — Nicole Brossard, *Accès à l'écriture*

THE FIRST EDITION OF *Picture Theory* (1982) has a design on the bottom right-hand corner of page 97, showing the corner of the page lifting to reveal a three-dimensional city, its highrises modelled in shimmering white outline against a dark grid. "Enter this book/city," suggests the picture, "and enter a virtual and three-dimensional world." The image corresponds to a densely written passage describing the vacationers' last night on the island, during which they negotiate the ninth and richest turn of the spiral: "une nuit parfaite"[1] (112):

> À l'autre bout de la nuit, j'allais ouvrir une bouteillle. Les cités convergeaient dans nos verres. Des femmes émergeaient de partout, l'architecture; la somme des lois tournait dans leurs yeux, la vélocité de leur vie, les formes qu'elles s'apprêtaient à prendre: chiffres, herbes, livres, lettres, spirale, première neige.[2] (112-13)

The scene contrasts two Brossardian conceptions of the modern city, two urban realities which co-exist. The first, defined in a 1981 text entitled "Pré(e)," is the "la ville . . . patriarcale jusqu'aux dents"[3] (5). The second is the urban environment in which radical lesbian women come together. "[L]es cités convergeaient une à une, convoquées par la fulgurante intuition que nous avions traversant l'histoire de l'art, sagittaires

---

1 a perfect night (84).
2 At the other end of the night, I was going to open a bottle. The cities were converging in our glasses. Women were emerging from everywhere, architecture: the sum(ma) of laws revolving in their eyes, the speed of life, the forms they are preparing to take on: numbers, grasses, books, letters, spiral, first snow (85).
3 the city . . . patriarchal to its teeth." (My translation.)

aériennes en voie de transformations"[4] (*PT* 113). Gazing into their glasses as if they were crystal balls, the five travellers witness Universal Man in the form of straight red arrows which inundate the patriarchal city, wounding women in their bodies and in their vision:

> chaque ville était un document qui abondait en flèches ... l'homme-flèche. . . . Les villes, l'orbe lunaire, black out, il nous fallait apprivoiser l'énergie pour éviter que s'installe dans nos membres et surtout dans nos regards, une mortelle immobilité pouvant faire croire à un renoncement.[5] (113)

Still in the virtual world of their glasses, the horizon is opened by a flash of lightning, and the women walk calmly, in spite of the arrows in their souls, into the virtual city of their feminist desire:

> Dans nos verres, un coup d'éclat ouvrant l'horizon sous nos yeux, à même mos corps en état de pensée, dans une position de tir, anticipation mentale, la flèche dans l'eau de l'âme, nous avancions calmement dans les rues désertes.[6] (113)

The flash of lightning that opens the horizon links this spatial traversal to the night voyage across the continent to the island, identifying it with the primary event. Louise Forsyth argues that the city, like the human being, is a transformative *topos* of concentrated energy: "la rencontre des femmes fait lever la page sur la cité des femmes"[7] (*Préface* 23. See also "Deconstructing Formal Space" 337). The city of women is the virtual site of freedom *to be* for the "[t]raversières, urbaines radicales, lesbiennes"[8] (105) of *Picture Theory*. The women walk into the city on page 97, which rises like a hologram above the streets of New York, Montréal, Buenos Aires, Cairo or Paris—its hieratic metonymy evoking the textual three-dimensionality of Brossard's vision.

---

4 The cities were converging one by one, called forth by the flashing intuition we had passing through the history of art, aerial sagittarians en route to transformation (85).

5 Each city was a document abounding in arrows ... arrow-man. . . . The cities, lunar orb, **black out**, we needed to tame energy in order to avoid the installation in our limbs and especially in our gazes, of a moral immobility able to make one believe in renunciation (85).

6 In our glasses, a flash opening the horizon under our eyes, our very bodies in a state of thought, in firing position, mental anticipation, the arrow in the water of the soul, we were advancing calmly through the deserted streets (85).

7 The encounters between women lift the page on the city of women. (My translation.)

8 Border crossers, radical city dwellers, lesbians (76).

Three-dimensionality is an important figure in Brossard's work of this period, and not only in association with the virtual three-dimensionality of the hologram. Everyday, ordinary reality also has three dimensions, and Brossard celebrates every woman's effort to live fully, at any given moment, in all three of them. She writes in the dedication to *La lettre aérienne* of her desire to understand patriarchal reality and its functions, "non pas pour elle-même mais pour ses conséquences tragiques dans la vie des femmes, dan la vie de l'esprit"[9] (9). In relating this dedication to the figure of three-dimensionality, we remember the patriarchal limitation of women's physical freedom, not only by extreme practices such as foot-binding and purdah, but wherever the ability of girls and women to exercise freely in three dimensions is constrained by regulations of propriety, safety and morality. In *Picture Theory*, the character of Judith Pamela accepts patriarchal law, unlike the five protagonists who practise extending women's horizons. Brossard writes,

> Il y a dans *La Lettre aérienne* dix ans de combat contre ce qui fait écran à l'énergie, à l'identité et à la créativité des femmmes. Dix ans de courbes, de graffiti, de ratures et d'écriture afin d'exorciser "le mauvais sort." Il a fallu me "colleter aux mots" pour que naissent de la bagarre bigarrée des émotions, le flamboiement des spirales et les femmes tridimensionelles qui alimentent mon désire et mon espoir.[10] (9)

These three-dimensional women who nourish desire and hope are related not only to the characters in *Picture Theory* but also to actual women fighting for women's rights and freedoms around the world. To such women, Brossard offers a mirror which, while it is as provisional as any other representation, is relatively accurate and a welcome relief from the unrelentingly negative portrayals of feminists in mainstream culture. In fact, *Picture Theory* is full of rather ordinary mirrors which reflect what is: as Brossard puts it, "si le patriarcat est parvenu à ne pas faire exister

---

9 not for its own sake, but for its tragic consequences in the lives of women, in the life of the spirit (35).

10 Ten years of anger, revolt, certitude, and conviction are in *The Aerial Letter*; ten years of fighting against that screen which stands in the way of women's energy, identity, and creativity. Ten years of curves, graffiti, erasures, and writing, in order to exorcise that "curse." I had to "come to grips with words," in order that, from the heated emotional struggle, the three-dimensional women who nourish my desire and my hope would spiral forth (35).

ce qui existe, il nous sera sans doute possible de faire exister ce qui existe"[11] (*RI* 87).

The figures of the mirror and of three-dimensionality are related to those of the hologram and the three-dimensional text. Narratology describes as three-dimensional any narrative text that includes discourse, or citation, because it implies multiple narrative levels or textual depth. The feminist reader of *Picture Theory* will see herself repeatedly in the mirror texts of the "discours autour de la table quotidienne"[12] (95). But *Picture Theory* extends narrative three-dimensionality by signifying holography in all three registers of fabula, story and text. Perspective becomes a function of reading and writing, while mirrors and embedded mirror texts play a key role as part of the holographic mechanism.

Mirror texts share important elements with the primary fabula, signifying the fabula to the reader as to the characters (*N* 146). An important contrasting mirror text is the fragment of Richard Wagner's *Die Walküre*, which serves also as a footnote to Oriana's operatic career. Wagner articulates clearly the principles of European patriarchy: the daughter is subject to patriarchal authority on the four levels of her body, her family, her state and her religion: she is dominated by her husband, father, king and god. Because she has rebelled, she is isolated from any community, even the natural one of her siblings:

Wotan

Did you not hear what I ordained?
J'ai exclu de votre troupe la soeur infidèle;
à cheval avec vous elle ne traversera plus les airs;
la fleur virginale se fanera,
un époux gagnera ses faveurs de femme;
désormais elle obéira à son seigneur et maître,
et, assise devant son foyer filant la quenouille,
elle sera la cible et l'objet de toutes les moqueries.
Si son sort vous effraie, alors fuyez celle qui est perdue!
Ecartez-vous d'elle et restez loin d'elle.
Celle d'entre vous qui oserait demeurer auprès d'elle
celle qui me braverait, prendrait le parti de la misérable,

---

11 If patriarchy can take what exists and make it not, surely we can take what exists and make it be (103).
12 Talk around the daily table (67).

cette insensée partagerait son sort: cette téméraire
doit le savoir![13] (54)

The narratological requirement that a mirror text share a common element with the main fabula is fulfilled by the rebellious figures of the out-
cast sister and the other, bold woman who stays close to her. Wotan's
ordained punishment of isolation images in reverse the feminist community of *Picture Theory*.

The talk around the daily table is the central mirror text and sign of
the novel, as Claire Dérive herself points out early in "L'émotion": "Nous
étions assises autour de la table et Claire Dérive disait que de nous voir
ensemble et ici retrouvées au bord de la mer, c'est un signe"[14] (96-97).
The women seated together in the house by the sea are a sign of the book
and a sign of social change, signifying that the break from patriarchal
meaning has been effected, and the second stage, the creation of the
imaginary territory or "vacance" to be filled with women's energies, is in
progress. The embedded conversations impact causally on the main fabula, producing the energy essential to the primary event. The narrative
technique of free indirect discourse blurs hierarchical embedding and
underlines the importance of feminist discourse as the irreplaceable
model and strategic occasion for the collective feminist practice of
semantic divergence in the spiral of political and personal change.

The overarching topic of conversation is, of course, women's trajectory
out of patriarchy, making the embedded conversations argumentative and
mirroring the intentions of the book as a whole. The conversations move
rapidly over a range of theoretical issues associated with the radical feminism of the 1980s, including the concept of matriarchy, the nature of

---

13   **Did you not hear what I ordained?**
J'ai exclu de votre troupe la soeur infidèle;
No more will she ride her horse through the air with you;
the virginal flower will wither,
a husband will win her womanly favours;
henceforth she'll obey her lord and master
and, seated at her hearth will ply the distaff,
she'll be the target and object of all mockery.
If her fate frightens you, then flee her who is lost!
Distance yourself, keep away from her.
One of you women who dare to stay near her
who will bravely defy me, take the side of the miserable wretch,
that rash woman will share her fate: that bold one must know it! (33)
14 We were seated around the table, and Claire Dérive said that to see us all here
together again, meeting at the seaside, was a sign (69).

patriarchy and the role of the patriarchal mother, and the resocialization of women's sexual desires. Claire is thinking about a key condition for the creation of the hologram:

> Bien qu'elle affirmait que le mot abstraction se glisse quelque part dans sa pensée, elle admettait pour le moment qu'il lui était difficile d'établir un lien direct entre le fait d'être cinq femmes dans une île et la notion même de ce que peut être une abstraction.[15] (97)

Her intuition of an abstraction refers to "l'abstraction vitale" (88) of May 16, which, I have argued, corresponds to Brossard's concept of turning away from negative memory in order to build on what is ecstacy, and new. It also recalls the abstraction through which women, as subjects of language, "lay claim to universality," as Wittig argues in "The Mark of Gender" (6). Claire develops her ideas further, relating *being* to *utopia*:

> à la source de chaque émotion, il y a une abstraction dont l'effet est l'émotion mais dont les conséquences dérivent la fixité du regard et des idées. Chaque abstraction est une forme potentielle dans l'espace mental. Et quand l'abstraction prend forme, elle s'inscrit radicalement comme énigme et affirmation. Avoir recours à l'abstraction est une nécessité pour celle qui fait le project, tentée par l'existence, de traverser les anecdotes quotidiennes et les mémoires d'utopie qu'elle rencontre à chaque usage de la parole.[16] (105)

The "je suis" of "La perspective" (76) and "des phrases complètes et abstraites liant la vie et la parole"[17] (96) are also Brossardian responses to this key issue of language and the access to undivided subjectivity.

While Claire's friends don't respond theoretically to her point, they respond in practice, each woman offering her own being, preoccupations and thought:

---

15 Even though she asserted that the word abstraction slipped its way somewhere into her thought, she admitted for the moment that it was difficult to establish a direct link between the fact of being five women on the island and the very idea of what could be an abstraction (69).

16 at the source of each emotion, there is an abstraction whose effect is the emotion but whose consequences derive from the fixity of the gaze and ideas. Each abstraction is a potential form in mental space. And when the abstraction takes shape, it inscribes itself radically as enigma and affirmation. Resorting to abstraction is a necessity for the woman who, tempted by existence, invents the project of going beyond routine daily anecdotes and the memories of Utopia she meets each time she uses language (77).

17 complete sentences, abstract ones, linking life and speech (69).

Oriana se mit alors à parler du temps tout en cherchant ses mots en français pour dire comment elle l'imaginait. Elle dit ne pas comprendre pourquoi, chaque fois que des femmes sont réunies, dans les films par exemple, le temps semble s'arrêter autour d'elles après les avoir figées ou changées en statues de sel chargées de symboles. Oriana, après que Danièle Judith l'eût interrompue pour dire matriarcat, continuait sa description du temps.[18] (97)

In speaking of the deathly effect of the patriarchal gaze on the bodies of women, Oriana refers to the myths of Lot's wife and Eurydice, each woman paralyzed by her husband's gaze. These classical myths, rewritten by Brossard as well as by Marlatt and Wittig, are central to lesbian rewriting of patriarchal mythology. The lesbian is able to lead her lover out of hell—unlike the male lover who betrays her and incorporates her death into a religious symbology. In *Picture Theory*, the taste of salt is a motif associated with the memory of ancient betrayal. Danièle interrupts Oriana with the talisman of matriarchy to charm away damage to the body and imagination. Later, however, she corrects herself, disassociating the concept of matriarchy from that of utopia: "Danièle Judith disait que le matriarcat est un mot d'anthropologie et qu'il ne peut pas être utilisé d'une manière contemporaine pour exorciser le patriarcat. Ce mot ne pouvait non plus servir à élaborer quelque utopie qui aurait rendu les femmes à leur genre"[19] (101). The developing political critique of lesbian utopianism, discussed in chapter 1, lies behind Danièle's qualifications of the word "matriarcat" as well as Michèle's and Claire's programmatic interventions with respect to ecstasy: "Je voulais dire que l'extase est une réalité en soi qui rend le temps éternel. Claire Dérive affirmait qu'il ne fallait pas confondre la nuit des temps, le temps patriarcal et l'extase"[20] (97).

---

18 Oriana then began to talk about time and the weather all the while searching for the words in French to say how she imagined it. She said that she did not understand why, each time certain women got together, in films for example, time seemed to stop around them after having frozen them or changed them into pillars of salt, loaded (with) symbols. After Danièle Judith had interrupted her to say matriarchy, Oriana continued her description of time (69).

19 Danièle Judith was saying that matriarchy is a word from anthropology and it cannot be used in a contemporary way to exorcize patriarchy. This word could not be used either to elaborate some Utopia that would have restored women to their gender (73-74).

20 I wanted to say that ecstacy is a reality in itself which makes time eternal. Claire Dérive affirmed that we mustn't confound time out of mind, patriarchal time and ecstacy (69).

In *Picture Theory*, ecstasy is related to utopia, and both are feminist issues. As Brossard explains, *La lettre aérienne* addresses a feminist question to the heart of "des séquences utopiques qui traversent nos pensées, nos paroles et nos gestes"[21] (9-10). The timelessness of ecstasy, Claire specifies, has nothing in common with the timelessness of women's non-being in patriarchal systems, as patriarchal darkness has nothing in common with night. To imagine otherwise is to identify pleasure with a masochistic annihilation: "de cette confusion naissaient des femmes suspendues et immobiles dans l'espace"[22] (97). Ecstasy is part of the utopian program because it is forward looking; it can provide a match for our glimpses of what is not, but what could be. Even Oriana's search for words corresponds to the creation of a screen sufficiently imbued with ecstatic elements that it will be able to interact eventually with the utopian screen. At issue is a quality of emotion:

> Nous étions assises autour de la table. . . . Je disais, avec dans la bouche un goût de sel, à propos de l'utopie en commençant par le mot femme que l'utopie n'allait pas assurer notre insertion dans la réalité mais qu'un témoignage utopique de notre part pouvait stimuler en nous une qualité d'émotion propice à notre insertion dans l'histoire. Avant que Claire Dérive parle d'abstraction, j'ajoutais que nous devions socialiser nos énergies de manière à n'en être point victimes ou encore pour éviter que nos ventres seuls soient méritoires comme une virilité mentale pouvant servir par la suite à meurtrir les corps pensants.[23] (101-102)

Michèle argues that women's energies must be resocialized in order for them to cease to live as victims—a radical argument made convincingly by Monique Wittig in "La pensée straight." Michèle might have added that such resocialization, if it is possible at all, could never take place in isolation but would require the complicity of others doing the same. Michèle's words metonymically interpellate the reorganized subjectivity of which she dreams. In order to effect the transformation of individual

---

21 the utopian sequences which traverse our thoughts, words and deeds (36).

22 from this confusion were born women suspended and immobile in space (69).

23 We were sitting around the table. . . . I said, with a taste of salt in the mouth, on the subject of Utopia beginning with the word woman that Utopia was not going to ensure our insertion into reality but that a Utopian testimony on our part could stimulate in us a quality of emotion favourable for our insertion into history. Before Claire talks about abstraction, I added that we ought to socialize our energies so that we would in no way be victims or again to avoid having our wombs alone praiseworthy as mental virility able to serve afterward for the murder of thinking bodies (73-74).

utopian experience into a new symbolic and historical organization of gender, women must generate a new libidinal economy. The ideal point of departure for such an enterprise is exactly where these characters are, around the table sharing language and energy. The repetition of the phrase "nous étions assises autour de la table"[24] (96, 101, 105, 107, 109), with its feminine "assises," underlines the round-table discussions as a motif in the novel, and a mirror for the readers who find themselves participating in a virtual reality there.

The circle around the table is also a healing circle, for the long-term destructive effects of the formation of female identity in the patriarchal family is also a feminist issue, as the characters' tearful memories of childhood make clear. Women are paralyzed in "le temps patriarcal," betrayed in many ways, as Mary Daly elaborates in chapter 4 of *Gyn/Ecology*, often by their own mothers who initiate them into patriarchal law. In the morning light of *Picture Theory*, Claire Dérive denounces the patriarchal mother:

> Le temps patriarcal ne s'est-il pas arrêté autour d'elles pour les confondre morbidement à la folie, à la mort et à la soumission. La mère est partout quand le temps s'arrête, la mère est pleine de secrets qui angoissent les filles laissées à elles-mêmes dans les ruines patriarcales: autos, pneus, ascenseurs, métros, verres brisés. L'âme en ruine, l'esprit de l'homme ne peut plus se concevoir autrement qu'en projetant la perte de sa déité dans les corps abstraits de quelques femmes isolément réunies, l'âme en ruines. Il y a là un manque à imaginer qui bien que n'étant pas nôtre, nous accable dans l'exercice même de nos fonctions mentales.[25] (97-98)

But the narrator testifies to the changing times: "Pour la première fois, comme ce matin devant la mer, je n'ai pas peur d'entendre les mots d'une autre femme"[26] (98). After *L'amèr*, in the transformative world of

---

24 We were seated around the table (69, 73, 77, 78, 81).

25 Didn't patriarchal time come to a stop around them merging them morbidly in madness, death and submission. The mother is everywhere when time stops, the mother full of secrets that cause anguish to girls left to themselves in the patriarchal ruins: cars, tires, elevators, subways, broken windows. The soul in ruins, the mind of man can no longer conceive itself differently except by projecting the loss of his deity on the abstract bodies of a few women reunited in isolation, soul in ruins. There is a lack of imag(in)ing in this which, although not ours, overwhelms us in the very exercise of our mental functions (70).

26 For the first time, as this morning in front of the sea, I was not afraid to hear the words of another woman" (70).

Picture Theory, Michèle can listen without fear to the words of another woman because, in this world, women no longer have anything to gain by initiating other women into patriarchal law.

In "L'émotion," the characters reach for words adequate to a shared experience of utopia/ecstasy freed from the patriarchy, and they depend on each other for a linguistic community that understands words the way they do. In Brossard's thought, the women are speaking with the same accent, having undergone a parallel process of semantic deviation so that, by the time they reach the spiralling world of *Picture Theory*, they are practised at articulating reality from multiple perspectives. "La perspective," which follows "L'ordinaire" but precedes the virtual production of "L'émotion," prepares the reader to participate in "L'émotion" by developing the double perspective first suggested in the fragmentary scènes blanches.

"La perspective" presents two scenes: the scene of the book, which reads Djuna Barnes's *Nightwood* as mirror text/intertext, and the love scene, which carries forward the abstraction and which reveals the narrator to herself. Claire's arrival, announced with great anticipation at the close of "L'ordinaire," is the beam of coherent light that transforms the holographic plate, the incoherent record of the first exposure, into the virtual three-dimensionality of the holographic image. The love scene between the narrator and Claire Derive puts "L'ordinaire" into a new perspective.

Perspective is traditionally thought to formalize a relationship between a work of art and an observer. The mathematical principles of one-point or central perspective, known to the architects of classical Greece but lost during the Middle Ages, were rediscovered by Renaissance architect Filippo Brunelleschi, and Leon Battista Alberti theorized and applied Brunelleschi's discovery of the vanishing point in his thesis *Della pittura* (1436). According to his "picture theory," all parts of a painting were to be constructed in rational relationship to each other and to the observer. The ideal observer's height and distance from the painting are established by the artist during the perspective construction, thus placing the viewer in a fixed position. This traditional one-point perspective is made obsolete by the three-dimensionality of the hologram, which permits a multiplicity of points of view.

Picture Theory interpellates a viewer/reader who develops new perspectives while engaged in the ongoing activity of reading. Whereas traditional perspective effectively transforms three-dimensional objects and spatial relationships in order to represent them on a two-dimensional plane or in flat relief, in *Picture Theory*, the printed page, imagined as a shallow relief of paper and ink, functions as a relay-transistor or screen for the reconstitution of a utopian and three-dimensional image. Brossard creates a place for the reader in the textual perspective, but it is no longer necessary for this place to be fixed because a hologram, like a "real" object, can be regarded from any situation without distortion of its vital characteristics.

The difficulties encountered in reading *Picture Theory* are guides for the developing perspectives of the reader. The hologram is to appear in the mind's eye of the reader, not as an image of woman, for images of women are everywhere and entirely co-opted, nor as a hologram of a woman, for such holograms already exist, and have changed nothing. The hologram is to appear like a wave of emotion evoked by the memory of utopia; it is to appear as interacting wave formations in the cervical cortex, resulting in a three-dimensional consciousness/memory/picture of "la femme intégrale": a generically female human being, with all ensuing consequences. In order to produce this desired effect, *Picture Theory* assembles the necessary elements: Claire Dérive, the love scene, the narrator who reconstitutes nothing, the mirror and the beam of coherent light which is split into two. The love scene will be holographed, and at the right moment, the hologram will be activated by the reader.

The split beam of light, necessary for three-dimensional perspective, is figured in a variety of ways. In la scène blanche and "La perspective" the text is diffracted into the parallel scenes of the carpet or love scene, the holographed scene (43) and the book (43). Concurrently, a double perspective on time is elaborated through alternate use of the present tense with the imperfect or the passé composé (65), and through the correlation between *changing consciousness* and *crossing the threshold*. The motifs of the "hall d'entrée" and the room filled with light, familiar from la scène blanche, guide the reader through the transformations of "La perspective." The split scene corresponds to the split beam of light; the passages in the present tense correspond to the reference beam and the passages in the past tense have been reflected off the love scene and carry that information forward to the future. Claire's cheek, offered to her lover, is a "mise en abyme" (65), but, as the section continues, the perspective appears more and more to be based on a vanishing point of light (88). The rose of light which Dante saw in paradise appears in aerial perspective: "/posture aérienne / l'apparence d'une rose double dans la clarté"[27] (69). Claire enters "le hall d'entrée," and then the forest, and the images turn to Dante, Wittig and the Joycean event of the book.

Parallel linguistic strategies model wave-front interaction throughout *Picture Theory*. Just before the achievement of the hologram, "Screen Skin Utopia" evokes the polysemy of words in the first-person, present tense: "La langue est fiévreuse comme un recours polysémique. Le point de non-retour de toute affirmation amoureuse est atteint. Je suis là où commence 'l'apparence magique,' la cohérence de mondes, trouée par d'invisibles spirales qui l'activent"[28] (188). The second paragraph, written in the pluperfect and imparfait tenses and in the third person, looks at the scene from a position in the future: "M.V. s'était redressée, avait lentement tourné la tête le regard pris entre le rebord de la fenêtre et l'horizon. Le poème hurlait opening the mind"[29] (188). As the mind opens, Michèle's gaze traverses the boundary of the window to reach that of the horizon. The temporal gymnastics implicate the deixis inherent in verb tenses, analyzed by Benveniste as one of the primary means through which subjectivity is created in language (see chapter 18). *Picture Theory* uses every tense in the French language to invoke every conceivable relationship a subject may have to time.

In addition, the text moves between English, French, Italian and sometimes Spanish. This is characteristic of Brossard's work, as testified by her long interest in linguistic plurality and translation, her fascination with what can be richly present in one language, yet absent from another. Translation, like thought, is understood to be "a complex act of passage which inflame[s] the mind" ("Nicole Brossard" 53). Because translation is always the site of an encounter between language, thought and meaning, it suggests the transcendent figure of the white centre, that sudden illumination of the mind which transforms consciousness.

Since the characters of *Picture Theory* are Québecoise, American and Italian-American, the encounter of languages in *Picture Theory* is realistically motivated; Claire, for example, speaks English as her mother tongue. But Brossard's "literary bilingual consciousness" is creative

---

27   /[A]erial posture
          the appearance of a double rose in the clarity (45).
28   Langu age is feverish like a polysemic resource. The point of no return for all
          amorous affirmation is reached. I am there where "the magical appearance" begins,
          the coherence of wor(l)ds, perforated by invisible spirals that quicken it (153).
29   M.V. had straightened herself up, slowly turned her head her gaze caught between the
          window ledge and the horizon. Le poème hurlait **opening the mind** (153).

because, as Bakhtin suggests, in the encounter of languages, "two myths perish simultaneously: the myth of a language that presumes to be the only language, and the myth of a language that presumes to be completely unified" (62, 68). In *Picture Theory*, the confusion of tongues is related to the creation of new discourse based not on the single origin of patriarchal law but on a double origin and all that it might represent for the development of a non-binary symbolic:

> Claire revenait avec le vin, hors d'elle, parlait bitch, dyke, sentait l'américaine à plein nez, ultra modern style new-yorkais. Stop it, Michèle, watch it, disait Florence très énervée pendant que je savais vouloir réaliser la fameuse synthèse de l'eau et de feu qui brûle la langue. I know, ça me trahit cette synthèse de la double origine, I knew, I know.[30] (112)

"I knew, I know" enacts the strategies of parallel verb tenses and the use of English, while naming the new perspective. "Cette synthèse de la double origine" is opposed to the single logos of phallogocentric vision. The creative chaos of circulating language elements is underlined by Oriana's speech, which slips from French to English to Italian to German: "Elle était tout genre à la fois d'une langue à l'autre[31] (111). Oriana, who of the five women is the character most marked by patriarchy, is helped in her progress towards a generically feminine mind by her polyglot origins.

Picture Theory ends on page 188 where it begins again in a new book, *Hologramme*, another figure of translation and another mirror text, a sign of utopia which re-enacts *Picture Theory* on the level of the hologram. The translation and re-enactment of a text within a text is a technique that Brossard has explored in *french kiss* (1974), *Le désert mauve* (1987) and *Aviva* (1985), exploiting, as she has explained, the "abundant use of synonyms, homonyms . . . rhymes and rhythm" ("Nicole Brossard" 54). Activating musically symbolic associations between words and things, Brossard creates an intertextual magnetism within her texts and from one text to the next. Certain words tend to evoke others as they do in translation or in any act of interpretation. Reading Brossard reading Brossard makes virtual both the musicality of her language and the flexibility of

---

30 Claire came back with the wine, beside herself, saying **bitch, dyke,** feeling American to the tip of her nose, ultra-modern New York style. **Stop it, Michèle, watch it,** said Florence very worked up while I knew I wanted to real-ize the celebrated **synthesis of** water and fire that burns the tongue. **I know,** that synthesis of the double origin betrays me, **I knew, I know** *(84).*

30 She was all genders at once in one language or another (83).

the intertextual alliances (*les connivences*) between the dominant figures in her work, including a radical reading of reading. Brossard has qualified the enthusiastic claims made for "écriture feminine" by specifying that writing which is "traversé," or "crossed," by feminist consciousness simply permits "another *reading* of reality and self" (personal interview with Nicole Brossard, June 8, 1988). Feminist desire to "metamorphose mental space" (43, 58) and "open the mind" (188) can result in the cortical realization of a three-dimensional virtual reality. This hologram will not be found in a holography museum, but between the leaves of a book, where it waits for the readers' gaze to illuminate lovingly or boldly traverse the body/screen/text, seeking the perspective that will reconstitute feminist desire.

CHAPTER 11

Intertextual Metanarrative

NOUS les FILLES   NOUS les FILLES
faudra bien qu'nous sortions des cuisines
qu'nous sortions des armoires des baignoires faudra bien qu'nous retrouvions la FORET les FILLES
faudra bien qu'nous retrouvions la FORET[1]
— (des FILLES homosexuelles à Marseille,
janvier 1975)

I HAVE SUGGESTED THAT the narrative fabula of *Picture Theory* must be read intertextually: the island passage recalls Sappho and her collaborators, chiasmatic structures echo classical odysseys, exiles and returns, and the quest itself is so overdetermined that it can scarcely be used. *Picture Theory* demands intertextual interpretation no less at the narrative levels of story and text. Brossard's "Notes" acknowledge Djuna Barnes, and "pasolini, homère, ashberry, joyce, wagner, daive, wittgenstein, gonzales, tunon"; give references for Claude Fléouter's *Le tango de Buenos Aires*, Wagner's *Die Walküre*, Carlos Cardel's *L'âge d'or du tango* and *Chansons d'un pays quelconque*; and credit, "en toute connaissance de cause et reconnaissance," Gertrude Stein's *Tender Buttons*, Michèle Causse's *Lesbiana* and Mary Daly's *Gyn/Ecology*. A footnote directs the reader to *Questions féministes*, No. 8, and thus to Monique Wittig, Christine Delphy, Hélène Cixous, Simone de Beauvoir and the other writers who brought Parisian feminism to life again in the 1970s (48). The fiction also requires some scientific literacy. *Picture Theory* as intertext presents a rich field for scholarship, and one that has not been neglected.

1

WE the GIRLS   WE the GIRLS
now we have to come out of the kitchens out of the closets out of the bathrooms now
we have to find the FOREST GIRLS now we have to find the FOREST
(some homosexual girls in Marseilles, January 1975)

169

Lorraine Weir describes the intertext which links Brossard's "nuit parfaite" with Bloom's wanderings through the Dublin night in Joyce's
Ulysses, pointing out too that "La pensée" presents "a series of virtuoso
inventions of Joycean themes and elaborations on the major *topoi* of the
novel" (346). Louise Forsyth, in the "Introduction" to the 1989 edition,
traces Brossard's radical displacement of the philosophy of Ludwig
Wittgenstein, from whom she took the title of *Picture Theory*; Forsyth also
reads the Brossardian elaborations on the tango.

What is the motivation for Brossard's intense intertextuality? Why an
intertextual strategy in a feminist utopian text? I have suggested that
intertextual writing may be an empowering genre choice for the culturally
marginalized writer. Western women, specifically, must deal with this, our
culture—having no other home ground. If canonical texts of European
cultures can be rearticulated from [+female] thetic horizons, the difference may enlighten women who find themselves defined by civilizations
which are and are not their own. This is, I believe, the position both of
Brossard and of the writer whom she has named as her predecessor,
Djuna Barnes.

The *Picture Theory/Nightwood* intertext introduces the reader to a
Western feminist project of rehabilitation: transformations of Barnes
open into *Picture Theory*'s evocation of Dante's *Divine Comedy*, our
exemplary narrative of spiritual liberation and transcendence. In the passage from book to book, Yeats's millennial spirals are encountered, and
culturally overdetermined motifs such as the Sphinx, angel, rose, forest
and guide are renegotiated. The Brossardian figures of the continent,
falaise, salt and hologram help to translate patriarchal signs into the language of a new millennium.

The "Notes" specify that all the citations in "Livre un" are from
Djuna Barnes's 1936 novel, *Nightwood*. *Nightwood* is first cited in
"L'ordinaire," as the narrator flies to Paris:

> La piste sur l'écran, une étrange linéarité dans la fuite de la peur.
> Le journal qu'on lit avant le décollage: bombe, or, mentalité. Il y a
> des territoires qui guettent les mémoires aériennes. Dans le hublot,
> les ustensiles font des reflets tautologiques: les villes me surpren-
> nent encore, répétées. Lumineuses. "Une image est une halte que
> fait l'esprit entre deux incertitudes*."[2] (45)

---

2 The strip on the screen, a strange linearity in the flight of fear. The newspaper you
   read before you take off: bomb, gold, mentality. There are territories lying in wait for
   aerial memories. In the porthole, the utensils make tautological reflections: the cities

Barnes's enigmatic definition of an image as "a stop the mind makes
between uncertainties" (111) is a favourite of Brossard's, as Forsyth
points out (*Préface* 26). In the context of *Picture Theory*, it is important to
note that Barnes's formula corroborates Wittgenstein's philosophical
proposition which is so central to this text: namely, that language can
create a *picture* of a reality which it cannot *describe*. These specialized
meanings given to the concepts of "picture" and "image" are comparable to Brossard's own metaphorical use of the hologram to "formuler
l'innommable"[3] (202). Claiming authenticity for no more than what it is,
the image, picture or hologram makes a modest claim by the standards of
history or philosophy. Yet the claim is a serious one, and in the cases of
Barnes and Brossard it is framed by an awareness of lesbian being cen-
sored by many so-called encyclopedic framings of culture and society.
Brossard's passage is curiously parallel to Marlatt's description of the
opening flight in *How Hug a Stone* where the threat of fear, an association
between the airline utensils and linear teleology, and the narrator's resistance to patriarchal closure on reality are also at issue. It is no accident
that Marlatt, Brossard and Barnes resist generic claims for completion,
nor that Barnes is explicitly acknowledged throughout *Picture Theory*,
although many other authors appear incognito, nor that the image pic-
tured in *Picture Theory* is that of a lesbian. In foregrounding *Nightwood*,
Brossard reverses patriarchal literary history's observable tendency to
forget about the openly lesbian author, Djuna Barnes. As *Picture Theory*'s
intertextual world is collective because built upon the work of others, so
Brossard has built into the foundations of *Picture Theory* her recognition
of her forebear. In her 1981 essay, "Djuna Barnes de profil moderne,"
and elsewhere, Brossard acknowledges how deeply Barnes's writing
nourishes her own, and it is perhaps for all these reasons that in *Picture
Theory*, as in *Amantes* (14), Brossard's characters are portrayed reading
Djuna Barnes.

Nightwood is the book of "the scene of the book." Near the end of
"L'ordinaire," Claire Dérive has promised to bring the book to Michèle
(58) and the book does finally appear, with Claire, at the opening of "La
perspective": "le livre, je l'ai tout de suite remarqué / sur la table, à
l'envers et ouvert / recto verso le seul objet virtuel"[4] (65). The lovers are

---

surprise me again, repeatedly. Luminous: "an image is a stop the mind makes
between uncertainties" (25).

3 formulate the "unnameable" (163).

4 the book, i noticed it at once / on the table, upside down and open / recto-verso the
only virtual object (41).

still talking about it in "L'émotion," when Claire comments that
"'Veilleur qu'en est-il de la nuit' est le plus beau chapitre"[5] (111). "La
perspective" recontextualizes a series of passages from *Nightwood*. The
first is that of "le plus étrange salon d'Amérique"[6] (68). In *Nightwood*,
this salon belongs to Nora Flood, an American lesbian, like Claire, who
has likewise inherited the house of her grandmother:

> The strangest "salon" in America was Nora's. Her house was
> couched in the centre of a mass of tangled grass and weeds. . . . It
> was the "paupers" salon for poets, radicals, beggars, artists, and
> people in love; for Catholics, Protestants, Brahmins, dabblers in
> black magic and medicine; all these could be seen sitting about her
> oak table before the huge fire, Nora listening, her hand on her
> hound, the firelight throwing her shadow and his high against the
> wall. Of all that ranting, roaring crew, she alone stood out. (50)

Nora's house in the weeds becomes Claire's house on the sea island, and
the "ranting, roaring crew" is transformed into a company of like-minded
women, who provide for each other a community that Nora desperately
lacks.

Barnes's mysterious formula for avoiding death, "Écartée de la
mort . . . de successifs bras de femmes,"[7] appears repeatedly in the love
scene of "La perspective" (72, 74, 82).

> en parallèle j'étais confrontée
> "écartée de la mort" dans l'ovale du miroir
> "de successifs bras de femmes" au seuil
> au sol recueillaient mon souffle
> là-bas igné mon corps
> trouvait à se déplacer jusqu'ici[8] (82)

Under the congruent gaze of Claire Dérive, Barnes's fictional proposition
signifies the virtual reality apprehended by Michèle, who discovers a triumphant formula in Nora's expression of despair.

---

5 "Watchman, what of the night?" is the most beautiful chapter" (83).
6 the strangest salon in America (44).
7 Moved out of death's way by the successive arms of women (48, 50, 58).
8 i was confronted parallel
   "moved out of death's way" in the oval of the mirror
   "with successive women's arms" on the sill
   on the soil women collecting my breath
   down there my body ignited
   found itself dis/placed right here (58).

In *Nightwood*, this proposition marks the moment when Nora abandons hope in her lesbian relationship:

> She closed her eyes, and at that moment she knew an awful happiness. Robin, like something dormant, was protected, moved out of death's way by the successive arms of women; but as she closed her eyes, Nora said "Ah!" with the intolerable automatism of the last "Ah!" in a body struck at the moment of its final breath. (64)

At this point in the story, Robin and Nora live together in the apartment that Nora purchases to be their home, in Paris, on the *rue du Cherche-midi*. As Robin goes out into the streets, night after night, Nora is tormented by images of her beloved "alone, crossing streets, in danger" (56); it seems that "all catastrophes ran towards her" (56). Nora then realizes that only "[i]n death would Robin belong to her" (58); the desire to keep Robin safely at home could only be fulfilled by her death. Much later, Nora will confess to the Doctor, that, "Once, when she was sleeping, I wanted her to die" (128, 144). Nora's night discovery of Robin and Jenny in each other's arms means, ironically enough, that Robin is safe from such an imagined possession-as-death, "moved out of death's way by the successive arms of women" (64).

In Barnes's text, the passage could be paraphrased to say that as long as Robin changes, she lives; it is, in this sense, a classic meditation on mutability. As the Baron elaborates later in the novel, "Our basic idea of eternity is a condition that cannot vary. It is the motivation of marriage. . . . [A] habit . . . is a form of immortality" (112). In Brossard's text, too, the passage figures a glimpse of immortality in the mirroring interplay of dimensions and realities, which exceed the framework of ordinary time. Brossard's characters, however, do not pay the heavy price of the characters in *Nightwood*, and immortality or eternity is translated not as death but as utopia or virtual reality.

These and other phrases from *Nightwood*, such as "une fièvre méthodique"[9] (*PT* 68; *Nightwood* 43), and "avec au coeur une crispation si passionnée / qu'elle rendait le septième jour immédiat"[10] (*PT* 79; *Nightwood* 52), transfer intact to Brossard's fiction, where they are wound into a very different narrative context and can be viewed from a positive perspective. Nora suffers for her love, which is made unbearable

---

9 a fever methodical (44).

10 with a muscle in her heart so passionate / that she made the seventh day immediate (55).

by alcohol abuse and by Robin's departure, but *Picture Theory* celebrates the love of Michèle and Claire, finding there a utopian emotion. Barnes's lesbian characters fail to communicate with each other, while in *Picture Theory* the lesbian characters are skilled communicators. *Nightwood* describes a relationship that brings the world to an end, but the love in *Picture Theory* is a vibrant beginning: "Je n'aurais à l'esprit que *l'idée* qu'elle puisse être celle par qui tout peut arriver"[11] (183). *Picture Theory* redirects *Nightwood*'s downward spiral, which closes in a night scene of "obscenity" (170) and despair; the women in *Picture Theory* spiral up into the dawn of history. Even Claire's name metamorphoses Nora's, a black (noir) flood refigured as clear, drifting water. Replacing the self-hatred which defeats Barnes's characters with the love and friendship of *Picture Theory*, Brossard reconfigures the dark forest that closes over Nora and Robin.

Barnes's symbolic "nightwood" is a key figure in Brossard's transformative intertext. Combining the qualities of forest and night, the nightwood of "The Possessed" harbours the monstrous mystery of origins; as the Doctor puts it, in his own messy congruity, "the sea is the night!" (93). Mieke Bal points out that a forest is always an overdetermined image: "The hero of a fairy tale has to traverse a dark forest to prove his courage. So there is a forest" (*N* 96). The forest is the matrix or female ground, and thus, ultimately, the opponent against which the generically masculine hero's action is inscribed. In *Nightwood*, at the close of the book, Nora is lost according to the terms of any patriarchal story, but she is true to her lesbian lover and to her gender. Brossard redeems the demonized image of the nightwood, transforming it into the perfect night, which is the matrix for the vacationers' ninth turn. In this way, Nora's end there can be reread as a triumphant one.

Drawn both from Barnes and from the broader cultural repertoire, the forest is among the most heavily overdetermined of signs. Traditionally, narrative structure accepts as isomorphic the forest and other *topoi* of exile and descent, such as the underworld, the desert and the dark night of the soul. *Picture Theory* suggests such a structure in the departure, descent, ascent and vision of "la nuit parfaite," which resembles or parodies the Western epic. In the spatially organized epic, the subject-hero's wanderings map the known universe in a revelation of a (patriarchal)

---

11 I would have in mind only *the idea* that she might be the woman through whom everything could happen (147).

world. On the last and perfect night, Brossard's characters traverse the island to encounter the decadent remnants of that world. The fourth wave of "L'émotion" sets in place intertextual motifs which signify the quality of their encounter: Joyce's Dublin, the desert sand, the Sphinx of Giza and the myth of Oedipus.

> je me débattais avec une émotion aussi forte, aussi pressante que des sables mouvants, qu'une mer de sable m'entraînant par les talons, jusqu'à ce que l'horizon ne soit plus qu'un reflet sur mon casque doré. Maintenant Claire Dérive parlait et c'est la nuit qui tombe sur nos épaules dans l'éclairage au-dessus de nos corps pensants. C'était de la nuit qu'elle parlait et pourquoi de Dublin quand elle disait ne pas croire en l'existence de cette ville.[12] (102)

The images signify the historic sweep of the patriarchal story which darkens the sunny, July day. Varieties of darkness and night, which recur in the ninth wave, include "le désert" (112), "les talons" (113), "Dublin" (112) and "la cité" (115). The golden helmet can be related to "une déesse" (114); "l'horizon" (115), as always, signifies the horizon of sense/meaning. "Les sables mouvants" and "les talons" are images from the Oedipal story: the sands of the Sahara Desert, which shift over the paws of the Sphinx, and the heels by which Oedipus as a baby was bound, and which gave him the name "swollen foot" (Graves, *The Greek Myths*, 13).

"[L]a nuit qui tombe sur nos épaules," particularly in the context of the desert and the Sphinx, recalls the dropping darkness of W.B. Yeats's "The Second Coming":

> . . . somewhere in the sands of the desert
> A shape with lion body and the head of a man,
> A gaze blank and pitiless as the sun,
> Is moving its slow thighs, while all about it
> Reel shadows of indignant desert birds.
> The darkness drops again; but now I know
> That twenty centuries of stony sleep
> Were vexed to nightmare by a rocking cradle
> And what rough beast, its hour come round at last,
> Slouches toward Bethlehem to be born? (402)

---

12 I was struggling with an emotion so strong, as urgent as quick sand, that a sea of sand carrying me away by the heels, until the horizon was only a reflection on my golden helmet. Now Claire Dérive was speaking and it is night falling on our shoulders in the light above our thinking bodies. It was night she was talking about and why talk about Dublin when she said she didn't believe in the existence of that city (74).

Yeats's celebrated poem expresses his theory that in the twentieth century a cycle, or historical gyre, is ending: "Turning and turning in the widening gyre / The falcon cannot hear the falconer; / Things fall apart; the centre cannot hold" (402). After two thousand years of Christianity, the pagan Sphinx, or rough beast, may be about to have a turn again.

In the spiral's collapse, Yeats sees bloodshed, anarchy and chaos, but Brossard, who associates bloodshed with the outgoing patriarchy (112), views with optimism the dissolution of the old coherence. Like Yeats, she announces that in the desert a mysterious form stalks history: "Le désert est grand, rempli de pyramides et de Hilton qu'une lumière blanche fait surgir. Une forme guette l'émotion, l'histoire. Surveille de près la structure et la matière qu'on lui réserve"[13] (112). In referring to the Sphinx in the context of a new epic order, both poets point to the Oedipal memory of man's triumph over the monster, embedded in the metaphorical rock where it is constitutive of generically masculine ego-identification. For Yeats, any movement of this old rock has a terrifying potential for savagery, but for Brossard, the breaking open is welcome and necessary. It is related to the figure of the cliff, which tells the story of history, and of the shifting continental plates which will bring the continents and islands into a new set of metaphorical relations. In "Screen Skin Too," she defiantly asserts that the (female) Sphinx was never overcome; the story that she was is a "scandale des temps."

> La falaise, le désert, la ville sur ordinateur devenaient continuité cosmique: Hilton —————————————— △ alors qu'aux pieds de la falaise, l'émotion se refermait comme un coquillage. La moindre fente. La Fente faisait un jour qui motivait M.V. dans chacune des surfaces qu'elle explorait avec la sensation de retrouver ses peines perdues dans l'horizon bleu des métaphores, là où régnait le Sphinx. Prise dans la pierre de l'effroi, M.V. était prête à devenir un buste de femme à la tête orageuse qui affolerait l'étranger lorsque la voyant paraître, il sentirait son pouls faiblir. Pulsion, pulsion, pulvérisant l'encrier, I smell ashes in the ink. L'énigme/sandales/scandale des temps. Ô mémoire patriarcale qui fit croire que la Sphinx pouvait être vaincue par un homme dont les talons dépassaient des sandales.[14] (165-66)

---

13 The desert is vast filled with pyramids and the Hilton which a white light causes to rise. A form is on the look out for emotion, story. Keep a close eye on the structure and the mater(ial) reserved for it (84).

14 Cliff, desert, the city on computer was becoming cosmic continuity: Hilton ———————— △ when at the feet of the cliff, emotion closed like a shell.

The Sphinx is not the only female spirit sleeping away the millennia cased in stone. The stony sleep of Brossard's Sphinx is paralleled by that of other sleeping female monsters, "des femmes dans la pierre"[15] (104) and the Medusa. M.V., petrified with fear, is about to become an adornment on Perseus' shield. "Le Sphinx" reigns on the blue horizon of patriarchal metaphor—blue because, from an aerial perspective, very distant objects appear blue. "La Sphinx" is supposed to have killed herself in despair, but in Brossard's spiralling night, the Sphinx in the desert is a journey station on the epiphanic horizon of sense. The image of the Cairo Hilton highlights the superimposition of these classical motifs upon a very contemporary scene.

The Sphinx exemplifies patriarchal overwriting on the palimpsestic manuscript of the perfect night. In this, it resembles "le casque doré,"[16] (102) signifier of Athena, goddess of the patriarchal triumph over women-identified religion. Infamously born from the head of Zeus without the aid of a woman, Athene kills Pallas, her Amazonian counterpart, and then controls the trace of her friend by taking her name. It is she who intervenes on behalf of Agamemnon, Apollo and Orestes against the Furies and Clytemnestra. Athena is a pre-eminent sign of patriarchal victory, but in *Picture Theory* her "picture" is abstracted out of its narrative context to become (only?) the image of a helmeted, female warrior. The pre-patriarchal Eumenides vacate the patriarchal niche where Aeschylus' Oresteian trilogy leaves them, to traverse the night sky: "C'était une nuit parfaite. C'était la nuit: traversée par la tendresse, les monstres et les exploits. C'était la nuit 'parcourant le ciel enveloppée d'un voile sombre, sur un char attelé de quatre chevaux noirs avec le cortège de ses filles, les Furies, les Parques' "[17] (112).

The tiniest slit. The Slit made one day that motivated M.V. in each of the surfaces she explored with the sensation of finding her lost pains again in the blue horizon of metaphors, where the Sphinx reigns. Caught in the stone of fright, M.V. was ready to become the bust of the woman with the tempestuous head who would frighten the stranger when seeing her appearing, he would feel his pulse weaken. Pulsion, pulsion, drive, pulverizing the ink well, **I smell ashes in the ink**. Enigma/sandals/scandal of time. Oh patriarchal memory that made people believe the Sphinx could be conquered by a man whose heels exceeded sandals (132).

15 women in the rough stone (76).
16 golden helmet (74).
17 It was a perfect night. It was night: shot through with tenderness, monsters and heroic exploits. It was night "travelling through the sky enveloped in dark veil, on a chariot harnessed to four black horses with the procession of her daughters, the Furies, the Parquae"* (84).
(* *Dictionnaire des symboles*).

To this company of goddesses, we must add Persephone (217), held half the year in Hades with her captor/husband, and Eurydice, whose ancient name means "far-seeing," and whom patriarchal mythology chose to leave behind forever in the underworld, reduced to a pillar of stone. Her fate resembles that of Medusa, also turned to stone, and of Lot's wife who, looking back towards Sodom and Gomorrah fiery with God's wrath, was turned into a pillar of salt. This woman, excluded from the renewed patriarchal contract, was left behind in Gomorrah with the taste of salt in her mouth. In defining utopia from women's experience, Brossard begins with God's interdiction against homosexual bonding between women, and Oriana, in a passage already discussed, asks for an explanation: "pourquoi . . . le temps semble s'arrêter autour d'elles après les avoir figées ou changées en statues de sel chargées de symboles"[18] (97). The narrator, specifying the utopian quality of emotion between women, arguing for the resocialization of women's desires, tastes the salt (102). According to the paradoxes encoded in *L'amèr*, the taste of salt is both the bitter awareness of ancient betrayals and the oceanic strength of the original and fruitful. *Sous la langue/Under Tongue* will add to this polysemic cluster the silky, salty *cyprine* of the goddess of love (n.p.), while Djuna Barnes's bogus gynecologist describes the vaginal passage through which most of us come into the world: "a moist, gillflirted way" (99). But the image is related, too, to the ashes that Florence tastes in a moment of discouragement with the feminist project: *"Puis brusquement Florence dit: 'Sometimes, Michèle, my mouth is full of ashes as if our kingdom had been burned down forever indescriptible, tu comprends.' D'un signe de tête, je ne voulais pas acquiescer"*[19] (206). The narrator tastes salt in her mouth, but will not acquiesce to ashes. There are ashes, but they are not in/on the tongue; they are in the (over-)writing, ashes in the ink (166).

Brossard's night-forest is an epic environment that enables the women to successfully encounter certain monstrous inventions of patriarchal writing and thus to change the course of fiction (116). In the nightclub located in the heart of the virtual city at the farthest end of the night, the women encounter the most blatant one, a fake woman. *Nightwood*'s Dr.

---

18 why . . . time seemed to stop around them after having frozen them or changed them into pillars of salt, loaded (with) symbols (69).

19 Then abruptly Florence says: "**Sometimes, Michèle, my mouth is full of ashes as if our kingdom had been burned down forever** indescriptible, tu comprends." With a sign of my head, I did not want to agree (167).

Mathew-Mighty-grain-of-salt-Dante-O'Connor, whose wisdom derives from his being "dead in the beginning" (152), appears in *Picture Theory* as the cross-dressed man who crackles like a machine: "I speak because I am dead. I speak because I want to reply to words" (115). Unlike Dr. Mathew, he is not a homosexual man, but a generic one with mastery of disguise and appropriation: "déguisé mais non travesti. Car le projet de cet homme était d'un autre ordre. Sa vie capital(e) l'emportait sur tous les jeux. Son enjeu: la terreur. Cet homme devant nous était porteur d'un mensonge subliminal générateur des passions meurtrières abbattant les femmes"[20] (114). As the dawn filters over the forested island, he disappears as do all the spectacles of the night which has yielded up its riches to the "filles studieuses" (116). The night is "parfaite et claire" (113); in fact, the women have passed "toute la nuit explorant au grand jour le dictionnaire, le contexte dans lequel les idées étaient formées puis renouvelées"[21] (116). Generic man's victory is Pyrrhic (113). The "nightwood" in which Robin and Nora are lost is transformed into "la forêt" of "La perspective" (73, 74, 75, 79, 87), a diffracted image of the forested island and the body of a beloved woman.

Brossard's polyvalent forest now recalls that other symbolic wood in which Dante, lost in the middle of his life, "came to himself" (I, 23). In *Picture Theory*, important elements of Dante's *La divina commedia* are renewed as a spiritual symbolic language. The special role of Dante's poem is suggested by the fact that "Oriana avait appris à lire dans *La divine comédie*"[22] (107); *The Divine Comedy* corresponds to the alphabet in which the new language will be written. Four Dantesque motifs are transformed into elements of Brossard's *Picture Theory*: the forest, the beloved guide, the river of light and the celestial rose. Brossard's text activates these motifs to relay Dante's sublime *au féminin*.

The dark wood in which Dante comes to his senses is feminine, *una selva*, and savage, harsh and dense.

---

20 Disguised but not travestied. Because the project of this man was of another order. His life, his capital(e) won out over all the games. His stake on the l/ine: terror. This man in front of us was the bearer of a subliminal lie generator of murderous passion slaughtering women (86).

21 All night long exploring in broad daylight the dictionary, the context in which ideas were formed then renewed (88).

22 Oriana had learned to read *The Divine Comedy* (79). My reading, however, depends upon an ambiguity lost in the tranlation—did she learn to read by reading Dante, or learn to read Dante?

Nell mezzo del cammin di nostra vita
   mi ritrovai per una selva oscura
   che la diritta via era smarrita.
Ah quanto a dir qual era è cosa dura
   esta selva selvaggia e aspra e forte
   che nel pensier rinova la paura!
Tant' è amara che poco è piu morte;

In the middle of the journey of our life, I came to myself within a
dark wood where the straight way was lost. Ah! how hard a thing it
is to tell of that wood, savage and harsh and dense, the thought of
which renews my fear! So bitter is it that death is hardly more. (I,
22-23)

Dante is guided out of this dark wood by his first guide, the poet Virgil.

Passage through Brossard's forest also marks a poet's coming to sense.
In "La perspective," the forest is a figure that links the love-making of
Michèle and Claire to the structures of the primary event and to the
historical/cultural context. In both *La divina commedia* and *Nightwood*,
the forest signifies the night, but Brossard transforms "la forêt" into a
motif for the body of the beloved and for the sexual energy that transforms that body into a utopic territory flooded with coherent light:

Claire Dérive pensait à la forêt quand elle
prenait des mots entre ses lèvres ma langue
qui lui allait réellement comme une peau
faisait en sorte que mon corps soit légèrement vêtu
devant elle pour que sa bouche entame d'instinct
de mémoire, corps à son ultime qui n'épargne
jamais le futur et la réalité qui s'en va[23] (73)

In this passage, the forest is a thought or a mental representation in the
mind of Claire Dérive which mirrors, at a critical moment, the empowering abstraction to which she has access through language. The transposition of the body of a woman into a three-dimensional expression of
virtual reality is made possible along the polysemic axis of *livre* and
lèvre, *langue* and *langue*, exciting sense. The lovers' resulting utopic or

---

23 Claire Dérive thought of the wood when she
took words between her lips my tongue
which really suited her like a skin
saw to it that my body was lightly dressed
in front of her so her mouth from instinct could start
from memory, body at its ultimate which never
spares the future and reality that passes (49).

virtual body exceeds matter—"saisie dans le matin clair par la clairvoyance/ des peaux prêtes à reproduire l'infini"[24] (73)—and thus exceeds the matrix of generic femininity defined by the womb caught in space and time. Alice Parker writes that Brossard displaces "the hermetically sealed female body, a paradigm of bounded space that has constituted materiality since Classical Greece" (*NBBW* 1). As the utopic body traverses frontiers to fill allspace with its virtual light, the forest is a polysemic thought unfolding all along the living and responsive surface of the continent.

Subsequent passages of "La perspective" develop these pictures, reiterating the constituent elements of Djuna Barnes's book, as well as the helmeted goddess, the forest traversed and the love-making of the two women. The diction underlines fluidity and excess, which joyously exceed limitations and control: "chaque fois plus nombreuse"[25] (74), "la source" (74), "l'inonde" (74), "la joie" (74), "les continents affluent" (75), "l'énergie même" (75), "traversant l'oubli la forêt jusqu'à la mer"[26] (75). The final passage of "La perspective" in which the figure of forest is evoked overflows with happiness and the sense of a mythically meaningful new beginning:

> Claire Dérive est entrée dans la forêt
> et les songes emportée par la vision
> du temps qui s'écoule entre ses lèvres
> elle entend la pluie qui danse sur son casque
> elle traverse la forêt ruisselante
> et déterminée comme l'est sa bouche
> Claire Dérive est dans la rosée
> l'horizon, allongée entre mes cuisses[27] (87)

---

24 caught in the clear morning by the clairvoyance/ of skins ready to reproduce the infinite (49).
25 each time more numerous (50).
26 continents abound, the self-same" energy, passing through oblivion the forest right to the sea (51).
27 Claire Dérive entered the forest
and dreams carried away by the vision
of time running out between her lips
she hears on her helmet the rain dancing
she goes through the forest dipping
and determined as is her mouth
Claire Dérive is in the dew
the herizon, lo(u)nging between my thighs (63).

Brossard's characters are not lost in the forest, but traverse it "jusqu'à la mer," or indeed to "des rives," which divide patriarchal reality from the real potentials of women. Insofar as it is a source of regeneration, this forest resembles that of Wittig's warrior women, or the "la grande FORET SAUVAGE" evoked in a 1975 manifesto authored by des FILLES homosex-uelles à Marseille. Brossard, on the other hand, never even hints that recuperation of the past might be a solution for women. Her water-drenched forest is an imaginative opening out of the body of a contempo-rary beloved, and the *vita nuova* to which it will give birth is infinitely gentle. In Brossard's new world, unlike Dante's, the patriarchal order "n'aura pas lieu"[28] (38); the hero and his generically feminine ground are simply no more.

Brossard's feminist variations on *The Divine Comedy* are comparable with those of Wittig, who foregrounds the relationship between the poet and guide in *Virgile, non* and earlier, in *Le corps lesbien*, which reconfig-ures Eurydice's voyage out of the underworld. In both texts, the relation-ship between the guide and the guided is an intense expression of release from an underworld of non-being into life as a whole subject. In *Le corps lesbien*, Wittig's narrator watches the back of her lover who does not turn around but instead accomplishes her successful exit from hell.

> J/e dirai seulement comment tu viens m/e chercher jusqu'au fond de l'enfer. Tu traverses à la nage la rivière aux eaux boueuses sans redouter. . . . J/e vois ton large dos l'un ou l'autre de tes seins quand tes mouvements te montrent *de profil.* . . . tu m//entraînes jusqu'à la surface où le soleil est visible. C'est là seulement là au débouché vers les arbres et la forêt que d'un bond tu m/e fais face et c'est vrai qu'en regardant tes yeux, j/e ressuscite à une vitesse prodigieuse.[29] (11-13) (My emphasis.)

---

28 The patriarchy shall not take place (18).

29 *I* shall recount only how you come to seek m/e in the very depths of hell. You swim across the muddy waters of the river . . . You sing without pause. The female guardians of the dead mollified close their gaping mouths. You obtain their permis-sion to bring m/e back as far as the light of the living on condition that you do not turn round to look at m/e. The march along the underground passages is inter-minable. *I* can see your broad back one or other of your breasts when your movements show you in profile. . . . you drag m/e to the surface of the earth where the sun is visi-ble. Only there at the exit towards the trees and the forest do you turn to face m/e with a bound and it is true that looking into your eyes *I* revive with prodigious speed (19-20).

"La perspective" also represents the guiding relationship as an erotic one, and Brossard's wording at times seems to recall Wittig's, for example, in the following passage:

> j'esquisse un geste de la main pour
> dire en voyant le tableau la stèle grise
> d'illusion, de perspective son dos momentanément
> lorsque nous quittons le hall d'entrée
> devant le tableau elle se tourne, je
> suis un relais l'intrigue si je désire
>
> Claire Dérive demandait hors-texte si
> or tel est le mouvement de la main
> quand des doigts elle touchait le livre agitée
> et me regardait *feindre* la douleur
> qu'effectivement la stèle, la toile, tissu blême
> alors Claire Dérive s'esquivait dos adoré[30] (67)

The "dos adoré" and the accent put onto the expression, "de profil" (105) are reminiscent of Wittig, while "la stèle grise" seems a sober *herme* marking an ancient route to the underworld. Brossard's text, however, views such images from a utopian perspective, which means that, for Michèle and Claire, hell is a "hall d'entrée" through which they pass as they enter a more important place; its traversal corresponds on the level of the fabula structure to the primary narrative event.

The passage out of the Inferno takes Dante to the "living green of the divine forest" of Purgatory (Canto XXVIII, 2), from where he is guided towards Paradise by his feminine guide, Beatrice. Dante's second forest more closely resembles the living forest of *Picture Theory*'s "La perspective," and, like Dante's passage through Purgatory, Brossard's forest traversal ends in a transcendent vision. While Claire as guide replaces both Beatrice and Virgil—like Virgil, she enters the forest; like Beatrice,

---

30 i sketch a gesture with my hand to
say when seeing the painting grey stele
of illusion, in perspective momentarily her back
when we leave the entrance
in front of the picture she turns around, i
am a relay the intrigue if i desire

Claire Dérive asked extra-textually if
this is not the movement of the hand
when agitated her fingers touched the book
and looked at me *feigning* pain
that effectively the stele, the canvas, livid tissue
then Claire Dérive slippped away adored back (43).

she guides the poet into Paradise—she is closer to Paradise than to the
Inferno, and closer to Beatrice than to Virgil. Claire and Beatrice are
both associated with light. In his final apostrophe to her in Canto XXXI
of the *Purgatorio*, Dante addresses Beatrice as the "splendour of living
light eternal" (O isplendor di viva luce etterna" II, 408-409), thus making clear the extent to which she shares the attributes of Paradise.

Dante's Paradise is imaged by the heavenly rose, the angel, the river
of light and the light of intellectual love:

> E vidi lume in forma di rivera
>   fulvido di fulgore, intra due rive
>   dipinte di mirabil primavera.
> Di tal fiumana uscìan faville vive,
>   e d'ogni parte si mettìen ne' fiori,
>   quasi rubin che oro circunscrive.
> Poi, come inebriate dalli odori,
>   riprofondavan sè nel miro gurge;
>   e s'una intrava, un'altra n'uscìa fori.

> And I saw light in the form of a river pouring its splendour between
> two banks painted with marvellous spring. From that torrent came
> forth living sparks and they settled on the flowers on either side,
> like rubies set in gold; then, as if intoxicated with the odours, they
> plunged again into the wondrous flood, and as one entered another
> came forth. (III, 432-435)

The vision of the river of light is transformed into that of the heavenly
rose, "rising above the light all round in more than a thousand tiers . . .
the eternal rose, which expands and rises in ranks and exhales odours of
praise to the Sun that makes perpetual spring" (III, 437). In his experience of Paradise, which is made possible by his love for Beatrice, Dante
is granted a vision unlimited by space and time (III, 443), and illuminated by the light of intellectual love:

> con atto e voce di spedito duce
>   ricominciò: 'Noi siamo usciti fore
>   del maggior corpo al ciel ch'è pura luce:
> luce intellettüal, piena d'amore;
>   amor di vero ben, pien de letizia;
>   letizia che trascende ogni dolzore. . . .

> Come subito lampo che discetti
>   li spiriti visivi, sì che priva
>   dall'atto l'occhio di più forti obietti,
> così mi circunfulse luce viva;

e lasciommi fasciato di tal velo
del suo fulgor, che nulla m'appariva.

[S]he began again with the voice and bearing of a guide whose task
is done: "We have come forth from the greatest body to the heaven
that is pure light,—light intellectual full of love, love of true good
full of joy, joy that surpasses every sweetness. . . ." Like sudden
lightning that scatters the visual spirits and deprives the eye of the
action of the clearest objects, a vivid light shone round about me
and left me so swathed in the veil of its effulgence that nothing was
visible to me. (III, 432-33)

In his description of Paradise, Dante sought to express the inexpressible:
"by the successive stages of his imagery, he strives to set the ultimate
realities of the spirit apart from all lesser experience" (III, 441). "Dante
suggests by sensible imagery the conditions of a super-sensible
world. . . . Sound and light have been the main ingredients of his marvellous effects . . . he achieves . . . the presentation of a world beyond the
perceptions of sense" (C.H. Grandgent, cited in Alighieri, III, 455).

The rose, the river of light and the light of intellectual love are equally
Brossardian motifs, and, like Dante, Nicole Brossard has embraced the
project of writing of what cannot be expressed because it lies beyond our
daily perspectives. The first occasion of la scène blanche addresses the
difficulty of this utopian writing: "nous voilà, l'horizon, jamais je ne
saurai narrer"[31] (40). Music and light are the medium, too, of Brossard's
marvellous effects: "comme en musique . . . une brûlure capable . . . de
faire surgir cette dimension autre / qui étonne soudain les lèvres au nom
de la brûlure / échapper à toute catégorie niant / l'espace même et toujours fluide de l'instant"[32] (69).

Dante's river of light is translated as the gaze of Claire Dérive which
twice floods the scene (88, 76): "*Claire Dérive est invisible quand elle /
inonde la scène de son regard et qu'elle / bouge lentement devant moi,
légèrement / dans la blanche matinée*"[33] (88). Like Dante's Paradise,
Brossard's utopia opens with an earthly dawn which is related to the
appearance of a rose and an angel:

---

31 there we were, the horizon, I will never be able to narrate (20).

32 as in music . . . a burn capable . . . of arousing / this other dimension astonishing
    suddenly lips in the name of the burn / to escape from all categories denying / space
    itself and always fluid the moment (45).

33 *Claire Dérive is invisible when she floods the scene / with her look and when she moves
    slowly in front of me, / lightly in the white morning* (64).

>dans la clarté, prête à commencer les gestes
>invisibles qui nous lient, une lecture attentive
>pousse les corps à agir
>   /posture aérienne
>l'apparence d'une rose double dans la clarté
>mortellement touchée ou traverse le savoir
>si l'ange s'offre à la réflexion dans la lumière
>miroir ardent.[34] (69)

Key words such as "touchée" and "l'apparence" weave into "La perspective" an evolving contemporary perspective on spiritual liberation, viewed by Dante as Paradise, but translated by Brossard as *being*: the being to which the subject, through abstraction, has access in language. Love and writing interface to propose the hologram of a scene which refigures Dante's images of the dawn, the light, the rose:

>*J'étais l'énergie sans fin, la sensation*
>*de l'idée, j'étais dans l'expression de*
>*l'utopie une femme touchée par l'appa-*
>*rence d'une rose. J'étais ce matin du 16*
>*mai, avec Claire Dérive, exposée à*
>*l'abstraction vitale*[35] (88)

Brossard calls upon the most traditional of romantic associations between the beloved woman and the rose. She is not the only writing lesbian to have done so; Adrienne Rich, in a passage which Brossard celebrates in *Amantes* (13), writes: "your strong tongue and slender fingers / reaching where I had been waiting years for you / in my rose-wet cave—whatever happens, this is" (32). Rich, like Judy Chicago, accesses the image of the rose by means of a visual association between women's sex and flowers, but Brossard's is an intertextual association. Brossard's rose, like her

---

34 in the clarity, ready to begin the invisible
    gestures linking us, an attentive reading
    pushes the bodies to act
                        /aerial posture
    the appearance of a double rose in the clarity
    fatally touched where knowledge passes
    if an angel presents reflection in the light
    burning mirror. i speak slowly
    detached from the words i pronounce invisible (45).
35 *i was energy without end, the sensation of the idea, i*
    was a woman touched by the appearance of a rose in
    Utopia's expression. i was this morning of May 16th,
    with Claire Dérive, exposed to vital abstraction (64).

angel, is an image remarkable not for its fresh tenor but rather for the
narrative context into which it is written, a context that recontextualizes
the meaning of the traditional symbol in the visionary terms of a feminist
utopia.

When Wittig, in *Virgile, non*, gets out of hell, she arrives at an earthly
paradise where lesbian angels on motorcycles are preparing to celebrate
an open-air banquet featuring the fruits of the earthly paradise.

> Des anges passent à présent portant sur leurs épaules des paniers et
> des caisses de fruits. Elles les disposent ensuite au centre de la
> cour dans des entassements géométriques. Il y a des cerises, des
> fraises, des framboises, des abricots, des pêches, des prunes, des
> tomates, des avocats, des melons verts, des cantaloups, des
> pastèques, des citrons, des oranges, des papayes, des ananas et des
> noix de coco. A un moment donné, un chérubin seins nus, sonne la
> trompette pour annoncer que tout est prêt pour la cuisine des
> anges.[36] (138)

Brossard's utopian angel has nothing of Wittig's campy comedy, but must
be interpreted in relation to two other Brossardian angels, the first of
which directs us back into a night-world reminiscent of Dr. Mathew-
Mighty-grain-of-salt-Dante-O'Connor. This is the world of the *portenos*,
Buenos Aires's poor.

As Forsyth has commented (*Préface* 12), M.V. cites Claude Fléouter in
underlining the correspondence between the *portenos*, the characters of
Picture Theory and women in general, particularly in the dangerous
night-world of prostitution:

> Dans les cafés et les *clandestinos* "tout un monde farouche qui ne
> doit rien à personne, qui vient là avec le fol espoir et le désespoir,
> les détresses et les passions qui embrasent parfois les nuits": plus
> tard, les femme s'appelèrent Lola la Petisa, Maria la Tero, la Mon-
> donguito, la China Bencecia et Madame Yvonne. Des noms de
> femmes qui vivaient comme dans des internats; la chambre la plus
> coûteuse s'appelait Los Angelitos "au-dessus du lit, le crucifix, des

---

36 Now angels pass, carrying baskets and bowls of fruit on their shoulders. Then they
   arrange them in the centre of the courtyard in geometric piles. There are cherries,
   strawberries, raspberries, apricots, peaches, plums, tomatoes, avocados, green mel-
   ons, cantaloupes, watermelons, lemons, pawpaws, pineapples and coconuts. At a
   given moment a bare-breasted cherub sounds the trumpet to announce that all is
   ready for the angels' kitchen (119).

images religieuses, des médailles en plâtre sont là comme pour souligner que la foi restera préservée."[37] (108)

To the fully aware irony of a prostitution that takes for itself the names of the angels, Brossard adds an association between angels and two little girls who lived in dormitories, and who grew up to become M.V. and Danièle Judith.

> Danièle Judith allongeait avec précision sa main vers la bouteille de vin, ses yeux bleus-bleus, d'autant plus que les larmes ce soir, lui donnaient un air d'ange et cela me renvoyait à mes cahiers d'ecolière, aux premières journées d'octobre, penchée sur mon pupitre, petite main d'artiste à l'oeuvre. *Los Angelitas*, celles qui écrivent dans les internats, signes pubiens, clair-obscur, à genoux, en pénitence, celles qui écrivent leur raison, leur instinctive révolte sur les médailles en plâtre.[38] (111)

The text reclaims the image of the angel by reinvesting it with the emotions of characters who embody human aspiration in feminist terms, solidarizing with girls coming face to face with the damaging effects of gendered socialization, and with women caught by prostitution who yet privately harbour laughter and innocence in their beds. In this way, Brossard is able to weave very traditional images into a metanarrative framework of feminist and spiritual liberation, using particularly Dante's version of a spiritual relationship in which the love of a woman is guide.

Brossard juxtaposes traditional images, replete with cultural memory, with the nearly empty symbols of virtuality, laser light, the hologram. She reinvents the baroque, with its spiralling curves, displacing classical restraint by an outrageous exuberance and reliable intellectual virtuosity. In *Picture Theory*, the love between Michèle and Claire, like that of

---

37 In the cafés and *clandestinos* "an entire fierce world that owes nothing to anybody, who comes there with mad hope and despair, distresses and passions that sometimes set these nights on fire"; later, the women were called Lola la Petisa, Maria la Tero, la Mondonguito, la China Benececia and Madame Yvonne. Women's names living as though in boarding schools; the most expensive room was called Los Angelitos "above the bec, the crucifix, some religious images, some plaster medals are there as if to underline that the faith will be maintained" (79-80).

38 Danièle Judith stretched out her hand with precision towards the bottle of wine, her blue, blue eyes, all the more so since the tears this evening gave her the airs of an angel and that sent me back to my school books, to the first days of October, hunched over my desk, artist's little hand at work. *Los Angelitas*, the girls who write in boarding schools, pubic signs, clair-obscure, on the knees in penitence, the girls who write their reason, their instinctive revolt on the plaster medals (83).

Dante and Beatrice, opens into a experience of paradise, so that the lesbian is signified within the dominant Western spiritual tradition, from a perspective that is no longer vulnerable to the charge of negativity. Like Daphne Marlatt, Brossard works out of an epistemology grounded in women's actual lives, and writes intertextually to refashion Western cultural histories for life in the next millennium.

PART FOUR

Afterword

CHAPTER 12

In the Feminine

Lorsque nous parlons de culture, il nous faut
nécessairement parler de codes, de signes,
d'échanges, de communications et de reconnaissance.   — Nicole Brossard, "De radical à
intégrales"

ÉCRITURE AU FÉMININ, as Barbara Godard specifies in her introduction
to *The Tangible Word*, "confronts the symbolic" and disrupts the binary
oppositions structuring normative discourse. The term itself and the writing it has come to represent can be distinguished from feminist writing,
defined by France Théoret as "manifestory, aiming at communication,"
and from *écriture féminine*, "characterized by stereotypes of femininity"
(15). For these and other reasons, the expression *au féminin* constitutes a
discursive acquisition of the feminist movement in Québec and, to a
more limited extent, in English Canada. The capacity of the term to
express symbolic confrontation—in fact, the mechanism for such confrontation—has to do with the term's origins, which are not in feminist
theory at all, but in grammar: *beau au féminin* is *belle*. Semantic range is
controlled; feminine essence is precluded, while the binary m/f gender
paradigm is explicitly evoked, but unbalanced, insofar as an expression
in the feminine affirms a [+female]-marked term in the place of the masculine generic.

In practice, *au féminin* means different things in different contexts.
The term appears in the title of a 1983 almanac for Québec homemakers,
Le livre au féminin, where it refers to women's traditional domain. The
use of *au féminin* and *au masculin* in two philosophical collections shows
how the expression works as a gender-point-of-view shifter: Corinne Gallant's *La philosophie . . . au féminin* (1984) and Benoîte Groult's *le
féminisme au masculin* (1977) both attest to the misogyny of much Western philosophy, and go on to consider feminist points of view. Gallant,

193

however, addresses sexist philosophy from her own, feminist point of view, while Groult acknowledges influential men such as John Stuart Mill, who argued in 1869 that the subordination of women was an obstacle to humanity's progress. In each case, *au féminin* or *au masculin* suggests a switch in perspective.

The expression *au féminin* became current in Québec's feminist discourse in the late 1970s or early 1980s. It appeared in a 1980 text by Nicole Brossard, "Mais voici venir la fiction ou l'épreuve au féminin," published in *La Nouvelle Barre du jour*, and gave its name to an important conference held in Montréal in 1982: "L'émergence d'une culture au féminin." Organized by Marisa Zavalloni, this conference brought together social scientists, philosophers and writers, including Nicole Brossard, Louky Bersianik, Michèle Causse, Mary Daly, Marisa Zavalloni, Françoise Collin and Andrée Michel, who worked through and across their disciplines to address the emergence of culture in the feminine. Nicole Brossard presented her theoretical text that most clearly outlines this project, "De radical à intégrales." The conference papers were eventually published as *L'emergence d'une culture au féminin* (1987), edited by Marisa Zavalloni.

The literal translation of *au féminin* as "in the feminine" gives us an expression which is less colloquial than the French but which maintains the grammatical reference. Lise Weil and Miranda Hay used it in the first English translation of "De radical à intégrales," published in *Trivia* 5 in the fall of 1984, and the expression appeared in print again when Daphne Marlatt coined it for the title of the Women and Words conference proceedings: *in the feminine: women and words/les femmes et les mots* (1985). Karen Gould's 1990 study, *Writing in the Feminine: Feminism and Experimental Writing in Quebec*, and Barbara Godard's more recent anthology, *Collaboration in the Feminine: Writings on Women and Culture from Tessera* (1994), would seem to indicate that the term is gaining ground, although Marlene Wildeman, in her influential 1988 translation of *La lettre aérienne*, preferred the more immediately accessible "female culture."

"In the feminine" is an accurate term which can displace problematic formulations such as "feminine writing" (*what* is feminine?) and "women's culture" (women as producers? audience? owners? and *which* women?). Referring to the disruption of the generic along the axis of gender, the expression doesn't make claims about ownership or content, but instead indicates that female will be the contextual default. In this sense, as I have suggested, the term refers to a female generic.

According to these definitions, are *How Hug a Stone* and *Picture Theory* written in the feminine? The short answer is "yes, but." Certainly both texts defy the masculine generic—quite strikingly, at the fabula level—and both establish woman-centred worlds in which the default human perspective is female. Both texts explore the symbolic terrain, experimenting with non-patriarchal figures, colours and codes.

Neither Marlatt nor Brossard uses the grammatical masculine generic when referring to people; both authors, however, also avoid the use of a feminine grammatical generic. Language is not allowed to erase any character's gender reality in these texts! Grammatically, therefore, neither text is written in the feminine.

Both texts establish a discursive female generic by representing a world in which women and women's points of view are constructed as default and normal. *How Hug a Stone* accomplishes this through the powerful focalization of the i-narrator. *Picture Theory* constructs a female generic in the context of a feminist discourse and as a result of the fact that the main characters are all women. The presence of John Dérive as a character marks the boundaries of the [+female] "normal" world of the novel's action. In other words, both *How Hug a Stone* and *Picture Theory* are written in the feminine at the story level, in relation to characters, emotions, plot and focalization.

At the textual level, both *Picture Theory* and *How Hug a Stone* are narrated through characters strongly marked as female; these texts are narrated in the feminine. Intertextually both Brossard and Marlatt draw on male authors (Joyce, Homer, Dames, Graves) as well as female (Barnes, Wittig, Woolf). The gender mix in the intertext perhaps indicates that while building culture *au féminin*—by virtue of a spiralling process of narrative accrual—feminist writers live in a generically male world, and must come to terms with their [+male] cultural heritage with its complex symbols, signs and codes.

How Hug a Stone and *Picture Theory* defy the masculine generic at the deepest level of narrative, the level of fabula structure, by generating subject-actants that cannot be male and deep narrative structures that cannot be described as quests. Both texts unequivocally contest the hero-obstacle opposition that is traditionally implicated in the production of m/f gender. *Picture Theory* constructs a [+female] subject actant embodied by a multiplicity of characters, none of which are male. The often-

repeated primary narrative event represents the [+female] subject actant
traversing the matrix of the continent, the island, "le hall d'entrée" and
the forest. "Le casque dorée" signifies classical heroism while contemporary science generates a post-relativity reading of the opposition
between energy and matter.

> Traversières, urbaines radicales, lesbiennes, aujourd'hui jour élec-
> trique, leur énergie prenait forme comme l'électricité par la struc-
> ture de la matière elle-même. Hier à l'origine, leur énergie n'avait
> été mise en évidence que par leurs propriétés attractives ou répul-
> sives. Maintenant dans l'orbe lunaire, elles avaient précédé la
> science de l'énergie.[1] (105)

Brossard's double strategy associates women with the active principle in
the binary opposition while demonstrating that the opposition itself is
outmoded. The narrative features a generically female actant at the fabula level, which means that, at the deepest level, *Picture Theory* is a narrative written in the feminine.

Brossard also theorizes the creation of a generic woman, a symbolic
alternative to the dominant Universal Man. Feminist investment in *woman*
(as outlined in "De radical à intégrales") leads to a condensation of inscriptions (131); in *hologramme*, the word attains perfect readability (223).
As *woman* is symbolically resituated, so the "abstraction pressentie" (183)
of full deictic subjectivity heralds the appearance of "le corps générique":

> (dans mon univers, l'utopie serait une fiction à partir de laquelle
> naîtrait le corps générique de celle qui pense). Je n'aurais pas à
> faire naître d'une première femme une autre femme. Je n'aurais à
> l'esprit que *l'idée* qu'elle puisse être celle par qui tout peut arriver.
> J'aurais tout en l'écrivant à imaginer une femme abstraite qui se
> glisserait dans mon texte, portant la fiction si loin que de loin, cette
> femme participant des mots, il faudrait la voir venir, virtuelle à
> l'infini, formelle dans toute la dimension de la connaissance, de la
> méthode et de la mémoire.[2] (183)

---

1 Border crossers, radical city dwellers, lesbians, today electric day, their energy took
  on form like electricity through the structure of matter itself. Yesterday at the origin,
  their energy had been made evident only in their properties of attraction or repulsion.
  Now in the lunar orb, they had gone ahead of the science of energy (76-77).

2 (In my universe, Utopia would be a fiction from which would be born the generic
  body of the thinking woman). I would not have to make another woman be born from a
  first woman. I would have in mind only *the idea* that she might be the woman through
  whom everything could happen. In writing it, I would have everything for imagining
  an abstract woman who would slip into my text, carrying the fiction so far that from

In fiction, in thought, in writing, in the night traversed by Michèle and Claire, "le corps générique s'apprête à souffler mots"[3] (178). Like "la femme intégrale," the generic woman is both singular and plural: *"je la vois venir les femmes synchrones au matin chaque fois plus nombreuse, élan vital"*[4] (205). She is generic, but she is a woman—in fact, in homage to Mary Daly, she is a crone. M.V. sends a coded message to M.W. (Wittig) to tell her that the abstract and universal can be embodied as [+female]: "My *m*ind is a *w*oman" (186).

In *How Hug a Stone*, Daphne Marlatt also constructs a [+female] generic, but implicitly, at the level of story, with the precision of the focalizer, i-narrator and implied author. Whereas Brossard is a metaphorical writer, a builder of (playful) philosophical systems, Marlatt is rarely metaphorical, writing poetry, prose and theory out of metonymy, particularity, connection. *How Hug a Stone* represents one woman's mind reaching intensely for full subjectivity in language, so that the text is written in the feminine at the story level. At the fabula level, however, Marlatt's strategy is to signify a gender-inclusive subject actant who acts as a sign for humanity. *How Hug a Stone* is written "in the human." The inclusion of Kit and the actantial role played by language are both critical to this development, as is the construction of parent-child relationships as fundamentally human. The text creates a powerful tension between the gender-inclusive human actant (which would tend to default to the male) and the female generic maintained at the levels of story and text by the [+female] i-narrator, focalizer and narrator. In this way, *How Hug a Stone* resists binary logic and its intolerance for in-between terms.

Both *How Hug a Stone* and *Picture Theory* feature feminist characters engaged in cultural analysis as they try to situate their lives in relation to a wider, symbolic field. In this way, Marlatt and Brossard each construct a feminist gaze toward the symbolic, in the field of which certain images—such as sacrifice and warfare—are rejected, while others reappear: memories, stones, colours, lesbians, spirals. "[B]lue joggers firmly planted on cement" (78). As Louise Dupré and others argue, the symbolic field is a feminist issue as long as women are weakly situated as human subjects (*L'amèr* 7). The symbolic is replete with an infinity of

---

afar, this woman participant in words, must be seen coming, virtual to infinity, formelle in every dimension of understanding, method and memory (147-48).

3 The generic body prepares to breathe words (144).

4 *I see her coming women syn-cronous in the morning each time more numerous, élan vital* (166).

images in addition to those of women and men. In the long term, women and their allies must confront, refashion and appropriate symbolic materials.

Women = darkness vs men = light is one of the binary oppositions linking m/f gender to the cultural equations goodness = light vs darkness = evil. These equations have a long and dishonourable history in the construction of sexist and racist ideologies. Some writers have been tempted to reverse the terms. Hélène Cixous, for example, writes:

> Le "Continent noir" n'est ni noir ni inexplorable: Il n'est encore inexploré que parce qu'on nous a fait croire qu'il était trop noir pour être explorable. Et parce qu'on veut nous faire croire que ce qui nous intéresse c'est le continent blanc, avec ses monuments au Manque. Et nous avons cru. On nous a figées entre deux mythes horrifiants: entre la Méduse et l'abîme. Il n'y aurait de quoi faire éclater de rire la moitié du monde, si ça ne continuait pas.[5] (RM 47)

European patriarchy *is* characterized historically by bright, male gods; however, as Claire specifies, we must not confuse "la nuit des temps" and "le temps patriarcal" (97). In *Picture Theory*, patriarchy is red: "écarlate" (113) and bloody (112). Brossard broadens the colour palette of the classical oppositions to include more colours; women are dark *and* light in her kaleidoscope. As women's energies take form, light intensifies in a perspective created by the new technological context. Light is an essential element in the hologram, but shadow is also required; plates require exposure to light and dark. Too much light is blinding (101), so Brossard suggests formulae such as "d'ombre et de lumière" (95), "l'obscure clarté" (95) and "clair-obscur" (111). Brossard's baroque style and holographic metaphor both lead away from the symbolic impasse of the light and the dark.

Marlatt's treatment of colour symbolism is wound up in her research into pre-patriarchal symbolic systems, discussed in chapter 7. As Gimbutas shows, Paleolithic colour symbolism is almost the reverse of the white/black binarism of Indo-European patriarchy; in particular, white is the colour of death, as it is today in some Asian cultures. *How*

---

5 *The Dark Continent is neither dark nor unexplorable.*—It is still unexplored only because we've been made to believe that it was too dark to be explorable. And because they want to make us believe that what interests us is the white continent, with its monuments to Lack. They riveted us between two horrifying myths: between the Medusa and the abyss. That would be enough to set half the world laughing, except that it's still going on (255).

Hug a Stone represents the caves, serpents and barrows of the earth mother, honouring her shades of glimmering brown, while the intertextual narrative of the poem distinguishes lessons from the past which can or cannot translate towards the future.

Questions about the origins of patriarchy and the kinds of pre-patriarchal cultures that might have preceded it are posed in feminist theory generally, and explored in both *Picture Theory* and *How Hug a Stone*. Brossard and Marlatt both reject solutions from the past, perhaps in response to the idealization of Neolithic goddess-worshipping societies expressed in certain currents of contemporary white feminism, for example, in the journal title, *Amazones d'hier, lesbiennes d'aujourd'hui*. It is idealistic to think that women can somehow remember their way back to an emancipated and pre-patriarchal consciousness, although the idea has a certain attraction that can be appreciated, for example, in this celebrated passage from Monique Wittig's *Les guérillères*:

> [I]l y a eu un temps où tu n'as pas été esclave, souviens-toi. Tu t'en vas seule, pleine de rire, tu te baignes le ventre nu. Tu dis que tu en as perdu la mémoire, souviens-toi. Les roses sauvages fleurissent dans les bois. Ta main se déchire aux buissons pour cueillir les mûres et les framboises dont tu te rafraîchis. Tu cours pour attraper les jeunes lièvres que tu écorches aux pierres des rochers pour les dépecer et les manger tout chauds et sanglants. Tu sais comment ne pas rencontrer un ours sur les pistes. Tu connais la peur l'hiver quand tu entends les loups se réunir. Mais tu peux rester assise pendant des heures sur le sommet des arbres pour attendre le matin. Tu dis qu'il n'y a pas de mots pour décrire ce temps, tu dis qu'il n'existe pas. Mais souviens-toi. Fais un effort pour te souvenir. Ou, à défaut, invente.[6] (126-27)

Wittig's narrator urges women to remember a pre-patriarchal time when they were strong and free, but the last three sentences of this passage, quoted in *Amantes* (45), are the ones that matter the most: when memory

---

6 There was a time when you were not a slave, remember that. You walked alone, full of laughter, you bathed bare-bellied. You say you have lost all recollection of it, remember. The wild roses flower in the woods. Your hand is torn on the bushes gathering the mulberries and strawberries you refresh yourself with. You run to catch the young hares that you flay with stones from the rocks to cut them up and eat all hot and bleeding. You know how to avoid meeting a bear on the track. You know the winter fear when you hear the wolves gathering. But you can remain seated for hours in the tree-tops to await morning. You say there are no words to describe this time, you say it does not exist. But remember. Make an effort to remember. Or, failing that, invent (89).

fails, we must invent. This is the conclusion of the narrator of *How Hug a Stone*, who "invent[s]" (15) a better story, "make[s] it up" (35). Brossard's characters also take care not to reconstruct the past and she herself, as I have argued, is consciously contemporary; "Rapportons-nous au présent," as she wrote in 1977 ("La tête qu'elle fait" 85).

On the other hand, both *How Hug a Stone* and *Picture Theory* feature chronological frameworks repeatedly interrupted by memory; in *How Hug a Stone*, the narrator attends to an increasingly distant past, while in *Picture Theory* linear chronology is confounded by memory, by the simultaneous presentation of events, by mythic motifs such as the millennial woman in the stone (104). "De mémoire, j'entame"[7] (35, 58, 167). This attention to the distant past has a political motivation: when one is thinking about patriarchy, it is very hard to get away from the prehistorical questions; and, in an environment where the feminist goal of ending patriarchy has been attacked as utopian, it is important to know that patriarchy, masculine/feminine (m/f) gender, and the universal man have not always dominated our symbolic systems.

Recent work in historical linguistics and archaeology demonstrates that non-patriarchal societies once existed in Europe. In Indo-European languages, m/f gender was a relatively late development which evolved in tandem with changing cultural and social realities. Hittite, the most ancient Indo-European tongue of which there is written evidence, categorizes nouns, adjectives and people not as masculine and feminine but as animate or inanimate. Scholars had thought that Hittite lost its m/f gender system, but Paul Brosman, Jr. demonstrates that Hittite must have separated from the parent tongue before m/f gender developed. He envisions a process of gender development which is not far different from that outlined by Karl Brugmann in 1893. Brugmann had suggested that the Indo-European feminine suffix −ā originally marked only collective and abstract nouns. He proposed that the feminine gender evolved in relation to semantic change in a noun like *gwena*, which shifted from "child-bearing" to mean "woman." Rocky V. Miranda offers further evidence in support of the concept that sometime around 4500 B.C.E., in those parts of Europe and Asia where Indo-European was spoken, binary m/f gender evolved. Brosman identifies three factors driving this evolutionary change: the arbitrary, grammatical form and semantic pull. Of these three, semantic pull would correspond to

---

7 From memory, I broach a subject (15, 37, 133).

changing social-symbolic status for women. This is linguistic evidence for the prehistorical formation of European patriarchy: as women's symbolic status shifted, language evolved a typological marking, a new gender category.

The argument that binary, patriarchal gender is old but not primordial has also been made in relation to etymological clusters within Indo-European languages. In "Amazon Etymology," linguist Susan Wolfe finds that concepts as female as "mother" are linked to universal notions such as matter, matrix and divinity. The word *Amazon* is cognate with *to be able, may, might* and *mighty*. In a series of articles published in 1980, Wolfe demonstrates that historical linguistics has been used to argue that hierarchical relations between the sexes are "natural" and concomitant with the evolution of the human species; she claims that scholars with strong patriarchal biases interpreted the data according to their expectations. In another 1980 article co-authored with Julia Penelope, the women use the same evidence as their ideological opponents to demonstrate the existence of a matriarchal, Amazonian culture in early Indo-European times.

Gwynne Dyer has also recently popularized the view that the human past is not as brutal as we have believed; he argues that the "original human tradition" was 30,000 years of co-operation and non-patriarchal gender relations, which freed us from "the isolation and anger of our primate past and create[d] a better social reality"; moreover, Dyer is convinced that patriarchy has now had its day:

> after 5,000 years when most human beings had to live like worker ants, building pyramids and palaces for their betters, we appear to be returning to [the original human tradition of cooperation]. With great difficulty, of course. . . . A growing mountain of evidence suggests that moral behaviour, cooperative behaviour, even love are as innate and natural to human beings as speech and the opposable thumb. We've had something like marriage since before we were fully human. We had the idea of equal rights long before we had politics. We are not chimpanzees. (29-30)

Dyer's arguments also support the conclusions of archaeologist Marija Gimbutas, the discoverer and scholarly champion of Old European culture—a non-patriarchal, pre-Indo-European Neolithic culture.

In one of her last articles, "The Social Structure of Old Europe, Parts 2 and 3" (1990), Gimbutas summarizes some of her most socially significant findings.

> The Cemetery evidence speaks of matrilineal, endogamous, and
> sex-egalitarian societies in all of Europe during 6500-4500 B.C.
> and into the 3rd millennium in the Aegean and Mediterranean areas
> and in Western Europe. Some deviation from this pattern is notica-
> ble only along the Black Sea coast at the end of the 5th millennium
> B.C. (253-54)

Men, women and children were buried collectively, with honour. Genetic
analysis proves that the societies were matrilineal, with girls and women
related, and adult males not. Sometimes the people buried together represent different racial groups, suggesting that this people did not dis-
criminate between races. There is no accumulation of wealth in graves,
but rather symbolic items. Megalithic henges, characteristic of Old European culture, were apparently built not as monuments to individual
power but as community "festival centres and meeting places, perhaps
also as grounds and courses for sports and games" (248). Gimbutas discusses the finds at one site in Neo Nikomedeia, in Macedonia, where a
temple inside a circular village contained outsize greenstone axes,
caches of flint blades, askoi (bird-shaped vases), a vase with a goddess
face on the neck and a Bird Goddess sculpture (257-58).

It is not utopian to argue that non-patriarchal cultures have contributed to Western civilization. Camille Paglia's assertion that "if civilization had been left in female hands, we would still be living in grass
huts" (38) is incorrect; in fact, the non-patriarchal architects of Old
European culture created the first European cities. One of the earliest of
these to be excavated, Çatal Hüyük, was an urban Neolithic settlement of
6,000 to 8,000 people, occupied between 6250-5270 B.C.E. Gerda
Lerner is right to argue that such settlements offer "hard evidence of the
existence of some sort of alternate model to that of patriarchy" (35). In
"The Linguistic Typology of the Old European Substrata in North Central
Europe," Martin E. Huld of California State University, Los Angeles,
begins a reconstruction of Old European languages that he finds to be
the source for our words "apple," "alder," "cat," "cannabis," "axe" and
"silver." These words, still so much a part of our world, may have origi-
nated in a non-patriarchal culture.

"Memory implies a relationship between past and present events,"
Jacques Barbizet suggests (149); words do too, and the same could be
said of stone. Geological memories of the distant past, stones are the oldest objects in our world, and stone fossils or carvings our primary source
of information about prehistory. Stones were already old in the Neolithic,
when European patriarchy was young. In *How Hug a Stone*, Marlatt is

paying attention to words, memories and stones: Neolithic megaliths and "squat stone mothers" (64); the lost mother, elusive as a bird: "rock-dove alone in the ruined palace crying, *ku? ku? ku? (qua?)* where have you gone? first love that teaches a possible world" (78). The transformation of *ku* into the Latin *qua*, "where, which way," reminds us that words, like stones, conceal a record of the past.

> what was familiar now is relic: *sweetshop, pillarbox.* clipped mono-syllables with a distinctive pitch pattern. remnants of Old English, even *moth, snake, stone.* Word henge to plot us in the current flow. without narrative how can we see where we've been? or, unable to leave it altogether, what we come from? (19)

Tracing the stories concealed in stones and words is the effort of memory to understand where we come from, because we cannot "leave it alto-gether." Navigating "in the current flow" towards an open-ended future, the narrator of *How Hug a Stone* takes her bearings on the horizon of memory and language.

Picture Theory associates stone with the static weight of patriarchal gender, which has petrified the Sphinx, Medusa, Eurydice and Lot's wife. In "L'émotion," on the day of the visit to the cliffs, the text opens into a meditation on what might lie concealed within the sedimentation of rock:

> Il y a des roches métamorphiques et des strates. Il y a la pierre. "La Polis, la Cité des Hommes est un tout dont le corps de pierre" citait de mémoire Florence Dérive. Il y a la pierre. Il en était donc ainsi au coeur de l'île, la pierre et l'eau, l'ardoise et la craie. Il y a des maîtres, des tableaux et des artisans. Il y a des caméras laborieuses et des mains qui travaillent. Il y a des femmes sculptées, des *mujeres* blanches, des jambes cassées, des fragments célèbres. Il y avait des femmes dans la pierre brute et la pierre "taillée de servitude de de ténèbres." Il y a la pierre parlante, les pierres de pluie. Il y avait des pierres percées et sonores. Il y a les falaises et la ville de pierre opaque. Il y avait au coeur de la pierre une femme qui disait moi millénaire translucide, gravée dans la pierre utopique.[8] (103-104)

---

8 There are metamorphic rocks and strata. There is stone. "The Polis, the City of Men is a totality whose body is stone" Florence Dérive quoted from memory. There is stone. So it was like this in the heart of the island, stone and water, slate and chalk. There are master masters, canvases and artisans. There are laborious cameras and working hands. There are sculpted, white *mujeres*, legs broken, famous fragments. There were women in the rough stone and the stone "cut by servitude and shadows." There are stones pierced and resonant. There are cliffs and the city of opaque stone. There was in the heart of the stone a woman saying me millenary translucid, graven in Utopian stone (75-76).

In the heart of the stone Brossard finds not only memories of women, but chalk and slate, the materials for an immanent writing of civilization's story. Women's emotion is preserved at the foot of this cliff, where it is being freed by a millennial erosion; writing appears, "une lithophanie à l'aspect changeant"[9] (165). Women's buried emotion is the light in the stone, released to become a component of the hologram:

> Météorites dans le text. Ouverture. M. V. ne cherchait-elle pas a tra-
> verser toutes les atmosphères, tous les climats, tous du sens dans la
> pierre. Elle cherchait à se rompre ce qui n'était écrit nulle part visi-
> blement dans la pierre et qui pourtant faisait sens et sens flamboy-
> ant dans le rouge des identités, infra p. 167. C'était donc cela
> qu'elle cherchait au coeur de la lettre aérienne, cela cette phospho-
> rescence dans la nuit comme une permanence féminine prenant
> relief dans la pierre. L'image est floue. Les mots lapidaires.[10]
> (147-48)

"Screen Skin" returns to the motif of "phosphorescence dans la nuit comme une permanence féminine prenant relief dans la pierre"[11] (148). The light burning in the stone, translated into lithophanic writing, con- tributes to the layered inscriptions on the screen, the white light of la scène blanche, the coherent light of the hologram. But the woman in the stone poses a question that is thousands of years old. "Translucide," some light passes through her but not enough to permit one to see clearly. She is a signal, but she is not a guide. We may want to look back at her, but we don't want to end up in her place.

The open-ended curve of the spiral expresses this movement of dou- bling back while moving forward, so characteristic of the feminist love affair with the long ago. There are reasons why this ancient symbol is sig- nificant in Canadian and Québécois feminist culture, providing a visual syntax for Dorothy Todd Hénaut's film, Les terribles vivantes, and a name for the Québécois journal, Spirale. The spiral, as Sir Theodore Andrea Cook argued eloquently in 1918, is a symbol of orderly growth and life;

---

9 [A] lithophany of changing appearance (131).
10 Meteorites in the text. Overture. Was not M. V. seeking to pass beyond all atmo-
    spheres, all climates, all sense in the stone. She was seeking to sunder what was
    nowhere visibl(y) written in the stone and yet which made sense and flamboyant
    sense in the red of (id)entities, infra p. 149. So that's what she was seeking in the
    heart of the aerial letter, that phosphorescence in the night like a permanent feminine
    presence taking on relief in stone. The image is fluid. Words lapidary (115).
11 That phosphorescence in the night like a permanent feminine presence taking on
    relief in stone (115).

its structure is fundamental to plants, shells and the human body, to the periodicity of atomic elements and to an animal's horns, to microscopic DNA (the double helix) and to the Andromeda nebula. The spiral's mathematical expression is the golden section or the divine proportion, as it has been called. *Picture Theory* reflects on these matters, as in this passage from "La pensée":

> Seule, silence. L'utopie n'a cessé de luire ce matin à travers la pensée que j'ai eue pour chaque mot. J'écrivais "c'est elle" comme l'on sait pour longtemps la forme prise par nos mains quand elles touchent doucement, exactement, éternelles empreintes, cette partition qui éblouit à travers l'instant dont chaque note emplit l'espace du nautile à la nébuleuse, spiralée—un sexe de femme c'est mathémathique.[12] (136)

The spiral is also prominent in Old and New Stone Age iconography: countless inscriptions in stone and clay, innumerable snail shells deposited at sacred sites. For a long time now, the spiral has been a symbol for life.

Brossard and Marlatt use the spiral to suggest the form of the stories they are telling, and Brossard's fabula in particular has a spiralling form. Both authors relate the image to the absence of a fixed origin for their characters' trajectories. The spiral, to use another Brossardian trope, has "aerial roots" (97) which begin in mid-air. This is the paradox of the mother who is not the origin: the theme of Sarah Dérive Stein in *Picture Theory* and one of the lessons learned in *How Hug a Stone*, when the narrator seeks coherence and origin, but learns instead that her story starts "in flight" (15). Her maternal uncle, Edrys's brother, drives the Dartmoor Hills, "furious" and "driven," asking, "who writes the text?" (33). The narrator learns that, like language and like families, the story has no origin and no centre: "memorial orbits of love, spasmodic, reaching far back in the blood—where there is a gap, a black hole somewhere" (34). We begin where "we happen" (15); with Brossard's "le moment venu" (41).

Finally, and most significantly, both authors use the spiral to suggest where they are going, as they follow its open-ended curve towards the

---

12 Alone, silence. Utopia has not stopped shining this morning through the thought I had for each word. I was writing "it is she" as one knows for a longtime the form taken by our hands when they touch softly, precisely, eternally imprinted this score which dazzles through the instant, whose each note fills the space of the nautilus in the nebula, spiralled — — — — a women's sex is mathematical. Geo mater (104).

horizon, beyond which lies the unknown. What is becoming of our human universe? The ruins of monumental forms litter the symbolic field, but today's far-seeing women are not looking back. They are looking towards the future. Brossard celebrates the complex unfolding of women's meanings, which spiral further and further away from the enclosing circle of one-way sense. "A tort ou à raison, nous associons la liberté au futur comme si les deux mots formaient un couple moralement compatible"[13] (*Baroque d'aube* 242). Marlatt's narrator watches pigeons climb the air of Trafalgar Square, "ruffled neck feathers ripple snakelike movement of the neck last vestige of dinosaurs" (79). She is thinking of evolution's gyres. Both poets trace an open-ended arc. The need to grow and evolve is one of the complex conditions necessary for human happiness. "Free we want to be where live things are" (79).

---

13 Rightly or wrongly, we associate freedom with the future as if the two words formed a morally compatible pair (my translation).

PART FIVE

Bibliography, Appendix and Index

Bibliography

Adrados, Francisco Rodriguez. "The Archaic Structure of Hittite." *The Journal of Indo-European Studies* 10, 1-2 (Spring/Summer 1982): 1-35.

Alberti, Leon Battista. *Della pittura*. 1436. *On Painting*. Trans. and intro. John R. Spencer. Westport, CT: Greenwood Press, 1966.

Alighieri, Dante. *The Divine Comedy of Dante Alighieri*. Trans. and comment John D. Sinclair. 3 vols. New York: Oxford University Press, 1961.

Althusser, Louis. *Lenin and Philosophy*. Trans. Ben Brewster. London: Monthly Review Press, 1971.

Anzaldúa, Gloria. *Borderlands/La Frontera: The New Mestiza*. San Francisco: Spinsters/aunt lute, 1987.

Bakhtin, M.M. *The Dialogic Imagination*. Trans. Michael Holquist and Caryl Emerson. Ed. Michael Holquist. Austin: University of Texas, 1981.

Bal, Mieke. *Narratology: Introduction to the Theory of Narrative*. Trans. Christine van Boheemen. Toronto: University of Toronto Press, 1985.

————. *On Story-telling: Essays in Narratology*. Sonoma, CA: Polebridge Press, 1991.

Barbizet, Jacques. *Human Memory and Its Pathology*. Trans. D.K. Jardine. San Francisco: W.H. Freedman, 1970.

Barnes, Djuna. *Nightwood*. New York: New Directions, 1937.

Baron, Denis. *Grammar and Gender*. New Haven, CT: Yale University Press, 1986.

Barthes, Roland. "Introduction à l'analyse structurale des récits." *Communications* 8 (1966): 1-27. "Introduction to the Structural Analysis of Narratives." In *Image—Music—Text*. Trans. Stephen Heath. New York: Hill and Wang, 1977.

————. *S/Z*. Trans. Richard Miller. New York: Hill and Wang, 1974.

Beck, Evelyn Torton, ed. *Nice Jewish Girls: A Lesbian Anthology*. Watertown, MA: Persephone Press, 1982.

Belenky, Mary Field, Blythe McVicker Clinchy, Nancy Rule Goldberger and Jill Mattuck Tarule. *Women's Ways of Knowing: The Development of Self, Voice, and Mind*. New York: Basic Books, 1986.

Bersianik, Louky. *L'Euguélionne*. Montréal: La Presse, 1976.

Benveniste, Emile. *Problèmes de linguistique générale*. Paris: Gallimard, 1966. *Problems in General Linguistics*. Trans. Mary Elizabeth Meek. Coral Gables, FL: University of Miami Press, 1971.

Black, Maria, and Rosalind Coward. "Linguistic, Social and Sexual Relations: A Review of Dale Spender's *Man Made Language*." *Screen Education* 29 (1981): 69-84.

Blake, William. *Milton*. Boulder, CO: Shambala, 1978.

Blau DuPlessis, Rachel. *Writing beyond the Ending: Narrative Strategies of Twentieth-Century Women Writers*. Bloomington: Indiana University Press, 1985.

Booth, Wayne. *The Rhetoric of Fiction*. 2nd ed. Chicago: University of Chicago Press, 1983.

Bourgeois, Louise. *Destruction of the Father, Reconstruction of the Father*. Ed. Marie-Lauare Bernadac and Hans-Ulrich Obrist. Cambridge, MA: MIT Press, 1998.

Brémond, Claude. *Logique du récit*. Paris: Seuil, 1973.

Brosman, Paul. "Designation of Females in Hittite." *The Journal of Indo-European Studies* 10, 1/2 (Spring/Summer 1982): 65-70.

————. "The Development of P.I.E. Feminine." *The Journal of Indo-European Studies* 10, 3/4 (Fall/Winter 1982): 253-72.

————. "The Hittite Gender of Cognates of P.I.E. Neuters." *The Journal of Indo-European Studies* 6, 1/2 (Spring/Summer 1978): 93-106.

————. "The Semantics of the Hittite Gender System. *The Journal of Indo-European Studies* 7, 3/4 (Fall/Winter 1979): 227-36.

Brossard, Nicole. "Accès à l'écriture: rituel langagier." In *La lettre aérienne*. Montréal: Remue-ménage, 1985. 131-42. "Access to Writing: Rites of Language." In *The Aerial Letter*. Trans. Marlene Wildeman. Toronto: The Women's Press, 1988. 139-47.

————. *Amantes*. Montréal: Quinze, 1980. Rpt. in *Amantes suivi de Le sens apparent et de Sous la langue*. Montréal: Hexagone, 1998. *Lovhers*. Trans. Barbara Godard. Montréal: Guernica, 1986.

————. *Baroque d'aube*. Montréal: Hexagone, 1995.

————. "De radical à l'intégrales." In *La lettre aérienne*. Montréal: Remue-ménage, 1985. 87-105. "From Radical to Integral." In *The Aerial Letter*. Trans. Marlene Wildeman. Toronto: The Women's Press, 1988. 103-20. "From Radical to Integral." Trans. Lise Weil and Miranda Hay. *Trivia: A Journal of Ideas* 5 (Fall 1984): 6-16.

————. "Djuna Barnes de profil moderne." In *Mon héroïne*. Montréal: Remue-ménage, 1981. 206.

_____. *french kiss: étreinte/exploration*. Montréal: Quinze/présence, 1974.

_____. *Installations*. Trois Rivières: Écrits des Forges, 1989.

_____. "Interview with Nicole Brossard on *Picture Theory*." Trans. Luise von Flotow-Evans. *Canadian Fiction Magazine* 47 (1983): 122-35.

_____. *L'amèr ou Le chapitre effrité: théorie/fiction*. Préface de Louise Dupré. 2nd corr. ed. Montréal: Hexagone, 1988. *These Our Mothers or: The Disintegrating Chapter*. Trans. Barbara Godard. Toronto: Coach House Quebec Translations, 1983.

_____. *La Nuit verte du Parc Labyrinthe*. Laval, QC: Éditions Trois, 1992.

_____. "La plaque tournante." In *La lettre aérienne*. Montréal: Remue-ménage, 1985. 11-28. "Turning-Platform." In *The Aerial Letter*. Trans. Marlene Wildeman. Toronto: The Women's Press, 1988. 37-51.

_____. "La tête qu'elle fait." *La Barre du jour* 56-57 (mai-août 1977): 83-92.

_____. *L'Aviva*. Montréal: nbj, 1985.

_____. *Le désert mauve: roman*. Montréal: Hexagone, 1987.

_____. "Mais voici venir la fiction ou l'épreuve au féminin." *La Nouvelle Barre du jour* (mai 1980).

_____. "Mémoire: hologramme du désir." *La parole métèque* 7 (1988): 6-8.

_____. "Nicole Brossard." Trans. Susanne de Lotbinière-Harwood. In *Contemporary Authors Autobiography Series*, Vol. 16. Ed. Hal May and Susan M. Trotsky. Detroit: Gail Research Company, 1993.

_____. *Picture Theory*. Montréal: Nouvelle Optique, 1982. 2nd ed. Préface de Louise H. Forsyth. Montréal: Hexagone, 1989. *Picture Theory*. Trans. Barbara Godard. Montreal: Guernica, 1991.

_____. "Pré(e)." *La femme et la ville, la Nouvelle Barre du jour* 102 (avril 1981): 5.

_____. *Sous la langue/Under Tongue*. Trans. Susanne Lotbinière-Harwood. Montréal: L'Essentielle; Charlottetown: Gynergy Books, 1987.

_____. "Synchronie." In *La lettre aérienne*. Montréal: Remue-ménage, 1985. 79-85. "Synchrony." In *The Aerial Letter*. Trans. Marlene Wildeman. Toronto: The Women's Press, 1988. 71-101.

_____. *un livre*. Montréal: Quinze, 1980.

Brossard, Nicole, with Daphne Marlatt. *Character/Jeu de lettres*. Montréal: nbj/writing, 1986.

_____. *Mauve*. Montréal: nbj/writing, 1985.

Brugmann, Karl. *Grundriss der vergleichenden Grammatik der indogermanischen* [Outline of the Grammatical Comparison of the Indo-European Languages]. Berlin, 1893; 2nd ed. Vol. 2 Strassburg: Trubner, 1906-11.

Bruner, Jerome. *Actual Minds, Possible Worlds*. Cambridge, MA: Harvard University Press, 1986.

————. "The Narrative Construction of Reality." *Critical Inquiry* 18, 1 (Autumn 1991): 1-21.

Bucher, Cornelius J. *Three Models on a Rocking-Horse: A Comparative Study in Narratology*. Tübingen: Gunter Narr Verlag Tübingen, 1990.

Butler, Judith. *Gender Trouble*. New York: Routledge, 1990.

Butling, Pauline. " 'From Radical to Integral': Daphne Marlatt's "Booking Passage." In *Inside the Poem*. Ed. W.H. New. Toronto: Oxford University Press, 1992. 167-73.

Cameron, Deborah. *Feminism and Linguistic Theory*. London: Macmillan, 1985.

Carman, Bliss. *Sappho: One Hundred Lyrics*. London: Chatto & Windus, 1921.

————. *Vision of Sappho*. [New York?]: Bliss Carman, 1903.

Carr, Brenda. "Between Continuity and Difference: An Interview with Daphne Marlatt." In *Beyond Tish*. Ed. Douglas Barbour. *West Coast Line* 25, 1. Edmonton: NeWest Press, 1991.

————. "Re-casting the Steveston Net: Recalling the Invisible Women from the Margins." *Line* 13 (1989): 83-95.

Caulfield, John H. "The Wonder of Holography." *National Geographic* 165, 3 (March 1984): 364-77.

Causse, Michèle. *Lesbiana*. Paris: Nouveau Commerce, 1980.

Cayley, David. *Prison and Its Alternatives*. In *Ideas*. The Canadian Broadcasting Corporation. June 17-28, 1996.

Chamberlain, Lori. "Consent after Liberalism? A Review Essay of Catharine MacKinnon's *Towards a Feminist Theory of the State* and Carole Paterman's *The Sexual Contract*." *Genders* 11 (Fall 1991): 111-25.

Chevalier, Jean-Claude, Claire Blanche-Benveniste, et al. *Grammaire Larousse du français contemporain*. Paris: Larousse, 1964.

Chodorow, Nancy. 1985. "Gender, Relation, and Difference in Psychoanalytic Perspective." In *The Future of Difference*. Ed. Hester Eisenstein and Alice Jardine. New Brunswick: Rutgers University Press, 1985. 3-19.

Chow, K.L., and Leiman, A.L. "Aspects of the Structure and Functional Organization of the Neocortex." *Neurosciences Bulletin* 8 (1970): 157-219.

Cixous, Hélène. "Le rire de la méduse." *L'arc* 61 (1975): 39-54. "The Laugh of the Medusa." Trans. Keith Cohen and Paula Cohen. In *New French Feminisms*. Ed. Elaine Marks and Isabelle de Courtivron. New York: Schocken, 1981. 245-65.

————. "Ô grand-mère que vous avez de beaux concepts! C'est pour mieux vous arrièrer, mon enfant! un colloque féministe à New York: le second sexe trente ans après." *des femmes en mouvements, hebdo* 1 (9-16 novembre 1979): 11-12.

―――――. "Poésie, e(s)t politique?" *des femmes en mouvements* 4 (novembre-décembre 1979): 29-32.

Cixous, Hélène, and Catherine Clément. *La jeune née.* Paris: Union Générale, 1975. *The Newly Born Woman.* Trans. Betsy Wing. Minneapolis: University of Minnesota Press, 1986.

Clarke, George Elliott. *Whylah Falls.* Winlaw: Polestar Press, 1990.

Conley, Katharine. "The Spiral as Möbius Strip: Inside/Outside *Le désert mauve.*" *Québec Studies* 18 (Spring/Summer 1994): 149-58.

Cook, Theodore Andrea. *The Curves of Life.* London: Constable, 1914; New York: Dover, 1979.

Corbett, Greville. *Gender.* Cambridge: Cambridge University Press, 1991.

Cornillon, Susan Koppelman, ed. *Images of Women in Fiction: Feminist Perspectives.* Bowling Green, KY: Bowling Green University Press, 1972.

Cortazar, Julio. *Blow Up and Other Stories.* Trans. Paul Black. New York: Collier, 1968.

Cotnoir, Louise. "S'écrire avec, dans et contre le langage." *Tessera* 1/*Room of One's Own* 8 (1984): 47-49.

Cranny-Francis, Anne. *Feminist Fiction: Feminist Uses of Generic Fiction.* New York: St. Martin's Press, 1990.

Culler, Jonathan. *The Pursuit of Signs: Semiotics, Literature, Deconstruction.* Ithaca, NY: Cornell University Press, 1981.

Daly, Mary. *Gyn/Ecology: The Metaethics of Radical Feminism.* Boston: Beacon Press, 1978.

Dames, Michael. *The Avebury Cycle.* London: Thames and Hudson, 1977.

Davey, Frank. *From There to Here.* Erin, Ontario: Press Porcepic, 1974.

―――――. "Words and Stones in *How Hug a Stone.*" *Line* 13 (Spring 1989): 40-46.

De Beauvoir, Simone. *Le deuxième sexe.* 2 vols. Paris: Gallimard, 1949.

de Lauretis, Teresa. *Alice Doesn't: Feminism, Semiotics, Cinema.* Bloomington: Indiana University Press, 1984.

―――――. *Technologies of Gender: Essays on Theory, Film, and Fiction.* Bloomington: Indiana University Press, 1987.

―――――. "The Essence of the Triangle or, Taking the Risk of Essentialism Seriously: Feminist Theory in Italy, the U.S., and Britain." *Differences: A Journal of Feminist Cultural Studies* 1, 2 (Summer 1989): 3-37.

Delgado, Richard, ed. *Critical Race Theory: The Cutting Edge.* Philadelphia: Temple University Press, 1995.

Delphy, Christine. "The Invention of French Feminism: An Essential Move." *Yale French Studies* 87 (1995): 190-221.

Derrida, Jacques. *Of Grammatology*. Trans. Gayatri Chakravorty Spivak. Baltimore: Johns Hopkins University Press, 1984.

Des femmes. "Pour la première fois, peut-être, en vacances." *des femmes en mouvements* (juin 1978): 41-42.

————. "la différence internée." *des femmes en mouvements* 2 (mai 1978): 13.

————. "la situation et notre politique." *le quotidien des femmes* (3 mars 1975): 1-3.

Des FILLES homosexuelles à Marseille. "La FORET." *Les femmes s'entêtent, Menstruel* 1 [1975?]: 4.

Dragland, Stan. *The Bees of the Invisible: Essays in Contemporary English Canadian Writing*. Toronto: Coach House Press, 1991.

Duff, Gail. *Country Wisdom: An Encyclopedia of Recipes, Remedies and Traditional Good Sense*. London: Pan Books, 1979.

Dumond, Val. *Sheit: A No-Nonsense Guidebook to Writing and Using Nonsexist Language*. Tacoma, WA: Dumond Publications, 1984.

Dupré, Louise. "Du propre au figuré." Introduction to Nicole Brossard, *L'amèr ou le chapitre effrité*. Montréal: Hexagone, 1988.

————. *Stratégies du vertige: trois poètes: Nicole Brossard, Madeleine Gagnon, France Théoret*. Montréal: Remue-ménage, 1989.

Dyer, Gwynne. "Millennium." In *Ideas*. The Canadian Broadcasting Corporation, June 17-28, 1996.

Editorial Collective of *Questions féministes*. "Variations on Some Common Themes." *Feminist Issues* 1, 1 (Summer 1980): 3-22.

Engels, Frederick. *The Origin of the Family, Private Property, and the State, in the Light of the Researches of Lewis H. Morgan*. Moscow: Progress Publishers, 1968.

Epstein, Julia. "Either/Or—Neither/Both: Sexual Ambiguity and the Ideology of Gender." *Genders* 7 (Spring 1990): 99-142.

Fallon, Mary. *Working Hot*. Melbourne: Sybylla Press, 1989.

Fenn, Ann, Ingeborg Hoesterey and Maria Tatar, eds. *Neverending Stories: Toward a Critical Narratology*. Princeton: Princeton University Press, 1992.

Forsyth, Louise. "Deconstructing Formal Space/Accelerating Motion in the Work of Nicole Brossard." In *A Mazing Space: Writing Canadian Women Writing*. Ed. Shirley Neuman and Smaro Kamboureli. Edmonton: NeWest, 1986. 334-44.

————. "Errant and Air-Born in the City." Introduction to Nicole Brossard, *The Aerial Letter*. Trans. Marlene Wildeman. Toronto: The Women's Press, 1988.

_____. Préface to Nicole Brossard, *Picture Theory: Théorie/Fiction*. 2nd ed. Montréal: Hexagone, 1989.

Freud, Sigmund. *The Standard Edition of the Complete Psychological Works of Sigmund Freud*. Trans. James Strachey in collaboration with Anna Freud. London: Hogarth, 1959.

Fuss, Diana. *Essentially Speaking: Feminism, Nature & Difference*. New York: Routledge, 1989.

Gallant, Corinne, ed. *La philosophie... au féminin*. Moncton: Éditions Acadie, 1984.

Gelfand, Elissa D., and Virginia Thorndike Hules. *French Feminist Criticism: Women, Language, Literature: An Annotated Bibliography*. New York: Garland, 1985.

Genette, Gérard. "Discours du récit: essai de méthode." In *Figures Trois*. Paris: Éditions du Seuil, 1972. *Narrative Discourse: An Essay in Method*. Trans. Jane E. Lewin. Ithaca, NY: Cornell University Press, 1980.

Gilbert, Sandra, and Susan Gubar. "Sexual Linguistics: Gender, Language, Sexuality." In *The Feminist Reader: Essays in Gender and the Politics of Literary Criticism*. Ed. Catherine Belsey and Jane Moore. New York: Basil Blackwell, 1989. 81-99.

Gilligan, Carol. *In a Different Voice: Psychological Theory and Women's Development*. Cambridge, MA: Harvard University Press, 1982.

Gimbutas, Marija. "An Archaeologist's View of *PIE in 1975." *The Journal of Indo-European Studies* 2, 3 (1974): 289-307.

_____. "The First Wave of Eurasian Steppe Pastoralists into Copper Age Europe." *The Journal of Indo-European Studies* 5, 4 (1977): 277-338.

_____. *The Goddess Civilization: The World of Old Europe*. San Francisco: HarperCollins, 1991.

_____. *The Gods and Goddesses of Old Europe 7000-3500 B.C.* London: Thames and Hudson, 1974.

_____. *The Language of the Goddess*. With a Foreword by Joseph Campbell. San Francisco: Harper & Row, 1989.

_____. "The Social Structure of Old Europe, Parts 2 & 3." *The Journal of Indo-European Studies* 18, 3/4 (Fall/Winter 1990): 225-84.

Godard, Barbara, ed. *Collaboration in the Feminine: Writings on Women and Culture from* Tessera. Toronto: Second Story Press, 1994.

_____. "Essentialism? A Problem in Discourse." *Tessera* 10 (Summer/été 1991): 22-39.

_____. "Theorizing Feminist Discourse/Translation." *Tessera* 6 (Spring/printemps 1989): 42-53.

————. "Translating Translating Translation." Introduction to France Théoret, *The Tangible Word*. Trans. Barbara Godard. Montréal: Guernica, 1991.

Gould, Karen. *Writing in the Feminine: Feminism and Experimental Writing in Quebec*. Carbondale and Edwardsville: Southern Illinois University Press, 1990.

Graves, Robert. *The Greek Myths*. 2 vols. Harmondsworth: Penguin, 1957.

————. *The White Goddess: A Historical Grammar of Poetic Myth*. London: Faber and Faber, 1961.

Grillo, Trina, and Stephanie M. Wildman. "Obscuring the Importance of Race: The Implications of Making Comparisons between Racism and Sexism (or Other -isms)." In *Critical Race Theory: The Cutting Edge*. Ed. Richard Delgado. Philadelphia: Temple University Press, 1995. 564-72.

Groult, Benoîte. *Le féminisme au masculin*. Paris: Denoël/Gonthier, 1977.

————. "Rencontre du dimanche 24 november 1985 avec l'écrivaine Benoîte Groult." *Dialogue de Femmes*. Privately printed (12 rue Georges Berger, 75017, Paris, France).

Gubar, Susan. "Sapphistries." In *The Lesbian Issue: Essays from Signs*. Ed. Estelle Freedman et al. Chicago: University of Chicago Press, 1982. 91-110.

Hacker, Marilyn. *Love, Death, and the Changing of the Seasons*. New York: Arbor House, 1986.

Hanafi, Rhoda. "When 'I' Speaks to 'You': The Literary Subject as an Effect of Pronominal Play in Two Works by Contemporary Women Writers." Master's thesis, University of British Columbia, 1987.

Handy López, Ian F. "White by Law." In *Critical Race Theory*. Ed. Richard Delgado. Philadelphia: Temple University Press, 1995. 564-72.

Heidegger, Martin. *Poetry, Language, Thought*. Trans. Albert Hofstadter. New York: Harper & Row, 1971.

Hendricks, William. "Methodology of Narrative Discourse." *Semiotica* 7 (1973): 163-84.

Houghton Mifflin Canadian Dictionary of the English Language, The. Ed. William Morris. Markham, ON: Houghton Mifflini, 1982.

Huld, Martin E. "The Linguistic Typology of the Old European Substrata in North Central Europe." *The Journal of Indo-European Studies* 18, 3/4 (Fall/ Winter 1990): 417-23.

Irigaray, Luce. *Ce sexe qui n'en est pas un*. Paris: Minuit, 1977. *This Sex Which Is Not One*. Trans. Catherine Porter. Ithaca, NY: Cornell University Press, 1985.

Jacobson, Roman. *Selected Writings*. 8 vols. The Hague: N.p, 1971-88.

Jagose, Annamarie. *Lesbian Utopics*. New York: Routledge, 1994.

Jardine, Alice, and Anne Menke, eds. *Shifting Scenes: Interviews on Women, Writing, and Politics in Post-68 France*. New York: Columbia University Press, 1991.

Jelinek, Estelle, ed. *Women's Autobiography*. Bloomington: Indiana University Press, 1980.

Johnson-Laird, Philip N. "How Is Meaning Mentally Represented?" In *Meaning and Mental Representations*. Ed. Umberto Eco, Marco Santambrogio and Patrizia Violi. Bloomington: Indiana University Press, 1988. 99-118.

Katz, Wendy. *Her and His—Language of Equal Value: A Report of the Status of Women Committee of the Nova Scotia Confederation of University Faculty Associations on Sexist Language and the University*, 1981.

Knutson, Susan. "Challenging the Masculine Generic." *Tessera* 4/*Contemporary Verse* 11, 2/3 (Spring/Summer 1988): 76-88. Rpt. *WS 200A: Women in Society: Past and Present*. Victoria, BC: University of Victoria, 1993.

————. " 'Imagine Her Surprise': The Debate over Feminist Essentialism." In *Collaboration in the Feminine: Writings on Women and Culture from Tessera*. Ed. Barbara Godard. Toronto: Second Story Press, 1994. 228-36.

————. "Nicole Brossard's Elegant International Play." In *Canada: Theoretical Discourse/Discours théoriques*. Ed. Terry Goldie, Carmen Lambert and Rowland Lorimer. Montréal: Association for Canadian Studies/Association d'études canadiennes, 1994. 187-202.

————. "Paleo-linguistics and Feminist Theory: Reading between the Lines in *The Journal of Indo-European Studies*." In *Centre for Language in Social Life Working Papers*. Ed. Sally Johnson and Jane Sunderland. Lancaster, U.K.: Lancaster University, 1998. 1-13.

————. "Protean Travelogue in Nicole Brossard's *Picture Theory*: Feminist Desire and Narrative Form." *Modern Language Studies* 27.3, 4 (Winter 1997): 197-211.

————. "Reading Nicole Brossard." *Ellipse* 53 (Spring 1995): 9-19.

————. "Writing Metanarrative in the Feminine." *Signature: A Journal of Theory and Canadian Literature* 3 (Summer 1990): 28-43.

Kristeva, Julia. *La révolution du langage poétique: l'avant-garde à la fin du XIXᵉ siècle: Lautréamont et Mallarmé*. Paris: Seuil, 1974. *Revolution in Poetic Language*. Trans. Margaret Waller. New York: Columbia University Press, 1984.

Labrosse, Céline. *Pour une grammaire non-sexiste*. Montréal: Remue-ménage, 1996.

Leach, Edmund. "Fishing for Men on the Edge of the Wilderness." In *The Literary Guide to the Bible*. Ed. Frank Kermode and Robert Alter. Cambridge, MA: Harvard University Press, 1987.

Le Doeuff, Michèle. "Colloque féministe à New York: *Le deuxième Sexe* trente ans après." *Questions féministes* 7 (février 1980): 103-109.

Leith, Emmett N., and Juris Upatnieks. "Photography by Laser." *Scientific American* 212, 6 (June 1965): 24-35.

Le livre au féminin: les réponses à vos questions. Boucherville, QC: Éditions Proteau, 1983.

Lemire Tostevin, Lola. "Daphne Marlatt: Writing in the Space that Is Her Mother's Face." *Line* 13 (Spring 1989): 32-39.

Lenin, V.I. *The State and Revolution*. Moscow: Foreign Languages Publishing House, 1917.

Lerner, Gerda. *The Creation of Patriarchy*. New York: Oxford University Press, 1986.

Lévi-Strauss, Claude. "Structural Study of Myth." *Journal of American Folklore* 68 (1955): 428-43.

Libreria delle Donne di Milano [Milan Women's Bookstore]. *Non credere di avere dei diretti: la generazione della libertà femminile nell'idea e nelle vicende di un gruppo di donne* [Don't Think You Have Any Rights: The Engendering of Female Freedom in the Thought and Vicissitudes of a Women's Group]. Turin: Rosenberg & Sellier, 1987. Cited in de Lauretis, 1989.

Linke, Uli. "Blood as Metaphor in Proto-Indo-European." *The Journal of Indo-European Studies* 13, 3/4 (Fall/Winter 1985): 333-76.

Lorber, Judith, and Susan A. Farrell, eds. *The Social Construction of Gender*. New York: Sage, 1991.

Lorde, Audre. "An Open Letter to Mary Daly." In *This Bridge Called My Back: Writings by Radical Women of Color*. Ed. Cherríe Moraga and Gloria Anzaldúa. New York: Kitchen Table Press, 1993. 95.

Lotman, Jurij. "The Origin of Plot in the Light of Typology." *Poetics Today* 1, 1-2 (1979): 161-84.

Lowry, Glen. "Risking Perversion & Reclaiming Our Hysterical Mother: Reading the Material Body in *Ana Historic* and *Double Standards*." *West Coast Line* 5, 25/2 (Fall 1991): 83-96.

Lyons, John. *Introduction to Theoretical Linguistics*. London: Cambridge University Press, 1977.

Lyotard, Jean-François. *La condition postmoderne: rapport sur le savoir*. Paris: Éditions de Minuit, 1979. *The Postmodern Condition: A Report on Knowledge*. Trans. Geoff Bennington and Brian Massumi. Manchester: Manchester University Press, 1984.

Mackenzie, D.A. *Scottish Folklore and FolkLife* (1935); cited in Dames 1977, 86.

Mallarmé, Stéphane. *Un coup de dés jamais n'abolira le hasard*. Neuchâtel: Messeiller, 1960.

Marks, Elaine, and Isabelle de Courtivron, eds. *New French Feminisms*. New York: Schocken, 1981.

Marlatt, Daphne. *How Hug a Stone*. Winnipeg: Turnstone, 1983. Rpt. in *Ghostworks*. Edmonton: NeWest, 1993. 129-87.

————. "In the Month of Hungry Ghosts." *The Capilano Review* 16/17, 2-3 (1979): 45-95. Rpt. in *Ghostworks*. Edmonton: NeWest, 1993. 75-128.

————. Letter to Frank Davey, June 15, 1966. "Correspondences: Selected Letters." *Line* 13 (Spring 1989): 32-39.

————. "Narrative in Language Circuits." *The Dinosaur Review* 7 (1986): 60-61.

————. *Salvage*. Red Deer, AB: Red Deer College Press, 1991.

————. *Touch to My Tongue*. Edmonton: Longspoon, 1984.

————. "When We Change Language. . . ." In *Sounding Differences*. Ed. Janice Williamson. Toronto: University of Toronto Press, 1993. 182-99.

————. "Writing Our Way through the Labyrinth." *Tessera* 2/*nbj* (1985): 45-49.

Marlatt, Daphne, and Betsy Warland. *Double Negative*. With negative collages by Cheryl Sourkes. Charlottetown: Gynergy Books, 1988.

Marlatt, Daphne, and Nicole Brossard. *Character/Jeu de lettres*. Montréal: nbj/writing, 1986.

————. *Mauve*. Montréal: nbj/writing, 1985.

Marlatt, Daphne, Barbara Pulling, Victoria Freeman, Betsy Warland and Ann Dybikowski, eds. *In the Feminine: Women and Words/Les femmes et les mots, Conference Proceedings 1983*. Edmonton: Longspoon Press, 1985.

Marlatt, Daphne, Sky Lee, Lee Maracle and Betsy Warland, eds. (The Telling It Book Collective). *Telling It: Women and Language Across Cultures*. Vancouver: Press Gang, 1990.

Martin, André, and Henriette Dupuis. *La féminization des titres et les leaders d'opinion: une étude exploratoire*. Québec: Gouvernement du Québec, 1985.

Matejka, Ladislav, and Krystyna Pomorska, eds. *Readings in Russian Poetics: Formalist and Structuralist Views*. Cambridge: M.I.T. Press, 1971.

McDermott, Patrice. *Politics and Scholarship: Feminist Academic Journals and the Production of Knowledge*. Chicago: University of Illinois Press, 1994.

McIntosh Snyder, Jane. *Sappho*. New York: Chelsea House, 1995.

Mehta, Gita. *A River Sutra*. New York: Vintage Books, 1993.

Meigs, Mary. *The Medusa Head*. Vancouver: Talon Books, 1983.

Miller, Casey, and Kate Smith. *The Handbook of Non-Sexist Writing*. London: Women's Press, 1980.

Miranda, Rocky V. "Indo-European Gender: A Study in Semantic and Syntactic Change." *The Journal of Indo-European Studies* 3, 3 (Fall 1975): 199-215.

Moi, Toril. *Sexual/Textual Politics: Feminist Literary Theory*. London: Routledge, 1985.

Moraga, Cherríe, and Gloria Anzaldúa, eds. *This Bridge Called My Back: Writings by Radical Women of Color*. Watertown, MA: Persephone Books, 1981. Rpt. New York: Kitchen Table Press, 1993.

Mordecai, Pamela, and Betty Wilson, eds. *Her True-True Name: An Anthology of Women's Writing from the Caribbean*. London: Heinemann, 1989.

Morgan, Lewis H. *Ancient Society, or Researches in the Lines of Human Progress from Savagery through Barbarism to Civilization*. London: Macmillan, 1877.

Nicholson, Linda J., and Nancy Fraser. "Social Criticism without Philosophy." In *Feminism/Postmodernism*. Ed. Linda J. Nicholson. New York: Routledge, 1990. 19-38.

Nourbese Philip, Marlene. *She Tries Her Tongue, Her Silence Softly Breaks*. Charlottetown: Ragweed, 1989.

————. "Whose Idea Was It Anyway?" *Tessera, Vers une narratologie féministe/Toward Feminist Narratology* 7 (Fall/automne 1989): 45-54.

Olson, Charles. *Selected Writings*. Ed. Robert Creeley. New York: New Directions, 1966.

Paglia, Camille. *Sexual Personae: Art and Decadence from Nefertiti to Emily Dickinson*. New York: Vintage Books, 1990.

Parker, Alice. *Liminal Visions of Nicole Brossard*. New York: Peter Lang, 1998.

————. "Nicole Brossard's Body Work: *Le corps impair*." Paper presented to N.E.M.L.A., Montréal, April 20, 1996.

Penelope, Julia. [a.k.a. Julia P. Stanley]. "Gender-Marking in American English: Usage and Reference." In *Sexism and Language*. Ed. Alleen Pace Nilsen et al. Urbana, IL: National Council of Teachers of English, 1977. 43-76.

————. "Paradigmatic Woman: The Prostitute." *Linguistic Society of America* (1973).

————. *Speaking Freely: Unlearning the Lies of the Fathers' Tongues*. Elmsford, NY: Pergamon Press, 1990.

Penelope, Julia [Stanley], and Cynthia McGowan. "Woman and Wife: Social and Semantic Shifts in English." *Papers in Linguistics* 12, 3-4 (1979): 491-502.

Penelope, Julia [Stanley], and Susan J. Wolfe [a.k.a. Susan Wolfe Robbins]. "Linguistic Problems with Patriarchal Reconstructions of Indo-European Culture: A Little More than Kin, a Little Less than Kind." *Women's Studies International Quarterly* 3 (1980): 227-37.

Penelope, Julia [Stanley], and Susan Wolfe Robbins. "Sex-Marked Predicates in English." *Papers in Linguistics* 11, 1-2 (1978): 487-516.

Pribram, Karl. *Languages of the Brain: Experimental Paradoxes and Principles in Neuropsychology*. Englewood Cliffs, NJ: Prentice-Hall, 1971.

Propp, Vladímir. *Morphology of the Folktale*. Ed. Louis A. Wagner. Trans. Laurence Scott. Intro. Alan Dundes. 2nd ed. rev. Austin: University of Texas, 1968.

The Province of British Columbia. *Communicating Without Bias: Guidelines for Government*. Victoria: Government of British Columbia, 1992.

_____. *Gender Neutral Language: Interim Guidelines for Government Communications*. Victoria: Government of British Columbia, 1991.

Raoul, Valerie. "Women and Diaries: Gender and Genre." *Mosaic* 22-23 (Summer 1989): 57-65.

Rich, Adrienne. *The Dream of a Common Language: Poems 1974-1977*. New York: Norton, 1978.

Ricouart, Janine. "De la spirale au baroque our La spirale de Nicole Brossard a-t-elle perdu le Nord?" Paper presented to N.E.M.L.A., Montréal, April 20, 1996.

Riley, Denise. "Commentary: Feminism and the Consolidations of 'Women' in History." In *Coming to Terms: Feminism, Theory, Politics*. Ed. Elizabeth Weed. London: Routledge, 1989. 134-39.

Robinson, David. *Sappho and Her Influence*. New York: Cooper Square, 1963.

Russ, Joanna. "What Can a Heroine Do? Or Why Women Can't Write." In *Images of Women in Fiction: Feminist Perspectives*. Ed. Susan Koppelman Cornillon. Bowling Green, KY: Bowling Green University Popular Press, 1972.

Shaktini, Namascar. "Displacing the Phallic Subject: Wittig's Lesbian Writing." In *The Lesbian Issue: Essays from Signs*. Ed. Estelle Freedman et al. Chicago: University of Chicago Press, 1982. 137-52.

Silveira, Jeanette. "Generic Masculine Words and Thinking." *Women's Studies International Quarterly* 3 (1980): 165-78.

Silverman, Kaja. *The Subject of Semiotics*. New York: Oxford University Press, 1983.

Spender, Dale. *Man Made Language*. 2nd ed. London: Routledge and Kegan Paul, 1985.

Spivak, Gayatri Chakravorty, with Ellen Rooney. "In a Word: Interview." *differences* 1, 2 (Summer 1989): 124-56.

Stein, Gertrude. *Bee Time Vine and Other Pieces (1913-1927)*. New Haven, CT: Yale University Press, 1953.

Stephens, Donald. *Bliss Carman*. New York: Twayne, 1966.

Stukeley, William. *Stonehenge, a Temple Restor'd to the British Druids: Abury, a Temple of the British Druids: Myth & Romanticism: A Collection of the Major Mythographic Sources used by the English Romantic Poets*. Ed. Burton Feldman and Robert Richardson. Rpt. New York: Garland, 1984.

Théoret, France. *Entre raison et déraison*. Montréal: Les Herbes Rouges, 1987.

————. "Speech in Defense of Women's Right to Existance!" In *The Tangible Word*. Trans. Barbara Godard. Montréal: Guernica, 1991.

Tomashevsky, Boris. "Thematics." In *Russian Formalist Criticism: Four Essays*. Trans. with intr. Lee T. Lemon and Marion J. Reis. Lincoln: University of Nebraska Press, 1965.

Tostevin, Lola Lemire. "Daphne Marlatt: Writing in the Space that Is Her Mother's Face." *Line* 13 (1989): 32-39.

Valverde, Mariana. *Sex, Power and Pleasure*. Toronto: The Women's Press, 1985.

Van Gennep, Arnold. *The Rites of Passage*. Trans. Monika Vizedom and Gabrielle Caffee. Intr. Solon Kimball. London: Routledge & Kegan Paul, 1960.

Vatcher, Faith, and Lance Vatcher. *The Avebury Monuments*. The Department of the Environment Official Handbook. London: Her Majesty's Stationery Office, 1976.

Wagner, Richard. *Die Walküre: Erster Tag aus der Trilogie: Derring des Nibelungen*. Mayence: B. Schott's Söhne, 1882.

Weed, Elizabeth. "Introduction: Terms of Reference." In *Coming to Terms: Feminism, Theory, Politics*. Ed. Elizabeth Weed. London: Routledge, 1989. xi-xxxi.

Weir, Lorna. "Anti-Racist Feminist Pedagogy, Self-Observed." *Resources for Feminist Research/Documentation sur la recherche feministe* 20, 3/4 (Fall/Winter 1991).

Weir, Lorraine. "From Picture to Hologram: Nicole Brossard's Grammar of Utopia." In *A Mazing Space: Writing Canadian Women Writing*. Ed. Shirley Neuman and Smaro Kamboureli. Edmonton: NeWest Press, 1986. 345-54.

Wildman, Stephanie, with Adrienne D. Davis. "Language and Silence: Making Systems of Privilege Visible." In *Critical Race Theory: The Cutting Edge*. Ed. Richard Delgado. Philadelphia: Temple University Press, 1995.

Williamson, Janice. "Sounding a Difference: An Interview with Daphne Marlatt." *Line* 13 (1989): 47-56.

Wilson, Thomas. *Arte of Rhetorique*. 1553. Rpt. Gainesville, FL: Scholars' Facsimiles and Reprints, 1962.

Wittig, Monique. "La pensée straight." *Questions féministes* 7 (février 1980): 45-54. "The Straight Mind." *Feminist Issues* 1, 1 (Summer 1980): 103-11.

––––––––. *Le corps lesbien*. Paris: Minuit, 1973. *The Lesbian Body*. Trans. David Le Vay. London: Peter Owen, 1975.

––––––––. *Les guérillères*. Paris: Minuit, 1969. *Les Guérillères*. Trans. David Le Vay. Boston: Beacon Press, 1985.

––––––––. *L'opoponax*. Paris: Minuit, 1964. *L'Opoponax*. Trans. Helen Weaver. New York: Simon and Schuster, 1966.

––––––––. "On ne naît pas femme." *Questions féministes* 8 (mai 1980): 75-84. "One Is Not Born a Woman." *Feminist Issues* 1, 2 (Winter 1981): 47-54.

––––––––. "The Mark of Gender." *Feminist Issues* 5, 2 (1985): 3-12.

––––––––. *Virgile, non*. Paris: Minuit, 1985. *Across the Acheron*. Trans. David Le Vay. London: Peter Owen, 1987.

Wittig, Monique, and Sande Zeig. *Brouillon pour un dictionnaire des amantes*. Paris: Bernard Grasset, 1976.

––––––––. *Lesbian Peoples: Materials for a Dictionary*. New York: Avon, 1979.

Women's Review of Books, The. Special Issue: *The French Connection* 3, 6 (1986).

Wolfe, Susan J. "Amazon Etymology." *Sinister Wisdom* 12 (Winter 1980): 15-20.

––––––––. "Constructing and Reconstructing Patriarchy: Sexism and Diachronic Semantics." *Papers in Linguistics* 13, 2 (1980): 321-44.

––––––––. "Gender and Agency in Indo-European Languages." *Papers in Linguistics* 13, 4 (1980): 773-94.

Woolf, Virginia. *A Room of One's Own*. 1929. Rpt. London: Granada, 1981.

––––––––. "The Intellectual Status of Women." *The New Statesman* (London, October 16 1920): 45-46. (Woolf is responding to Desmond MacCarthy's ["Affable Hawk"] review of Arnold Bennett's *Our Women* and Otto Weininger's *Sex and Character, The New Statesman* [London, October 9, 1920]).

––––––––. *Women and Writing*. Ed. Michèle Barrett. New York and London: Harcourt Brace Jovanovich, 1979.

Wright, Ellea. "Text and Tissue: Body Language: Interview with Daphne Marlatt and Betsy Warland." *Broadside: A Feminist Review* 6, 3 (1986): 4-6.

Yeats, William Butler. *The Variorum Edition of the Poems of W.B. Yeats*. Ed. Peter Allt and Russell Alspach. New York: Macmillan, 1957.

Zavalloni, Marisa, ed. *L'emergence d'une culture au féminin*. Montréal: Saint-Martin, 1987.

Zimmerman, Bonnie. "The Politics of Transliteration: Lesbian Personal Narratives." *Signs* 9, 4 (Summer 1984): 663-82.

Appendix: Daphne Marlatt's Bibliography*

Michael Dames, *The Avebury Cycle*.
Vatcher and Vatcher, *The Avebury Monuments*.
Robert Graves, *The White Goddess*.
The American Heritage Dictionary.
Françoise Sagan, *Scars on the Soul*.
The Manchester Guardian Weekly, Vol. 124, Nos. 25, 26; Vol. 125, Nos. 1, 2.
Daily Mail, Friday June 26, 1981 ("Nott's Navy Blues").
Gail Duff, *Country Wisdom*.
A.A. Milne, *Now We Are Six*.
Welcome to London: A Collins Travel Guide.
Dr. Fortescue-Ffoukes, *A Short History of Poltimore* (Pamphlet).

* This bibliography was included in the manuscript submitted to Turnstone Press for publication, currently held in the Literary Manuscripts Collection of the National Library of Canada.

The following books are also mentioned in Marlatt's notebooks for *How Hug a Stone*:

J. Fowles, Barry Brukoff, *The Enigma of Stonehenge*.
W.H. Stukeley, *A Temple Restored to the British Druids*.
Leon Stover and Bruce Kraig, *Stonehenge: The Indo-European Heritage*.

Index

actantial analysis, 38, 56-59, 63-65, 76, 91, 115, 134, 136, 145, 196

Alberti, Leon Battista, 164

Althusser, Louis, 40, 57, 116

Amazones d'hier, lesbiennes d'aujourd'hui, 199

androgyny, 7, 85-86

Antonioni, Michelangelo, 146

Anzaldúa, Gloria, 9, 19

Apollo, 5, 48, 177

Aristotle, 16, 115

Arthur (King), 43

Ashbury, John (ashberry), 169

Athene, 177

au féminin, v, xii, 14, 126 (figure), 179, 192-206

Avebury, v, xi, 54-55, 60, 62-63, 65, 68-74, 70 (figure), 95-96, 99-108

Bakhtin, M.M., 93-94, 167

Bal, Mieke, 36-39, 54-58, 61, 65, 67-68, 81, 90-91, 153, 158, 174

Barbizet, Jacques, 202

Barnes, Djuna, xi, 119-20, 169, 170-174, 178, 180, 195

Barney, Natalie, 118, 119-120

Baron, Denis, 24

Barthes, Roland, 35, 39, 55

Beatrice, 183-184

Beck, Evelyn Torton, 19

Benveniste, Emile, 80-84, 93, 166

Bersianik, Louky, 4, 24, 199-200, 194

Beyond Tish, 6

Bibliothèque, Marguerite Durand, xii, 10n

binary opposition, 6-8, 21, 24-26, 29-30, 34-36, 38, 41-45, 47, 55, 65, 81, 119-121, 134, 167, 193, 196-198, 200

bird(s), 48, 63, 71, 73-74, 92, 103, 107, 109, 202, 206

Black, Maria, 25-26, 31

Black Mountain Poetics, 19

Blais, Marie-Claire, 119-120

Blake, William, 92-93

Blau DuPlessis, Rachel, 39-41

Blow-Up, 145-146

Booth, Wayne, 38

Bourgeois, Louise, 136

Bowles, Jane, 119-120

brain, v, xi, 16-17, 122-123, 125, 126 (figure), 127, 129-135, 166

Brémond, Claude, 34, 38, 53-55, 61

Bronze Age, 77, 96

Brookes, Romaine, 119-120

Brosman, Paul Jr., 200-201

Brugman, Karl, 200

Bruner, Jerome, 33

Brossard, Nicole, xi, xii, 3, 4, 6, 9-10, 13-19, 22, 32-33, 43, 46, 49-50, 89, 113-189, 137, 193-206; "Accès à l'écriture," 138, 155; *Amantes*, 119-120, 191, 200; *Aube à la saison*, 114; *Aviva*, 167; *Baroque d'aube*, 114, 206; "De radical à intègrales," xi, 13-18,